The Heart of the Matter

By Pierre Teilhard de Chardin

THE HEART OF MATTER
TOWARD THE FUTURE
ACTIVATION OF ENERGY
BUILDING THE EARTH
CHRISTIANITY AND EVOLUTION
HOW I BELIEVE
HUMAN ENERGY
HYMN OF THE UNIVERSE
LET ME EXPLAIN
LETTERS FROM A TRAVELLER
MAN'S PLACE IN NATURE
ON LOVE
THE DIVINE MILIEU
THE FUTURE OF MAN
THE MAKING OF A MIND
THE PHENOMENON OF MAN
THE VISION OF THE PAST
EARLY MAN IN CHINA

Pierre Teilhard de Chardin

The Heart
of the Matter

Translated by René Hague

A Harvest Book • Harcourt, Inc.
A Helen and Kurt Wolff Book
San Diego   *New York*   *London*

The essays "La Nostalgie du front,"
"La Grande Monade," "Mon Univers,"
"Note pour servir á l'évangélisation des temps nouveaux"
and "Les Noms de la Matiére" first appeared in the
French editions of *Ecrits due temps de la guerre,*
© 1965 by Editions Bernard Grasset.

Library of Congress Cataloging-in-Publication Data
Teilhard de Chardin, Pierre.
The heart of the matter.
(A Harvest book.)
Translation of Le coeur de la matiére.
"A Helen and Kurt Wolff book."
"Chronological list of works": p.
Bibliography: p.
Includes index.
1. Matter — Addresses, essays, lectures.
2. Cosmology — Addresses, essays, lectures.
3. Christianity — Philosophy — Addresses, essays, lectures.
4. Paleontology — Addresses, essays, lectures. I. Title
B2430.T373C5813 1979b   230'.2   79-24527
ISBN 0-15-602758-5

Printed in the United States of America

B D F H J I G E C A

CONTENTS

FOREWORD

At the head of this thirteenth and last volume of Père Teilhard's essays stand two as yet unpublished writings of key importance: *The Heart of Matter* and *The Christic*. These are followed by a number of shorter pieces which have come to light; these are printed in chronological order.

The Heart of Matter was written in 1950. Here Père Teilhard exposes the very foundations from which arose the whole structure of his work. 'I have tried,' he says, 'to describe in a sort of autobiography the general process and the principal stages of "the emergence of the picture".' So, almost at the very end of his life, Teilhard turns back and distinguishes with unmistakable clarity the two converging roads along which he has travelled: the road of Science and the road of Religion. And in so doing he sees, and allows us to see, the unity of his whole life.

We cannot read such an essay without being reminded of Bergson's *Philosophical Intuition*: '. . . the more we seek to make ourselves at home in a philosopher's thought, the more his teaching becomes transfigured for us. In the first place, its complexity grows less. Then we see how one part fits into or leads into another. Finally the whole comes together at one single point, which we feel we might be able to come closer and closer to, even though we can never hope to reach it.'[1]

The main themes emphasized in *The Heart of Matter* – the Cosmic or the Evolutive, the Human or the Convergent – are subordinate, we shall find, to another theme which embraces them both: the Christic or the Centric. At the peak of his thought Teilhard finds himself faced with God alone. It is then that he writes his *Prayer to the ever-greater Christ*, a prayer as yet unequalled, whether for its mystical depth, the width of its underlying scholarship, or the beauty of its language.

After reading these pages we might well be inclined to think that Teilhard had said his last word; but *The Christic* was still to come. At the beginning of this – dated in the month before his death – he explains his purpose: 'It is now many years since I tried, in *The Mass on the World* and *Le Milieu Divin*, when my views on these matters were not yet correctly focused or fully developed, to pin down in words my sense of dazzled wonder. Today, after forty years of continual thought, it is still the same fundamental vision that I feel I must put down and share with others in its mature form, for this one last time.'

Providentially, *The Christic* is at hand to fill the gap caused by Père Teilhard's religious obedience. He had, in fact, planned a second part of *The Phenomenon of Man*, which would have completed the first part by the addition of the Phenomenon of Religion, but his religious superiors had then ordered him to confine himself to the strictly scientific field.[2]

In the great symphony of Teilhard's writing, *The Christic* provides the coda to the last movement: and we may well consider how the resonance of those notes has endured since his death.

Translation into twenty-two languages has spread his writings into practically every country in the world. Any number of books and articles have been written, whose aim has been closely and thoroughly to examine various aspects of his thought, and these have helped to illuminate its internal coherence and to correct mistaken interpretations.

Even so, although Pierre Teilhard de Chardin wished and hoped to open up a road into the future which all men would hasten to follow, we have to admit that only a select few live with a clear awareness of an accelerated and irreversible evolution and of mankind's imminent transition into the era of synthesis. Nevertheless we should not overlook the progress that has been made since his day.

In palaeontology, Professor Jean Piveteau, of the Institut de France, has shown, as against G. G. Simpson, how effectively

Teilhard's influence has directed palaeontology along new paths, particularly in relation to palaeoneurology. Teilhard would have been delighted by the important discoveries that have been made since his day, some of which have been discussed by his learned colleague in his *Origine et Destinée de l'Homme*.

In biology, Professor Pierre Grassé has been actively engaged in biological investigations which he has recently described in his masterly *L'Evolution du Vivant*. What he says there confirms Teilhard's views on evolution.

Again in the field of evolution, Professor François Meyer has dealt impressively with the problem of the growing speed of change in relation to time in his *La Surchauffe de la Croissance*.

In *Le Macroscope* Dr Joël de Rosnay, the young Director of Development at the *Institut Pasteur*, provides a comprehensive method of synthetic vision.

Teilhard would have been entranced by these advances in science and would have recognized how they fitted into the hyper-physics he was opening up.

Nor should we forget the discoveries that have been made by W. Dement, N. Kleitman, M. Jouvet, O. Petre-Quadens, and so many others in the field of the Physiology of Dreams. Père Teilhard was very keenly interested in the problem of the awakening of consciousness, which was the central theme of his thought about man and the world. We may well hope for further investigation in the light of which the hypotheses he put forward may be tested.

Although Pierre Teilhard was not a specialist in philosophy, metaphysics and theology, nevertheless the work he did in these fields remains of cardinal importance: as is illustrated by his *Creative Union, The Struggle against the Multitude, A Metaphysic of Union*, essays to which the first volume of his *Journal* provides valuable complementary material.

Teilhard turned away from Scholasticism because its categories had ceased to be an apt medium for describing the world as we see it today; here he has been followed by such contemporary philosophers and theologians as Bernard Lonergan and Karl Rahner.

On the other hand, we can distinguish a certain convergence between Teilhard's thought and that of Whitehead, who worked with Russell and became Professor of Philosophy at Harvard. Whitehead, it is true, did not know Teilhard, but we know from one of the latter's notebooks that he intended to read *Science and the Modern World*.

However that may be, a comparison of their cosmological views brings out some points of evident kinship. Both emphasized the evolutive character of reality and the organic relationship of all events.

For Whitehead as for Teilhard, our universe has a spiritual centre. It is a universe governed by a freedom which God respects; but while, for Whitehead, the universe is evolving towards an ill-defined unification, for Teilhard it is eschatological and the consummation of its unity coincides with a fullness of maturity which brings about the final return of Christ.

A similar kinship is apparent in the massive volume edited by Professor Ewert Cousins, *Process Theology*, which reprints Ian Barbour's excellent paper 'Whitehead and Teilhard de Chardin'.

In the same way, we can foresee that Père Teilhard's theological views will continue to afford a wide field of study. Any number of books have already been written about this aspect of his thought, and his influence has been reflected in many publications of all sorts, among which we may include, in the first place, some of the documents of the Second Vatican Council. 'The period dominated by scholasticism', writes Bernard Lonergan, 'has reached its term. Catholic theology is in process of being re-structured' (*Method in Theology*, New York, 1972, p. 271). And it is already evident that this restructuring will not be accomplished without taking into account the problems raised by the work of Teilhard.

The great task that now awaits us is to continue Père Teilhard de Chardin's thought in the field of science, philosophy and theology beyond the limits that circumstances imposed upon him. If we do this – and only if we do this – the work he started will reach its full development and produce the fruit he hoped it would bear.

N. M. Wildiers
Dr in Theology

1. In *The Creative Mind*, trans. Mabel L. Adison, New York, 1946.
2. When Père Teilhard went to live in America, his religious superior allowed him full liberty to write what he pleased, and asked him to let him have copies of what he wrote.

THE HEART OF MATTER

INTRODUCTION
The Burning Bush

> At the heart of Matter[1]
> A World-heart,
> The Heart of a God.

In spite of certain appearances of strictly rigorous argument, the considerations that follow make no attempt to work out a designedly coherent structure – a philosophy of the real. Rather do they aim at describing a direct psychological experience – with just that amount of hard thinking behind it that will enable it to become intelligible and communicable without losing the objective, indisputable value of a document that reflects life.

What I shall try to do in the pages printed here (hoping that my own 'case' may make it possible for many other similar cases to be recognized or even to be brought into being) is quite simply this: to show how, starting from the point at which a spark was first struck, a point that was built into me congenitally, the World gradually caught fire for me, burst into flames; how this happened all *during* my life, and *as a result of* my whole life, until it formed a great luminous mass, lit from within, that surrounded me.

Within every being and every event there was a progressive expansion of a mysterious inner clarity which transfigured them. But, what was more, there was a gradual variation of intensity and colour that was related to the complex interplay of three universal components: the Cosmic, the Human and the Christic – these (at least the first and the last) asserted themselves explicitly in me from the very first moments of my existence, but it has taken me more than sixty years of ardent effort to discover that they were no more than the successive heraldings of, or approxi-

mate outlines of, one and the same fundamental reality . . .

Crimson gleams of Matter, gliding imperceptibly into the gold of Spirit, ultimately to become transformed into the incandescence of a Universe that is Person – and through all this there blows, animating it and spreading over it a fragrant balm, a zephyr of Union – and of the Feminine.

The Diaphany of the Divine at the heart of a glowing Universe, as I have experienced it through contact with the Earth – the Divine radiating from the depths of a blazing Matter: this it is that I shall try to disclose and communicate in what follows.

Les Moulins, 15 August 1950

I. THE COSMIC, OR THE EVOLUTIVE

Preliminary Note: The Sense of Plenitude

When I look for my starting point, for a clue to lead the reader through these pages, for an axis that will give continuity to the whole, I find that the first thing I have to do is to give a picture of, and briefly describe, a particular psychological disposition or 'polarization'; it is certainly common to all men (although not always formally recognized by them), and for want of a better name I shall call it the *Sense of Plenitude*. However far back I go into my childhood, nothing seems to me more characteristic of, or more familiar in, my interior economy than the appetite or irresistible demand for some 'Unique all-sufficing and necessary reality'. To be completely at home and completely happy, there must be the knowledge that 'Something, essential by nature' exists, to which everything else is no more than an accessory or perhaps an ornament. To know and endlessly to enjoy the aware-ness of this existence – I must indeed confess that if ever in past years I have been able to recognize my own self and follow my own development, it has been only by picking up this note or

PART I

tint, or particular flavour, which it is impossible (once one has experienced it) to confuse with any other spiritual emotion, whether joy in knowledge or discovery, joy in creation or in loving: and this not so much because it is different from all those emotions, but because it belongs to a higher order and contains them all.

The Sense of Plenitude, the Sense of Consummation and of Completion: the 'Pleromic Sense'.

Throughout all that I shall call in turn and indifferently 'Sense of Consistence', 'Cosmic Sense', 'Sense of the Earth', 'Sense of Man', 'Christic Sense', everything that follows will be simply the story of a slow unfolding or evolving within me of this fundamental and 'Protean' element which takes on ever richer and purer forms.

This is no fictitious or imaginary story; it is a real process at work, biologically guided and guaranteed for me as such by the identity my consciousness can clearly apprehend beneath all the metamorphoses and extensions of the operative psychological substratum.

And, let me add, it is a singularly significant operation in as much as, while destined to culminate upon what is highest in the direction of Spirit, it started in the first place (as I know by evidence and direct proofs) from what is most tangible and most concrete in the Stuff of Things, later to make its way into and conquer everything.[2]

a. The Appeal of Matter[3]

I was certainly not more than six or seven years old when I began to feel myself drawn by Matter – or, more correctly, by something which 'shone' at the heart of Matter. At the age when other children, I imagine, experience their first 'feeling' for a person, or for art, or for religion, I was affectionate, good, and even pious: by that I mean that under the influence of my mother, I was devoted to the Child Jesus. I shall return later, in Part III, to the essential part that this element played later in my life.

In reality, however, my real 'me' was elsewhere.

And to see that 'me' properly, you would have had to watch me as – always in secrecy and silence – without even any idea that there could be anything to say about it to anyone – I withdrew into the contemplation, the possession, into the so relished existence, of my 'Iron God'. *Iron*, mark you. I can still see, with remarkable sharpness, the succession of my 'idols'. In the country there was the lock-pin of a plough which I used to hide carefully in a corner of the yard. In town, there was the hexagonal head of a metal bolt which protruded above the level of the nursery floor, and which I had made my own private possession. Later, there were shell-splinters lovingly collected on a neighbouring firing-range . . . I cannot help smiling, today, when these childish fancies come back to my mind; and yet I cannot but recognize that this instinctive act which made me *worship*, in a real sense of the word, a fragment of metal contained and concentrated an intensity of resonance and a whole stream of demands of which my entire spiritual life has been no more than the development.

The real point, however, is: Why *Iron*? and why, in particular, *one special* piece of iron? (It had to be as thick and massive as possible.) It can only have been because, so far as my childish experience went, nothing in the world was harder, heavier, tougher, more durable than this marvellous substance apprehended in its *fullest* possible form . . . *Consistence*: that has undoubtedly been for me the fundamental attribute of Being. When this initial apprehension of the Absolute in the form of the Tangible is arrested prematurely in its growth, so that it becomes barren, you get dwarfism, and it is this that produces the miser or collector. Providentially, in my case the seed was destined to grow. But until this very day (and so, I feel, it will be until the end) this primacy of the Incorruptible, that is to say of the Irreversible, has never ceased, and never will cease, indelibly to characterize my predilection for the Necessary, the General, the 'Natural' – as opposed to the Contingent, the Particular and the

Artificial: and, as we shall be seeing, this disposition for a long time obscured for me the supreme values of the Personal and the Human.

Already this was the Sense of Plenitude, sharply individualized and already seeking for satisfaction in grasping a definite Object in which the Essence of Things could be found *concentrated*.

It was precisely what, after many years of experience and thought, I was to begin to discern in an evolutive Pole to the World!

It is a long way, however, from a piece of iron to Omega Point . . . And I was gradually to find, to my cost, to what a degree the Consistence of which I then dreamed is an effect not of 'substance' but of 'convergence'. I so well remember the pathetic despair of the child who one day realizes that Iron can become scratched and pitted – and can rust. '*Quo tinea non corrumpit*'.

And then, to comfort myself, I looked for things that would take its place. Sometimes it would be a blue flame (at once so material, so impossible to grasp and so pure) flickering over the logs on the hearth; more often some more transparent or more finely coloured stone: quartz or amethyst crystals and, best of all, glittering fragments of chalcedony such as I could pick up in the countryside. On those occasions it was essential, of course, that the cherished substance should be resistant, impervious to attack and *hard*!

There was an imperceptible transition, but one which was later to have an immense importance for my spiritual evolution: for it was precisely through the gateway that the substitution of Quartz for Iron opened for my groping mind into the vast structures of the Planet and of Nature, that I began, without realizing it, truly to make my way into the World – until nothing could satisfy me that was not on the scale of the Universal.

This is how it happened.

b. The Appearance of the Universal

At the very beginning of my conscious life, let me repeat, in my efforts to attain and grasp the 'solidity' to which my innate demand for Plenitude impelled me, I tried above all to capture the essence of Matter by looking for it in its most closely-defined and concentrated, and heaviest, forms; in this attempt I clung, of course, to what then seemed to me to be the queen of substances (in that case, Iron) – but in so doing I was greatly concerned to grasp this precious being in forms as sharply demarcated and *compact* as possible.

Then it was that my newly born attraction to the world of 'Rocks' began to produce the beginning of what was to be a permanent broadening of the foundations of my interior life.

Metal (such metal as I could find at the age of ten) tended to keep me attached to objects that were manufactured and so mere pieces. Mineral, on the other hand, set me on the road towards the 'planetary'. I woke up to the notion of 'the Stuff of Things'. And that famous Consistence, which I had hitherto looked for in the Hard and the Dense, began in a subtle way to emerge in the direction of an Elemental permeating all things – whose very ubiquity would produce incorruptibility.

Later, when I was studying geology, it might well have appeared that all I was doing was seriously and successfully to consider the chances of a career in science. In reality, however, during the whole of my life there was but one thing which would irresistibly bring me back (even at the expense of palaeontology) to the study of the great eruptive masses and continental shelves: that was an insatiable desire to maintain contact (*a contact of communion*) with a sort of universal root or matrix of beings.

The truth is that even at the peak of my spiritual trajectory I was never to feel at home unless immersed in an Ocean of Matter . . .

So it was that the Sense of Consistence led to the awakening and expansion of a dominant and triumphant Sense of the Whole.

Over about twenty years of my life (from my leaving home for boarding-school until I began my theology at Hastings in Sussex) I can distinctly recognize in my memories the unbroken trail that marks this profound transformation. During this time, as I shall have to explain, the material object of my secret joy may well have varied with my age; moreover, there was an important break in my life: my entry into the Society of Jesus. But I now see that these different events were no more than minor superficial ripples on the fundamental current constituted by my awakening to the Cosmic Sense and the Cosmic Life. This was a powerful interior process, in the course of which I found that I was gradually being invaded, impregnated and completely re-cast as the result of a sort of psychic metamorphosis into which, it would seem, there passed the brightest of the energies released by my arrival at puberty.

It would be difficult for me to work out again, or at least to explain in some detail, the complicated story in which, at that time of my life, the various threads were formed and began to be woven together into what was one day to become for me the fabric of the Stuff of the Universe.

Nevertheless, at this point in my analysis I must enumerate the more important strata whose successive individualization or accretion helped at that time to provide my Sense of the Whole with its chief components.

First of all, of course, and forming the solid permanent core of the system, was my taste for geology: the primacy of material matter, 'Matter-Matter', expressed in Mineral and Rock. I shall not re-analyse here, what I have mentioned earlier, this primordial modality of my Sense of Plenitude; but I could not explain, or follow myself, the vicissitudes of my psychic evolution if I did not emphasize once again the central position invariably occupied by my passionate study of the science 'of Stones', throughout the whole of my spiritual embryo-genesis.

Thus, between the ages of ten and thirty, at the heart of my absorbing interests and of my secret delights lay a continued and increased contact with the Cosmic 'in the solid state'. Already, however, in a semi-subordinate way, there was the newly emerged attraction towards vegetal and animal Nature; and, deep below, there came one day, at the end of that period, my initiation into the less tangible – but how stimulating! – magnitudes disclosed by the investigations of Physics. On either side of Matter stood Life and Energy: the three columns that supported my interior visions and felicity.

Because of its apparent fragility (a point I shall have to return to when I speak of Man) the living World greatly worried and disconcerted me as a child. On the one hand, when I thought of Plants and Animals, to the knowledge of which I was being initiated by my country life and my father's taste for natural history, I felt quite certainly drawn towards them by my constantly watchful 'Sense of Plenitude'. On the other hand, I had to justify to myself the interest aroused in me by objects so shockingly lacking in consistence and so perishable as a flower or an insect[4]; and so I created for myself (or did I discover in myself?) certain mysterious equivalent values whose psychological connection is not perhaps immediately obvious but which gave me just the same feeling of intense satisfaction. For the Solid and Incorruptible, I substituted the New and the Rare. So far was this carried that for years, as I now smile to remember, the pursuit in zoology and palaeontology of 'the new species' became one of the most important pivots around which my interior life revolved. It was a dangerous tendency, I must confess, for there could have been a risk of being dragged into the morass of collections and collecting for their own sake – had it not been for two safeguards: in the first place I retained my dominant Sense of the Universal, and even as I felt the glow of satisfaction as I put my hand upon a really treasured specimen, that sense enabled me to experience fundamentally only a delight in a more intimate contact (or a contact I imagined to be such) with what would later become for me 'the Biosphere'. Secondly, there was the decisive effect made upon my mind, at the right moment, by my introduction to physics and physicists.

It was only for three years, in Jersey – and then for another three years, in Cairo (1906–8) – that I studied (so far as I could) and taught (so far as my incompetence allowed me) a pretty elementary physics: the pre-quanta, pre-Relativity, pre-atomic-structure physics. This means that in this field I am, so far as technical knowledge goes, no more than an amateur – a layman. And yet I find it difficult to express how much I feel at home in precisely this world of electrons, nuclei, waves, and what a sense of plenitude and comfort it gives me. The Consistent, the Total, the Unique, the Essential of my childhood dreams – the vast cosmic realities (Mass, Permeability, Radiation, Curvatures, and so on) through which the Stuff of Things is disclosed to our experience in a form which is patient at the same time of being indefinitely reduced to elements and indefinitely expressed in geometrical terms – that mysterious Gravity (whose secret I ingenuously promised myself, at the age of twenty-two, that I would one day dedicate myself to unlocking): it was surely there that I met those very 'archetypes' which, as we shall be seeing, I still use, even when I come to the Christic itself, when I try to express for my own satisfaction precisely what I mean.

Linking the Animal World and the Energy-World lies the common underlying foundation of the Rock-World. From above this firmly cemented whole there flooded over me a first wave of the exotic, which sometimes affected me like a rich tapestry and sometimes seemed to bring me an invigorating draught of a new atmosphere. This was the East. I caught glimpses of it, and drank it in avidly, with no concern for its peoples and their history (which had not yet begun to interest me) but under the attraction of its light, its vegetation, its fauna and its deserts. Such, when I was about twenty-eight years of age, was the some-what muddled spiritual complex within which my passionate love of the Universe was smouldering without as yet the power to burst into open flame.

The truth is that, without realizing it, I had at that time come to a standstill in my awakening to Cosmic Life, and I could not start again without the intervention of a new force or a new illumination. A dead end: or perhaps I should say a subtly hidden tendency to drift towards a lower form (the commonplace, facile form) of the pantheist Spirit, the pantheism of effusion and dissolution. For, if the initial call that I had heard was in fact coming from Matter, then (someone kept whispering within me) why should I not look for the essence of Matter, for its 'heart', precisely in that direction in which all things are 'ultra-material-ized': that is to say, look for it just where I had found the incredibly *simple* and inclusive realities to the discovery of which I had ultimately been led by the Physics of Energy and the Ether (for we still retained that term in those days)? In other words, if I was to escape from the ruthless fragility of the Multiple, why should I not take my stance at an even deeper level and burrow, so to speak, below it?

It was thus that there tended insidiously to become rooted in me the concern and preference (completely eastern, beneath their scientific garb) for a *common substratum* of the Tangible – Element of all elements – Support of all substances – which, by a process of relaxation and diffusion, might be directly grasped, *beyond* every determination and every form.

This meant possession of the World by self-surrender, by passivity, by disappearing within a Formless that knows no boundaries – a movement that could be seen as 'centrifugal communion', inspired by the instinct for self-extension and self-distension, operating below all particulate plurality and delimita-tion, on the scale of, and homogeneous with, the total Sphere . . .

If I was to be All, I must be fused with all.

Such was the mystical act to which, following so many Hindu poets and mystics, I would logically have been driven by an innate, ungovernable need to attain self-fulfilment by accession not, indeed, *to others*, but to become *the Other* – had it not been that just at the appropriate moment the idea of Evolution ger-minated in me, like a seed: whence it came I cannot say.

c. The Discovery of Evolution

It was during the years when I was studying theology at Hastings (that is to say, immediately after I had experienced such sense of wonder in Egypt) that there gradually grew in me, as a *presence* much more than as an abstract notion, the consciousness of a deep-running, ontological, total Current which embraced the whole Universe in which I moved; and this consciousness continued to grow until it filled the whole horizon of my inner being.

What were the influences or what was the sudden jerk that caused this feeling to appear and drive its roots so deeply into me; how did the process develop and what were its stages? Those are questions that I would find very difficult to answer. I can remember very clearly the avidity with which, at that time, I read Bergson's *Creative Evolution*. But apart from my failure in those days correctly to understand what he meant by Duration,[5] I can now see quite clearly that the only effect that brilliant book had upon me was to provide fuel at just the right moment, and very briefly, for a fire that was already consuming my heart and mind. And that fire had been kindled, I imagine, simply by the coincidence in me, under 'monist' high tension, of the three inflammable elements that had slowly piled up in the depths of my soul over a period of thirty years. These were the cult of Matter, the cult of Life, and the cult of Energy. All three found a potential outlet and synthesis in a World which had suddenly acquired a new dimension and had thereby moved from the fragmented state of static Cosmos to the organic state and dignity of a Cosmogenesis.

At first, naturally enough, I was far from understanding and clearly appreciating the importance of the change I was undergoing. All that I can remember of those days (apart from that magic word 'evolution', which haunted my thoughts like a tune: which was to me like an unsatisfied hunger, like a promise held out to me, like a summons to be answered) – all that I can remember is the extraordinary solidity and intensity I found then in the

English countryside, particularly at sunset, when the Sussex woods were charged with all that 'fossil' Life which I was then hunting for, from cliff to quarry, in the Wealden clay. There were moments, indeed, when it seemed to me that a sort of universal being was about to take shape suddenly in Nature before my very eyes. Already, however, I was no longer trying, as I had tried earlier, to apprehend and pin down the Ineffable Ambience by looking towards some 'ultra-material'. I was already turning my eyes towards some 'ultra-living'. I had experienced a complete reversal of my Sense of Plenitude, and since those days I have constantly searched and progressed in that new direction.

Let me draw attention a little more closely to this discovery and to the way in which I retraced my steps.

Until that time my education and my religion had always led me obediently to accept – without much reflection, it is true – a fundamental heterogeneity between Matter and Spirit, between Body and Soul, between Unconscious and Conscious. These were to me two 'substances' that differed in nature, two 'species' of Being that were, in some incomprehensible way, associated in the living Compound; and it was important, I was told, to maintain at all costs that the first of those two (my divine Matter!) was no more than the humble servant of the second, if not, indeed, its enemy. Thus the second of the two (Spirit) was by that very fact henceforth reduced for me to being no more than a Shadow. In principle, it is true, I was compelled to venerate this shadow but, emotionally and intellectually speaking, I did not in fact have any live interest in it. You can well imagine, accordingly, how strong was my inner feeling of release and expansion when I took my first still hesitant steps into an 'evolutive' Universe, and saw that the dualism in which I had hitherto been enclosed was disappearing like the mist before the rising sun. Matter and Spirit: these were no longer two things, but two *states* or two aspects of one and the same cosmic Stuff, according to whether it was looked at or carried further in the direction in which (as Bergson would have put it) it is becoming itself or in the direction in which it is disintegrating.

Those phrases, 'to become itself' or 'to disintegrate', were still, of course, terribly vague, and it would be several decades before they acquired a precise meaning in my mind; but in their own way they sufficed to confirm me permanently in an attitude or choice which was to govern the whole of my interior develop- ment and whose chief characteristics may be defined in these simple words: the primacy of Spirit or, which comes to the same thing, the primacy of the Future.

Strictly speaking, no doubt, the mere fact of having seen the disappearance of the alleged barrier that separates the Within of things from the Without – or even of having realized that once we have knocked down that wall we find that an experientially and tangibly recognizable current runs from what is least conscious in Nature to what is most conscious – that mere fact, I must admit, would not by itself suffice to establish beyond question an absolute superiority of the Animate over the Inani- mate – of Psyche over Soma. Is there any reason, in fact, why the Cosmos should not swing at will first to one pole and then to the other? Or, after a certain number of oscillations, why should it not finally and unalterably settle down in the Matter position? . . . Surely these could be two of any number of evolutionary formulas?

These various problems were inevitably to present themselves to me later on, and I can see that I solved them at least for my own personal needs. What I find remarkable is that they did not occur to me at the very beginning. It may have been the impact of the clarity of my own instinct (for it seemed so obvious that I could not be mistaken in attributing to the cosmic movement that I had just discovered the highest degree of creative value and permanence); or it may have been an ill-defined anticipation of Evolution's psychic conditions or demands (which I was to learn later from the study of Human Energy): in any case, I never really paused for a moment to question the idea that the progressive Spiritualization of Matter – so clearly demonstrated to me by

Palaeontology – could be anything other, or anything less, than an *irreversible* process. By its gravitational nature, the Universe, I saw, was falling – falling forwards – in the direction of Spirit as upon its stable form. In other words, Matter was not ultra-materialized as I would at first have believed, but was instead metamorphosed into Psyche. Looked at not metaphysically, but genetically, Spirit was by no means the enemy or the opposite pole of the Tangibility which I was seeking to attain: rather was it its very heart.

It was to take me a whole lifetime to appreciate (and even then, alas, by no means completely) the unendingly constructive and at the same time revolutionary effect this transposition of value (this change in the very notion of Spirit) produced upon my understanding, upon my prayer and action.

Meanwhile, my interior position was as follows. By the direct leap I had taken from the old static dualism, which I found para-lysing, to emerge into a Universe which was in a state not merely of evolution but of *directed evolution* (that is, of *Genesis*) I was obliged to make a complete about-turn in my fundamental pur-suit of Consistence. Until that time, as I said earlier, my guiding Sense of Plenitude tended to point and settle down in the direction of the 'extremely simple' (in other words, of what cannot be broken down into physical components). In future, since the unique and precious essence of the Universe had assumed for me the form of an 'Evolutive' in which Matter was transformed into Thought as an extended consequence of Noogenesis, I found myself inevitably, and paradoxically, obliged to identify the extreme Solidity of things with *an extreme organic complexity*. Yet how could what was most corruptible become, as a result of synthesis, the supremely Indestructible? Because I had not yet perceived 'the biological laws of Union' and recognized the amazing attributes of a universal Curvature, I was still uncertain of the solution to that problem; but I no longer doubted but that the supreme happiness I had formerly looked for in 'Iron' was to be found only in Spirit.

Already, in fact, reassurance was at hand: two immense living Unities were beginning to rise over my inner horizon – unities of planetary dimensions in which I could distinguish, precisely as an effect of an excess of combination and organicity, the emergence within the Stuff of the cosmos of an extraordinary capacity for 'consolidation by complexification'.

In one of these my many varied experiences as a biologist in the field and in the laboratory were gradually coming together to form a naturally harmonious pattern. This was the Earth's living envelope – the Biosphere.

And the other was totalized Mankind – the Noosphere. But the price I would have to pay for this, if I was to bring it finally and sharply into focus, was no less than the spiritual shock of the War.

II. THE HUMAN, OR THE CONVERGENT

Today Man (or, to speak more correctly, the *Human*)[6] forms the pivot upon which the whole structure of my interior Universe rests, around which its links are formed and it coheres and moves. Yet the Human was far from occupying this cardinal position in my picture of the world immediately and without resistance.

As a result of the awakening in me of the notion of Evolution, Spirit (as I have just related) had, in my view, supplanted the Mineral and the Atomic in their dignity as the immutable and all-embracing essence of the Universe. But this *Spirit*, vaguely conceived as some sort of opposite pole to the physicist's Energy, was still, in my mind (and was so to remain for a long time)[7] without any precise structure: two innate and obstinate prejudices prevented me from facing and coming to terms with the fact (obvious though it was) that if the World does indeed represent an organo-dynamic system which is in process of psychic interiorization, then it is through the Flesh, by process of Hominization, that Noogenesis operates.

On the one hand there was the reaction I mentioned earlier

when I was speaking of my first relationship with Nature: the physico-chemical instability of organic substances in general, and of the human body in particular,[8] continued, in spite of all the intellectual evidence to the contrary, to obscure emotionally my need for consistence.

On the other hand there was a new obstacle: the more the primacy of the Cosmic asserted itself in my mind, and the more I felt its appeal, the more, by contrast, did the Human confuse and disturb me by the preponderance assumed at its level by 'the individual', 'the accidental', 'the artificial' . . . In Man, did not the Plural inevitably, and disastrously, break through and tear apart the Universal and the Total? . . . It was not merely that the trees prevented me from *seeing* the wood – the wood hardly even seemed to *subsist* behind them.

Putting it in rather cut and dried terms, I can, I think, reduce to *three* the stages I had to go through in turn, between the ages of thirty and fifty years, before I could overcome these two forms of inner reluctance and so at last become fully conscious of the extraordinary cosmic wealth concentrated in the Phenomenon of Man:

The first stage introduced me to the notion of human Planetarity (the existence of a Noosphere and the disposition of its contours).

The second disclosed to me more explicitly the critical transformation undergone by the Stuff of the cosmos at the level of Reflection.

And the third led me to the recognition of the Noosphere's accelerated drift towards ultra-human states, under the influence of psycho-physical convergence (or Planetization).

a. The Reality of the Noosphere

It was only, if I am not mistaken, in an article on Man, written about 1927[9] (that is, after my first visit to China), that I first allowed myself – on the model of Suess's Biosphere – to use the term Noosphere for the Earth's thinking envelope. But although the word appeared in my writings at that comparatively late date, it was ten years earlier that the vision itself had germinated in my mind through prolonged contact with the huge masses of mankind that were then facing one another in the trenches of France, from the Yser to Verdun.

The atmosphere of 'the Front': it was, I am quite sure, from having plunged into that atmosphere – from having been soaked in it for months and months on end – and precisely where it was at its most dense and heavily charged, that I ceased to notice any break (if not any difference) between 'physical' and 'moral', between 'natural' and 'artificial'. The 'Human-million', with its psychic temperature and its internal energy, became for me a magnitude as evolutively, and therefore as biologically, real as a giant molecule of protein. 1 was later to be astonished on many occasions to find in my own circle that those who could not agree with me suffered from a complete inability to understand that precisely because the individual human being represents a *corpuscular magnitude* he *must* be subject to the same development as every other species of corpuscles in the World: that means that he *must* coalesce into physical relationships and groupings that belong to a higher order than his. It is, of course, quite impossible for him to apprehend these groupings directly *as such* (because they are of the order of $n+1$),[10] but there are many indications that enable him to recognize perfectly well their existence and the influences they exercise. This gift or faculty of *perceiving*, without actually *seeing*, the reality and organicity of collective magnitudes is still comparatively rare:[11] but I have no doubt at all (as I said earlier) that it was the experience of the War that brought me this awareness and developed it in me *as a sixth sense*.[12]

Once I had acquired this complementary sense, what emerged into my field of perception was literally a new Universe. By the side of (or above) the Universe of large Masses, I saw (what I shall speak of later) the Universe of large Complexes. Looking at the Earth, my first instinct would originally have been to give particular consideration to what was most central and heaviest (the Barysphere, we might say). As things were, my attention and my interest (still guided by the same fundamental need for Solidity and Incorruptibility) were gradually and almost imperceptibly climbing up from the extremely simple central core of the Planet to its ridiculously thin, but dauntingly active and complex, peripheral layers. It was not merely that I found no difficulty in apprehending, more or less intuitively, the organic unity of the living membrane which is stretched like a film over the lustrous surface of the star which holds us. There was something more: around this sentient protoplasmic layer, an ultimate envelope was beginning to become apparent to me, taking on its own individuality and gradually detaching itself like a luminous *aura*. This envelope was not only conscious but thinking, and from the time when I first became aware of it, it was always there that I found concentrated, in an ever more dazzling and consistent form, the essence or rather the very Soul of the Earth.

b. *The Stuff of the Noosphere*

During a first phase of my apprehension, the feature in the Noosphere which most attracted my attention was what I would call, if I may, 'its surface tension'. This is a most exceptional – indeed, a unique – example in the field of our observation of a living magnitude, planetary in dimensions, which is strictly and exclusively self-totalizing. At the bottom we see (as we do in every 'sphere') ubiquity and solidarity; but above there is something more, there is organic unity of operation.

The oneness, or *Unicity*, of man stretched like a veil over the confused multitude of living beings: this astounding singleness in cohesion was in itself sufficient to catch and fascinate my passion for the Cosmic-apprehended-in-its-extreme-forms. Nevertheless it was only a first approximation in the story of my discovery of the Human – or (which may seem a better way of expressing it) it was a first break-through which illuminated in three stages the very nature of the Stuff of the Noosphere considered from the point of view of its underlying structure.

Deep down, there is in the substance of the cosmos a primordial disposition, *sui generis*, for self-arrangement and self-involution.

As we proceed, we find that a certain degree of vitalized Matter's physico-chemical arrangement brings a critical point 'of Reflection', which releases the whole train of the specific properties of the Human.

Finally, as a result of Reflection, we find a demand for, and a germinating principle of, complete and final incorruptibility, which permeates the very marrow of the Noosphere.

I mentioned earlier the curiously seductive power that the phenomena of gravity exerted on my mind while I was still very young. Was it by mere chance that the place of this mysterious energy, whose study was technically beyond my powers, was taken by another entity, as wide in its embrace and as powerful in its attraction, which gradually became apparent to me in a field that was both easier for me to work in and closer to the very axis of Cosmogenesis? This was no longer universal 'attraction' gradually drawing around itself the cosmic Mass – but that as yet undiscovered and unnamed power which forces Matter (as it concentrates under pressure) to arrange itself in ever larger molecules, differentiated and organic in structure. Beyond and above the *concentration-curve* I began to distinguish the *arrangement-curve* . . . not the gentle drift towards equilibrium and rest, but the irresistible 'Vortex' which spins into itself, always in the same direction,[13] the whole Stuff of things, from the most simple to the most complex: spinning it into ever more comprehensive and more astronomically complicated nuclei. And the result of this structural torsion is an increase (under the influence of interiorization) of consciousness, or a rise in psychic temperature, in the core of the corpuscles that are successively produced.[14]

The fantastic whirl of electrons, nuclei, atoms, extends into, ramifies and intensifies, unseen, in the deepest recesses of cells and cellular structure.

In that fundamental maelstrom I have for thirty years always seen but one thing: the deceptive superficial tranquillity of vitalized Matter simplifying, developing its essence, becoming transfigured.

Vitalized Matter: the fragile thing, whose apparent insignificance had always until that time disturbed and disappointed my yearning to worship.

Vitalized Matter: the delicate foam that floats precariously on the surface of the planetary crucible . . .

. . . And then suddenly I saw in you the very consistency of the World; it was welling up in you like sap, through every fibre, it was leaping up like a flame.

And as that happened, everything was bathed in light; my eyes had acquired a new sensitivity and I saw in things an ordered pattern which fitted the dual scale of values and of Time.

For in the first place, if Life is no longer what it might have appeared to be before this change, an anomaly, an accident, an exception – if, instead, it is simply the manifestation, reaching its peak in one particular spot, of a fundamental tide inherent in Matter – then, the minuteness of the quantity of organic substance at present scattered throughout space ceases in any way to detract from its *quality*. The rarity, in fact, of living beings is of no importance, if that rarity is only the effect and the visible expression of the difficulties which the play of chance presents to the emergence of a complexification-force which is under pressure everywhere in the Universe.

But there is a further point: as soon as I had recognized and accepted the great bio-physical principle of 'maximum arrangement' in Matter – which does not contradict, but rather complements or even dominates the mechanical principle of 'least effort' – as soon as I had done that, I could see quite clearly that once life has established a foothold somewhere in the World we might expect to see it not only expand but (as a result of ultra-complexification) reach the highest degree of intensity upon our vitalized planet. It was this that explained the persistent and irreversible rise of Cerebration and Consciousness over the surface of the Earth that runs through the geological eras. It was this, again, that showed me the full significance of the hominizing phenomenon of Reflection: Reflection, the 'cosmic' critical point which at a given moment is inevitably met and traversed by all Matter as soon as it exceeds a certain degree of psychic temperature and organization. Reflection: the transition (which is like a second birth) from simple Life to 'Life squared'. Reflection: the necessary and sufficient property that explains the marked discontinuity – the 'take-off' we might almost say – that we can observe experientially between Biosphere and Noosphere.

Matter is the matrix of Spirit. Spirit is the higher state of Matter.

These two propositions became the real axis of my inner vision and progress, and in them the word *spirit* was henceforth to bear a precise and concrete meaning. Spirit had become the *clearly defined term of a defined operation*.

Nowadays I might well come up against Freud's Unconscious or any one of the philosophical, artistic or literary theories of intuition that have become so fashionable since the First World War. At that time my position was firmly and permanently established: I had seen, once and for all, that when the World is left to itself it does not fall in the direction of obscurity; with all its vastness and all its weight it falls forward in equilibrium, towards the light. And in future nothing can make me swerve from this irrevocable conviction that it is in the form, I do not say of Concepts, but of *Thought* that the Stuff of things gradually concentrates in the pure state, in a cosmic peak: and this it does in its most stable form, which means in the form that has become the most completely irreversible.

However, if this is to be correctly understood, it calls for some elaboration; and for this I must now turn not to some bygone period of my life but rather to the most advanced stage of my inner exploration in search of the Heart of things.

c. The Evolution of the Noosphere

There is, fortunately, an ever increasing number of persons who can overcome certain ingrained intellectual habits and certain anatomical illusions and are beginning to distinguish a Noosphere which is like a halo around the Biosphere; but even among these, agreement is far from being reached as yet on the question of determining whether this 'corona' of *reflective* peri-terrestrial substance has, or has not, finished its planetary evolution.

Now, it is precisely on this crucial question of a *standstill* in anthropogenesis that, in the course of these last years, I have come to take up a decisive attitude: driven to it by the full force of the evidence I find within myself.

It is already a long time (cf., for example, *How I Believe*) since I noted how clearly Mankind (as we can see from the vestiges of its non-organization) discloses the possibility, and so the imminence of, some state of higher unification. *A priori* (judging, that is, from its potentiality for ultra-arrangement) we could say that hominization is still going on.

Very well: since 1939, it is the reality of this organo-psychic current that has constantly been apparent to me, in the light of the facts, with growing clarity. And this has had the result of giving a definitive form to, and a definitive goal for, my innate yearning for Plenitude and Consistence.

If we were to believe those who preach a certain sort of 'common sense', we would say that the process of cosmic involution from which the human zoological type emerged towards the end of the Tertiary came to a complete standstill some thousands of years ago. Could Mankind, they are continually asking us, produce anything superior to Beethoven or Plato? On the contrary, is my answer: how can we fail to see that the process of convergence from which we emerged, body and soul, is continuing to envelop us more closely than ever, to grip us, in the form of – under the folds of, we might say – a gigantic planetary contraction?

The irresistible 'setting' or cementing together of a thinking mass (Mankind) which is continually more compressed upon itself by the simultaneous multiplication and expansion of its individual elements: there is not one of us, surely, who is not almost agonizingly aware of this, in the very fibre of his being. This is one of the things that no one today would even try to deny: we can all see the fantastic anatomical structure of a vast phylum whose branches, instead of diverging as they normally do, are ceaselessly folding in upon one another ever more closely, like some monstrous inflorescence – like, indeed, an enormous flower folding-in upon itself; the literally global physiology of an organism in which production, nutrition, the machine, research, and the legacy of heredity are, beyond any doubt, building up to planetary dimensions; the increasing impossibility of the individual's attaining economic and intellectual self-sufficiency – although we recognize all this, why is it that we are still, for the most part, obstinately blind to the cosmogenic (or, more correctly, 'noogenic') significance of the phenomenon? Why, in other words, do we not recognize in the accelerating totalization against which we are struggling, sometimes so desperately, simply the normal continuation at a level above ourselves of that process which generates Thought on Earth? Why do we not see that it is a continuing process of Cerebration?

Technology and Socialization combined have forced us to recognize that man's *vision* is being enlarged in certain fields (particularly in that of pure Science); but we are still refusing to accept the possibility of continuing improvement, passed on from one generation to another, in the actual *organ* of this vision. It was from this obstinate prejudice, from this persistent illusion, that I one day found I had completely shaken myself free. That, thirty or forty thousand years ago, the individual power to feel and think reached its peak – at least for the time being – that is a possibility. But that Hominization in its essence (that is, the concentration upon itself of global terrestrial Psychism) should now have come to a final halt: to my mind, that is formally contradicted by the fantastic spectacle, staring us in the face, of a rapidly rising *collective Reflection*, moving in step with an increasingly unitary organization.

We have only to look around us to see how complexity (under compression) and psychic 'Temperature' are still rising: and rising no longer on the scale of the individual but now on that of the planet. This indication is so familiar to us that we cannot but recognize the objective, experiential, reality of a directionally controlled transformation of the Noosphere 'as a whole'.*

Zoologically and psychologically speaking, Man can at last be seen in the cosmic integrity of his trajectory, on which, however, he is still at only an embryonic stage – if we look ahead we can already see the outlines of a wide fringe of ULTRA-HUMAN.

Writing in the year 1950, I can say that the evolution of my inner vision culminates in the acceptance of this evident fact, that there is a 'creative' tide which (as a strict statistic consequence of their increasing powers of self-determination) is carrying the human 'mega-molecules' towards an almost unbelievable quasi 'mono-molecular' state; and in that state, as the biological laws of Union[15] demand, each *ego* is destined to be forced convulsively beyond itself into some mysterious *super-ego*.

For a long time now (in fact, ever since the moment when I saw the balance of the World reversed from what lies behind to what lies ahead) I have always had a feeling that at the head of Cosmogenesis there stands a Pole, not simply of attraction, but of *consolidation* – and that means a Pole which imparts the quality of *irreversibility*.

And so finally this mysterious focal point – which is made possible or even demanded by a maturing of man that cannot biodynamically reach its final critical point of Ultra-Reflection unless it is fostered and carried along by a growing hope of immortality – this mysterious focal point of Noogenesis became experientially real for me. In one single and irresistible movement, as the result of convergence, the Incorruptible of which I had

* Teilhard uses the English words, 'as a whole'.

38

always dreamed was *simultaneously* becoming universalized and personalized.

The 'piece of iron' of my first days has long been forgotten. In its place it is the Consistence of the Universe, in the form of Omega Point, that I now hold, concentrated (whether above me or, rather, in the depths of my being, I cannot say) into one single indestructible centre, WHICH I CAN LOVE.

III. THE CHRISTIC, OR THE CENTRIC

Preliminary Note: the Reflection or Revelation of Omega Point

The discovery of Omega brings to a close what I might call the natural branch of the inner trajectory I followed in my search for the ultimate consistence of the Universe. As we have just seen, it was not simply in the vague direction of 'Spirit' but in the form of a well-defined supra-personal focal point that a Heart of total Matter was disclosed to my experiential quest. Had I been an unbeliever and left entirely to the promptings of my Sense of Plenitude, I think that my inner exploration would have led me to the same spiritual peak; and it is even possible that a close rational study of the cosmic properties of Omega ('the complex unit in which the organic sum of the reflective elements of the World becomes irreversible within a transcendent Super-ego') would belatedly have led me, in a final stage, to recognize in an incarnate God the true Reflection, on our Noosphere, of the ultimate nucleus of totalization and consolidation that is bio-psychologically demanded by the evolution of a *reflective* living Mass.

To be completely Man, it may well be that I would have been obliged to become Christian.

But all this is gratuitous assumption.

The fact is, fortunately for me, I was born right into the Catholic 'phylum'; and that means into the very centre of the privileged zone in which the ascending cosmic force of 'Complexity-Consciousness' joins the descending (and so drawing up to itself) flood of personal and personalizing attraction which is introduced between Heaven and Earth by the influence of Hominization.

The result of this was that in step with the spontaneous evolution in me of the innate (or 'chromosomic') cosmic sense analysed above (Sections 1 and 2), another process (inaugurated in this instance *by upbringing*) has never ceased to operate in my mind and heart: by this I mean the awakening of a certain *Christic Sense*. In recording, as I now must, the phases of this process I shall have once again to return to my childhood memories.

The cosmic sense and the christic sense: these two axes were born in me quite independently of one another, it would seem, and it was only after a long time and a great deal of hard work that I finally came to understand how, through and beyond the Human, the two were linked together, converged upon one another, and were in fact one and the same.

a. The Heart of Jesus

For all its unitive and 'communicant' power, and for all the emotional charge that from the very beginning resulted from that power, my contact with, and consciousness of, the Universe was bound, if left on its own, never to go beyond a certain comparatively low degree of intimacy and warmth. Moving along the cosmic and biological road, Omega Point always lay just outside my grasp; this was because of a logical reconstruction which presented me with a 'deduced and conjectural' Entity rather than one entered into and experienced. A meeting of Centre with Centre, of Heart with Heart, these were anticipated rather than realized. On my part, no doubt, there was an effort of passionate intensity – but as yet there was no real love. In consequence there was a whole world between the two concerned.

It called for a spark to fall upon me, if the glow was to burst into flame.

That spark, through which 'my Universe', as yet but *half* personalized, *was to attain centricity by being amorized*, that spark undoubtedly came to me through my mother: it was through her that it reached me from the current of Christian mysticism and both illuminated and inflamed my childish soul.

Later, I was often to be astonished at seeing the extreme difficulty that many well disposed minds (many hungry minds, even) found in conceiving the mere *possibility* of a super-hominized love.

This was far from being the case with me.

Was this simply the effect of my earliest upbringing? Or was it, perhaps, the result of a certain 'psychic mutation' which gradually makes the Noosphere sensitive to the influences of Omega in the vicinity of the Christian axis? Or was it both at the same time?

Those are questions I cannot answer.

All I know is, that thanks to a sort of habit which has always been ingrained in me, I have never, at any moment of my life, experienced the least difficulty in addressing myself to God as to a supreme SOMEONE. So true is this that I now understand that a certain 'love of the Invisible' has always been active in me,[16] parallel to the 'congenital' cosmic sense which, as we have seen, is the 'backbone' of my inner life.

This appetite was a gift to me from Heaven, and after it had first, working undetected, nourished my *innate* appetite for the Earth it ultimately came out into the open and effected a confluence with it. And this it did through a process of *universalization*, whose first two phases may be described, as I remember them, as a 'materialization', soon to be followed by an 'energizing', of the notion of divine Love.

To take the 'materialization' of Divine Love first.

Biologically speaking, how could it have been otherwise in my case?

Sucked in with my mother's milk, a 'supernatural' Sense of the Divine had flowed into me side by side with the 'natural' Sense of Plenitude. Each of these two appetites strove to be exclusive, but neither could wipe out the other. The only conceivable result of their conflict, therefore, was an assimilation of the supernatural (the less primitive and, genetically speaking, the more external) by the natural. And the only way in which the assimilation could be effected was by an interior adjustment of the Divine to the Evolutive: that is to say, an adjustment to the psychological law, proper to my nature, of being unable to worship anything except from a starting-point in the Tangible and Resistant.

My progress in this direction was made easier by the fact that 'my mother's God' was primarily, for me as much as for her, the *incarnate* Word. This sufficed for the establishment of a first contact, through the Humanity of Jesus, between the two halves of my fundamental being, the 'Christian' and the 'pagan'. It was precisely in that contact, however, that there reappeared the difficulty I have already mentioned of perceiving 'the Consistence of the Human'.

How strange and ingenuous are the reactions that take place in the brain of a child! I can remember so well (see below, note 8) witnessing for the first time the distressing sight of a lock of hair being burnt up in the fire, and how my disappointment with the Organic instantaneously reacted on the very person of Christ . . . If I was to be able *fully to worship* Christ, it was essential that as a first step I should be able to give him 'solidity'.

And it was at this point in the story of my spiritual life that there emerged (and now I must beg my reader to suppress his smile) the central, seminal, part played by the 'devotion' with which my mother constantly sustained me: devotion to the Heart of Jesus, little though she suspected the transformations that were to be effected in it by my insatiable yearning for cosmic Organicity.

Everybody knows the historical background of the cult of the

Sacred Heart (or of the Love of Christ): how it was always latent in the Church and then in the France of Louis XIV assumed an astonishingly vigorous form, which was at the same time oddly limited both in the object to which it was directed ('Reparation') and in its symbol (the heart of our Saviour, depicted with curiously anatomical realism!).

The remains of this narrow view can still, unfortunately, be seen today, both in a form of worship which is always obsessed by the idea of sin and in an iconography which we must needs deplore without too much vexation. For my own part, however, I can say that at no time has its influence held the least attraction for my piety.

For the pious person of the seventeenth century the 'Sacred Heart' was, in effect, 'a part' (both material and formal) of Jesus – a selected, detached, part of the Redeemer: as happens when we isolate and enlarge *some detail* of a picture in order to be able to admire it more conveniently. My own experience was quite different. The moment I saw a mysterious patch of crimson and gold delineated in the very centre of the Saviour's breast, I found what I was looking for – a way of finally *escaping* from everything that so distressed me in the complicated, fragile and individual organization of the *Body* of Jesus. It was an astounding release! Not by a mere adjustment of the aperture (as in a camera), but as an effect of convergence and concentration, the whole physical and spiritual reality of Christ was visibly condensed for me into a well-defined, compact object from which all accidental and restrictive particularity disappeared: the first approach of a Christic beyond Christ, disclosing a remarkable homology between this new 'milieu' and the Metallic or Mineral which, at that very same time, were dominant in me – on the other side of the wall that still ran across my soul.

It would be difficult for me to convey how deeply and forcefully, and with what continuity (long before the notion of the 'Universal-Christ' became explicitly coherent in me) my religious life in the pre-war years developed under the sign of the

Heart of Jesus, *understood in this way*, and with the sense of wonder it aroused in me. At that time, the more I tried to pray, the more deeply did God 'materialize' for me in a reality that was at once spiritual and tangible; in that reality, though as yet I hardly guessed it, the great synthesis was beginning to be effected in which my life's whole effort was to be summed up: the synthesis of the Above with the Ahead.

It was the immersion of the Divine in the Corporeal: and an inevitable reaction brought the transfiguration (or transmutation) of the Corporeal into an incredible Energy of Radiation.

In a first stage, my mother's Christ was in some way 'de-individualized' for me into a form that was 'substantially' hardly representational. But then came a second stage when this humano-divine 'solid' (like my earlier piece of iron, and under the same psychic pressure) lit up and exploded from within. There was no longer a patch of crimson in the centre of Jesus, but a glowing core of fire, whose splendour embraced every contour – first those of the God-Man – and then those of all things that lay within his ambience.[17]

I was still not yet 'in theology' when, through and under the symbol of the 'Sacred Heart', the Divine had already taken on for me the form, the consistence and the properties of an ENERGY, of a FIRE: by that I mean that it had become able to insinuate itself everywhere, to be metamorphosed into no matter what; and so, *in as much as it was patient of being universalized*, it could in future force its way into, and so amorize, the cosmic Milieu in which at exactly the same moment I was (through another half of myself) engaged in making my home.

b. The Universal Christ

On one side – in my 'pagan' *ego* – a Universe which was becoming personalized through convergence.

And on the other side – in my Christian ego – a Person (the Person of Christ) who was becoming universalized through Radiation.

By each of these two roads, that is to say, the Divine was joining itself, through all Matter, to all the Human, in the direction of the infinity of the ages lying ahead . . .

It is in this confluence, through complementary channels, of Heaven and the World, that the advances (and, I must not forget to add, the conflicts) of my interior life have continually been realized: always, moreover, as the years go by, with ever greater clarity and passion.

Let us try, then, to understand both the advances and the conflicts.

1. The Conflicts

Speaking in general terms we may say that until quite recent times, and in the West, mysticism (even Christian mysticism) has never doubted but that God must be looked for only 'in heaven', that is to say in more or less direct and profound discontinuity with 'here below'.

To be spiritualized = to be de-materialized.

Such was (and such, in a static Cosmos, *had* to be) the basic equation that expresses Holiness.

Yet all the time (as we have seen) the natural movement of my thought had been carrying me not, indeed, in the opposite direction to, but athwart this traditional orientation. For me, Matter was the matrix of Consciousness; and, wherever we looked, Consciousness, born of Matter, was always advancing towards some Ultra-Human. In other words, a *second species of Spirit* was emerging – and this species was no longer directly above our heads – it lay transversely, appearing, we might say, on the horizon . . . In the inmost depths of my soul[18] a struggle, between the God of the Above and a sort of new God of the Ahead was, through structural necessity, being produced by the definitive co-existence and the irresistible meeting in my heart of the cosmic Sense and the Christic Sense.

I can look back and distinguish the first traces of this opposition in my years at school, when I remember my pathetic attempts to reconcile the evangelism (over-narrow, we must admit) of the *Imitation*, on which I drew for my morning prayers, with the attraction I found in Nature. Later, as a 'junior' in Jersey, I seriously considered the possibility of completely giving up the 'Science of Rocks', which I then found so exciting, in order to devote myself entirely to so-called 'supernatural' activities. And if I did not at that time 'run off the rails', it is to the robust common sense of Père T. (the novice-master)[19] that I owe it. In the event, Père T. confined himself to assuring me that what the God of the Cross was looking for in me was the 'natural' expansion of my being as well as its sanctification – without explaining how or why. What he said, however, was enough to leave me with a firm grasp of both ends of the line. And so I emerged from that trial unscathed. Gradually, through the synthesis which is effected by experience, detachment and attachment, renunciation and development, automatically came together as one within me: and this was realized in a deliberate change of direction to the *transverse*. I explained the theory of this, about 1927, in the first chapter of *Le Milieu Divin*.

Nevertheless, theory is still a long way from practice.

Even today I am still learning by experience the dangers to which – by an inner law and necessity – he is exposed who finds himself led away from the well-beaten but now under-humanized path of a certain traditional ascesis, as he seeks in the direction of Heaven for a road (a road which is not a mean but a synthesis) where the whole dynamism of Matter and Flesh is directed into the genesis of Spirit.[20]

Supposing a man, in all sincerity of heart, has one day made up his mind to do what *every* man who seeks for holiness will increasingly find himself obliged to do: that is, to allow the ascensional Faith in God and the forward-driving Faith in the Ultra-human to react freely upon one another in the depths of his being – then such a man will at times be unable to shake off a feeling of terror. He will not be able to hold back, but he will be frightened by the novelty, the boldness and at the same time the paradoxical potentialities of attitudes that he finds himself, intellectually and emotionally, obliged to adopt if he is to be faithful to his fundamental aim: which is to attain Heaven by bringing Earth to its fulfilment.

To Christify Matter: that sums up the whole venture of my innermost being . . . a grand and glorious venture; (and I still tremble often, even as I pursue it) – but I found it impossible not to hazard myself in it, so powerful was the force with which the levels of the Universal and the Personal came together and gradually closed up, over my head, to form one single vault.

2. Conflict becomes Progress

Christ. His Heart. A Fire: a fire with the power to penetrate all things – and which was now gradually spreading unchecked.

At the root of this invasion and envelopment I can distinguish, I believe, the rapidly increasing importance that was being assumed in my spiritual life by the Sense of 'the Will of God': fidelity to the divine Will, by which I mean fidelity to a *directed and realized* omnipresence, which can be apprehended both actively and passively in every element of the World and in all its events. Although at first I did not precisely realize the bridge by which this eminently Christian attitude connected my love of Christ and my love of Things, nevertheless I have always, ever since the first years of my religious life, gladly surrendered myself to this active feeling of communion with God through the Universe. It was a decisive emergence of this 'pan-Christic' mysticism, finally matured in the two great atmospheres of Asia and the War, that was reflected in 1924 and 1927 by *The Mass on the World* and *Le Milieu Divin*.

A decisive emergence, let me repeat – and one that I could at that time regard as complete. In fact, however, it still lacked something that was needed for its full release.

Let me explain what this was.

Today, when I re-read the so undisguisedly fervent pages of *Le Milieu Divin*, I am astonished to find how fully all the essential features of my Christo-cosmic vision were already determined at the time I wrote the book. On the other hand, I note with some surprise the vagueness and fluidity of the picture of the Universe that I still had in those days.

It is true that as a basis for the pan-communion by which I was then obsessed and intoxicated, I already possessed a World made up of organically woven elements and organically linked layers. But this enveloping organicity, the specific foundation of the Christic Diaphany, still existed for me, both spiritually and sensibly, in a form that I can only describe as diffuse. At that time, about 1930, the Convergence of the cosmos, with its whole train of consequent ideas (the Law of Complexity-Consciousness, the Confluence of human branches, the existence of an Omega Point at the head of Noogenesis) – none of that had as yet become distinctly clear to me. My then 'Weltanschauung' did not go far beyond a vast Plurality, whose nebula was illuminated by, but not yet concentrated in, the rays of the divine Star.

It was to be the task and the never-ending delight of the next twenty years to see, as I looked around me, how – step by step, and in step with one another – the two Densities came to reinforce one another: the Christic Density, and the cosmic Density of a World whose 'communicant power' I could see constantly rising as its 'convergent power' also rose.

At first, if I was to 'mould and experience' Christ in all things, all that I had at hand for this purpose was only the *detail* of events and beings. Gradually, as my mind came to understand the reality of the one vast psychogenic involution of the whole of Matter upon itself, so each new circle that I traced out in this fantastic spiral was to give solidity to the divine Ascendancy and to make me more tangibly conscious of its grasp.

Not in a metaphysical but in a *physical* sense, the Energy of Incarnation was to flow into, and so illuminate and give warmth to, ever wider and more tightly encircling forms of embrace.

And this led up to the moment when the upper term of that movement was reached, and it became possible to discern a wonderful confluence: no longer merely in a vague way between Christ and Matter, but between a Christ who was distinctly seen as 'evolver' and a cosmic Centre which was positively attributed to Evolution.

Thus I reached the Heart of the universalized Christ coinciding with the heart of amorized Matter.

c. The Divine Milieu

As a result of the particular structure of a mind polarized simultaneously in the plane of Heaven and in that of Earth, there was a danger, as we have seen, that two tendencies might cause the progress of my evolution to deviate as it advanced. If I followed the eastern and pagan line, I might allow my being to relax and dissolve into the universal Sphere. Or I might do the exact opposite and try to escape from that Sphere by tearing myself away or making a sharp cleavage. These were my Scylla and Charybdis, retrogressive materialization or dehumanizing spiritualization; and if, by the grace of God, I managed to avoid them both, it was because the day came when I saw that a World *which had already been recognized as essentially convergent* offered a third road towards Unity: and the right road, too. This consisted in reaching, at the heart of the cosmic Sphere, the mysterious double point where the Multiple, now completely ordered in its own organic structure, is reflected upon itself and so emerges from within into a Transcendent.

Here we move into what is indeed a remarkable, an astonishing, region where the Cosmic, the Human and the Christic meet and so open up a new domain, the *Centric*; and there the manifold oppositions which constitute the unhappiness and anxieties of our life begin to disappear.

Under the irresistible pressure of a planet that is contracting upon itself, we constantly feel, in ourselves and all around ourselves, a heightening of the antagonism between the 'tangential' forces that make us dependent upon one another, and the 'radial' aspirations that urge us towards attaining the incommunicable core of our own person. We recoil from the prospect of an inevitable totalization which threatens to imprison us in a sort of 'secondary Matter' made up of a mass of accumulated determinisms. We are terrified, too, when we see that mechanization may bring an end that is as much to be dreaded as a death through disintegration and return to 'Prime Matter'.

It is like a dream; we feel that we are caught up in the gyrations of some infernal circle.

And yet, it is from this very nightmare, in fact, that we are awoken by the first rays of a universal Centre of convergence and attraction, in which the bonds that make us one whole reach the upper limit of their complexity and then tend to merge into the magnetic force that pulls our *ego* ever more rapidly into what lies ahead. This is the miraculous effect that is specific to the Centric, which does not dissolve nor subordinate the elements it brings together, but personalizes them. And this because its way of absorbing them is constantly to 'centrify' them more and more. We may, indeed, say that at these high latitudes of the Universe Totalization reduces the Multiple to the One by synthesis, and so acts as a liberating agent. In other words, Matter becomes Spirit at just the same pace as love begins to spread universally.

From the first moment, of course, when, to my inner eye, 'the Gold of Spirit' replaced 'the Crimson of Matter' and started to swing towards 'the Incandescence of Some One', the World had begun, at least as a logical consequence, to affect me emotionally as a blaze of fire. By the mere appearance at the peak of Evolution of the Personal, the Universe was *potentially* becoming for me something that loved and could be loved. Even so, it called for nothing short of the coincidence of Christ with Omega Point for my eyes to be opened, in an explosion of dazzling flashes, to the astonishing phenomenon of a general global conflagration – the effect of *total amorization*.

Love . . . since all time, this strange force has puzzled and fascinated the masters of human thought by its ubiquity, its fiery vigour and the infinitely variegated spectrum of the forms it assumes; but I now see that it is only in the Christo-centric area of a noogenetic Universe that it is released in the pure state and so displays its astonishing power to *transform* everything and *replace* everything.

From the point of view of the convergent Evolution to which sixty years of varied experience and of thought has introduced me and in which I am now at home, the whole cosmic Event may be reduced in its essence to one single vast process of arrangement, whose mechanism (that is, the use of the effects of Large Numbers and the play of Chance) is governed by statistical necessity: so that at every moment it releases a given quantity of events that cause distress (failures, disintegrations, death . . .) There are *two sides* to this operation, the *constructive* and the *destructive*; and when Christ is installed at Omega Point it is both these two sides that are covered and permeated by a flood of unitive force. In one great surge, Cosmogenesis becomes personalized, both in the things it adds, which *centrify us for Christ*, and in the things it subtracts, which *draw us out of our own centres onto him*; thus it suddenly takes on, even in its most inexorable and most veiled determinisms, the form of a contact at innumerable points with a supreme Pole of attraction and completion. A current of love is all at once released, to spread over the whole breadth and depth of the World: and this it does not as though it were some super-added warmth of fragrance, but as a fundamental essence which will metamorphose all things, assimilate and take the place of all . . .

For a long time Science has made us familiar with the idea that all physical energy, if traced back evolutively 'to the bottom', tends to dissipate into heat within a World that has lost tension and vitality. Is it not most remarkable that an integral Energetics of the Universe should lead us in the end to a concept that exactly matches and complements our former idea? If it is taken to its limit in the direction of a cosmic pole of unification, everything we experience and even everything we see displays a singular 'bias' for *transforming itself* into love. This means that while love seemed initially to be no more than the charm, the allure, and then, later, the operative essence of all spiritual activity, it tends gradually, as experienced by us, to become the chief part of that activity – and finally its only, and supreme, form.

Sola caritas . . .

When all is said and done, I can see this: I managed to climb up to the point where the Universe became apparent to me as a great rising surge, in which all the work that goes into serious enquiry, all the will to create, all the acceptance of suffering, converge ahead into a single dazzling spear-head – now, at the end of my life, I can stand on the peak I have scaled and continue to look ever more closely into the future, and there, with ever more assurance, see the ascent of God.

d. Towards the Discovery of God, or an Appeal to Him who Comes

For a long time, absorbed in the delight of seeing how every single thing around me was simultaneously centred, consolidated and amorized, I confined my attention to one thing only in the vast phenomenon of Classification which the coincidence of the World and God disclosed to me; and that was the rise within my own self of the forces of Communion. Everything was directed towards the intensification of the Stuff of the cosmos, so that in that Stuff the Presence of God might be intensified for me. I can see quite clearly how the inspiration behind 'The Mass on the World' and *Le Milieu Divin* and their writing belong to that somewhat self-centred and self-enclosed period of my interior life.

The reason for this was that by one of those odd effects of inhibition that so often prevent us from recognizing what is staring us in the face, I failed to understand that as God 'metamorphized' the World from the depths of matter to the peaks of Spirit, so in addition the World must inevitably and to the same degree 'endomorphize' God. As a direct consequence of the unitive process by which God is revealed to us, he in some way 'transforms himself' as he incorporates us. So, it is no longer a matter of simply seeing Him and allowing oneself to be enveloped and penetrated by Him – we have to do more: we have *pari passu* (if not first of all) to disclose Him (or even, in one sense of the word, 'complete' Him) ever more fully. Such, today, seems to me the essential step to be taken by hominized Evolution, and such its essential concern.

All around us, and within our own selves, God is in process of 'changing', as a result of the coincidence of his magnetic power and our own Thought. As the 'Quantity of cosmic Union' rises, so his brilliance increases and the glow of his colouring grows richer. There at last we recognize, and can express in words, the Great Event, the Great Tidings.

Ever since my childhood an enigmatic force had been impelling me, apparently in conflict with the 'Supernatural', towards some Ultra-human; and in trying to pin it down I had become accustomed to regard it as emanating not from God but from some rival Star. All I had to do, then, was to bring that Star into conjunction with God and dependence upon Him.

The time had now come when I could see one thing: that, from the depths of the cosmic future as well as from the heights of Heaven, it was still God, it was *always the same God*, who was calling me. It was a *God of the Ahead* who had suddenly appeared athwart *the traditional God of the Above*, so that henceforth we can no longer *worship fully* unless we superimpose those two images so that they form *one*.

A new Faith in which the ascensional Faith that rises up towards a Transcendent, and the propulsive Faith that drives towards an Immanent, form a single compound – a new Charity in which all the Earth's dynamic passions combine as they are divinized: it is this, I now see with a vision that will never leave me, that the World is desperately in need of at this very moment, if it is not to collapse.

Classical metaphysics had accustomed us to seeing in the World – which it regarded as an object of 'Creation' – a sort of extrinsic product which had issued from God's supreme *efficient power* as the fruit of his overflowing benevolence. I find myself now irresistibly led – and this precisely because it enables me both to act and to love in the fullest degree – to a view that harmonizes with the spirit of St Paul: I see in the World a mysterious product of completion and fulfilment for the Absolute Being himself.[21] It is no longer *participated Being of extra-position and divergence*, but *participated Being of pleromization and convergence*. It is the effect, no longer of creative Causality, but of creative Union.

At the same time, too, I see that it is Christ who first makes himself 'cosmic' and then in some way makes himself 'absolute'.

There is an objection that we more and more often hear raised by Gentiles against Christians: that, by the very fact of the inter-position of Jesus between Man and God, our notion of God is arrested and, we might say, atrophied in its developments. As a result, they say, Christianity no longer stimulates the need to worship, for the modern mind, but rather paralyses it. How often have I myself come close to believing this – and how often, quite apart from that, have I not heard it said!

It is as though we believed in a Christ who diminished the stature of God . . .

How quickly, however, and how permanently, that fatal suspicion vanishes the very moment we become sensitive to the mysticism of today and so perceive that precisely because of those characteristics that would at first appear to confine him too strictly to the particular, *an historically incarnate God* is on the contrary the only God who can satisfy not only the inflexible laws of a Universe in which nothing is produced or appears except *by way of birth*, but also the irrepressible aspirations of our own mind.

For the basic truth is:

If we say 'God of the Above'+'God of the Ahead', what does

this new equation, fundamental to all Religion in the future, give us if not an ultimate whose dimensions are 'theocosmic', that is *christic*?

In a system of Creative Union, it is not only the Universe but God himself who is necessarily 'Christified' in Omega, at the upper limits of Cosmogenesis. In other words, 'evolved' Monotheism, around which all that is best in the Earth's religious energies undoubtedly seems to be concentrating, is moving to its logical and biological fulfilment in the direction of some Pan-Christism.

With no limit to his capacity for being extended and adapted to the World's new dimension and, in addition, with an inexhaustible charge of evolutive energy for our hearts – so there is growing in our firmament, to the scale of and at the demand of the *Ultra-human*, a true *Super-Christ*, in all the radiance of *Super-Charity*.

Prayer to the Ever-Greater Christ
Because, Lord, by every innate impulse and through all the hazards of my life I have been driven ceaselessly to search for you and to set you in the heart of the universe of matter, I shall have the joy, when death comes, of closing my eyes amidst the splendour of a universal transparency aglow with fire . . .

It is as if the fact of bringing together and connecting the two poles, tangible and intangible, external and internal, of the world which bears us onwards had caused everything to burst into flames and set everything free.

In the guise of a tiny babe in its mother's arms, obeying the great law of birth, you came, Lord Jesus, to swell in my infant soul; and then, as you re-enacted in me – and in so doing extended the range of – your growth through the Church, that same humanity which once was born and dwelt in Palestine began now to spread out gradually everywhere like an iridescence of unnumbered hues through which, without destroying anything, your presence penetrated – and endued with supervitality – every other presence about me.

And all this took place because, in a universe which was disclosing itself to me as structurally convergent, you, by right of your resurrection, had assumed the dominating position of all-inclusive Centre in which everything is gathered together.

A fantastic molecular swarm which – either falling like snow from the inmost recesses of the Infinitely Diffuse – or on the other hand surging up like smoke from the explosion of some Infinitely Simple – an awe-inspiring multitude, indeed, which whirls us around in its tornado! . . . It is in this terrifying granular Energy that you, Lord – so that I may be able the better to touch you, or rather, who knows? to be more closely embraced by you – have clothed yourself for me: nay, it is of this that you have formed your very Body. And for many years I saw in it no more than a wonderful contact with an already completed Perfection . . .

Until that day, and it was only yesterday, when you made me realize that when you espoused Matter it was not merely its Immensity and its Organicity that you had taken on: what you did was to absorb, concentrate, and make entirely your own, its unfathomable reserves of spiritual energies.

So true is this that ever since that time you have become for my mind and heart much more than He who was and who is; you have become *He who shall be.*

For some of your servants, Lord, the World, our New World – the world of nuclei, of atoms and genes – has become a source of constant anxiety: because it seems to us now so mobile, so irresistible, and so big! The increasing probability (to which we conspire to close our eyes) of other thinking planets in the firmament . . . the unmistakable rebound of an evolution that has become capable, through planetary effort, of governing its own direction and speed . . . the rising over our horizon, as an effect of ultra-reflection, of an Ultra-human . . . all this seems frightening to a man who, as he still shrinks from flinging himself into the great ocean of Matter, is afraid that he may see his God burst asunder in the acquisition of a new dimension . . .

Yet can anything, Lord, in fact do more for my understanding and my soul to make you an object of love, the only object of love, than to see that you – the Centre ever opened into your own deepest core – continue to grow in intensity, that there is an added glow to your lustre, at the same pace as *you pleromize yourself* by gathering together the Universe and subjecting it ever more fully at the heart of your being ('until the time for returning, You and the World in You, to the bosom of Him from whom You came')?

The more the years go by, Lord, the more I believe that I can see that in myself and in the world around me the most important though unvoiced concern of modern Man is much less a struggle for the possession of the World than a search for a way of escaping from it. The agony of feeling that one is imprisoned in the cosmic Bubble, not so much spatially as ontologically! The fretful hunt for a way out for Evolution – or, more exactly, for its point of focus! In the modern world, that is the sorrow, the price to be paid for a growing planetary Reflection, that lies heavy, but as yet hardly recognized, on the soul of both Christian and Gentile.

As mankind emerges into consciousness of the movement that carries it along, it has a continually more urgent need of a Direction and a Solution ahead and above, to which it will at last be able to consecrate itself.

Who, then is this God, no longer the God of the old Cosmos but the God of the new Cosmogenesis – so constituted precisely because the effect of a mystical operation that has been going on for two thousand years has been to disclose in you, beneath the Child of Bethlehem and the Crucified, the moving Principle and the all-embracing Nucleus of the World itself? Who is this God for whom our generation looks so eagerly? Who but you, Jesus, who represent him and bring him to us?

Lord of consistence and union, you whose *distinguishing mark* and *essence* is the power indefinitely to grow greater, without distortion or loss of continuity, to the measure of the mysterious

Matter whose Heart you fill and all whose movements you ultimately control – Lord of my childhood and Lord of my last days – God, complete in relation to yourself and yet, for us, continually being born – God, who, because you offer yourself to our worship as 'evolver' and 'evolving', are henceforth the only being that can satisfy us – sweep away at last the clouds that still hide you – the clouds of hostile prejudice and those, too, of false creeds.

Let your universal Presence spring forth in a blaze that is at once Diaphany and Fire.

O ever-greater Christ!

CONCLUSION

The Feminine, or the Unitive[22]

The living heart of the Tangible is the Flesh. And for Man the Flesh means Woman.

Ever since my childhood I had been engaged in the search for the Heart of Matter, and so it was inevitable that sooner or later I should come up against the Feminine. The only curious thing is that in the event it was not until my thirtieth year that this happened: so powerful was the fascination that the Impersonal and the Generalized held for me.

It was, therefore, a strange time-lag.

On the other hand, it was rewarding, because the new energy entered into my soul at the very moment, on the eve of the war, when my Sense of the Cosmos and Sense of Man were emerging from their childhood; thus there was no longer any danger that it might divert or dissipate my forces. Instead, it was superimposed, at just the right moment, on a world of spiritual aspirations whose vastness, still a little lacking in warmth, needed only that energy in order to ferment and become completely organized.

As I tell the story in these pages of my inner vision, I would be leaving out an essential element, or atmosphere, if I did not add in conclusion that from the critical moment when I rejected many of the old moulds in which my family life and my religion had formed me and began to wake up and express myself in terms that were really my own, I have experienced no form of self-development without some feminine eye turned on me, some feminine influence at work.

When I say this, you will understand, of course, that I mean simply that general, half-worshipping, homage which sprang from the depths of my being and was paid to those women whose warmth and charm have been absorbed, drop by drop, into the life-blood of my most cherished ideas.

In such a matter it is impossible for me to use exact language or to draw an exact picture, – on the other hand, what I can speak about with certainty is a double conviction that progressively asserted itself in me from my contact with facts; let me, now that I can write with all the serenity and impartiality that come with years, tell you about this.

In the first place, it seems to be indisputable (both logically and factually) that there can be for man – even if he be devoted to the service of a Cause or of a God, and however great that devotion – no road to spiritual maturity or plenitude except through some 'emotional' influence, whose function is to sensitize his understanding and stimulate, at least initially, his capacity for love. Every day supplies more irrefutable evidence that no man at all can dispense with the Feminine, any more than he can dispense with light, or oxygen, or vitamins.

Secondly, however primordial in human psychism the plenifying encounter of the sexes may be, and however essential to its structure, there is nothing to prove (indeed, the opposite is much more true) that we yet have an exact idea of the functioning of this fundamental complementarity or of the best forms in which it can be effected. We have a marriage that is always polarized, socially, towards reproduction, and a religious perfection that is always represented, theologically, in terms of separation: and there can be no doubt but that we lack a third road between the two. I do not mean a *middle* road, but a higher, a road that is *demanded* by the revolutionary transformation that has recently been effected in our thought by the transposition of the notion of 'spirit'. For the spirit that comes from dematerialization, we have seen, we have substituted the spirit that comes from synthesis. *Materia matrix.* It is no longer a matter of retreating (by abstinence) from the unfathomable spiritual powers that still lie dormant under the mutual attraction of the sexes, but of conquering them by sublimation. Such, I am ever more convinced, is the hidden essence of Chastity, and such the magnificent task that awaits it.[23]

Both those assertions fall into place and are justified if we look at them from the following point of view:

In my interpretation of Noogenesis, I have so far emphasized the phenomenon of individual super-centration, which causes the consciousness of the corpuscular to fold back upon itself and thence rebound in the form of Thought. But now an essential complement to this great cosmic event of Reflection becomes apparent to the informed eye, and it takes the form of what we might call 'the Break-through into Amorization'. Even after the flash of illumination in which the individual is suddenly revealed to himself, elementary Man would remain but half complete if he did not come into contact with the other sex and so, under the centric attraction of person-to-person, explode into flame.

First, we have the appearance of a *reflective monad*, and then, to complete it, the formation of an *affective dyad*.

And, *after that*, and only after that (that is, starting from this first spark) all that we have described follows in sequence – the gradual and majestic development of a Neo-cosmic, of an Ultra-human, and of a Pan-Christic . . .

All three not only illuminated in their very roots by Intelligence, but also impregnated throughout their entire mass,

as though bonded by a unifying cement,

by the Universal Feminine.

Paris, 30 October 1950

As a vindication of what has been said above, it may be useful, I believe, to reproduce here two pieces that are particularly representative of my state of mind at the very time (the war period) when my inner vision was being aroused into its definitive form.

The first of these was written on the eve of the attack on Douaumont (October, 1916) and is extracted from one of 'Three stories in the style of Benson'.[24]

The second, printed here in its entirety, dates from the summer of 1919, and was written in Jersey.

Both express more successfully than I could today the heady emotion I experienced at that time from my contact with Matter.

1. Christ in Matter

'My friend is dead, the man who drank from all Life as from a hallowed Spring. His heart consumed him with fire within. His body has vanished in the Earth, before Verdun. Now I can repeat to myself some of the words by which he initiated me into the intense vision which brought light and peace to his life.

'You wish to know,' he would say to me, 'how the mighty and multiple Universe came to assume for me the form of Christ? That was something that happened gradually; and intuitions that so remould our spirit are difficult to analyse in words. Still, I can try to tell you about some of the experiences that allowed the light of day to pour into my soul, from below – as though a curtain were being raised in successive jerks.'

The Picture
'. . . At that time,' he began, 'my mind was concerned with a

problem that was half philosophic and half aesthetic. Suppose, I used to think, that Christ should deign to appear here, in the flesh, before my very eyes – what would he look like? Most important of all, in what way would he fit himself into Matter and so be sensibly apprehended? How would he impinge on the objects around him? And I felt that there was something vaguely distressing, something that grated on me, in the idea that the Body of the Lord could be jostled in the world-scene by the multitude of inferior bodies without the latter's noticing or recognizing by some perceptible change the Intensity that brushed against them.

Meanwhile, my eyes had unconsciously come to rest on a picture that represented Christ with his Heart offered to men. This picture was hanging in front of me, on the wall of a church into which I had gone to pray. And, continuing my line of thought, I could not see how it could be possible for an artist to represent the sacred Humanity of Jesus without giving him this over-exact physical definition, which seemed to cut him off from all other men: without giving him a face whose expression was too individual – a beautiful face, no doubt, but beautiful in a particular way which excluded all other types of beauty.

I was worrying and wondering about all this; and I was still looking at the picture when the vision began.

(Indeed, I cannot be certain exactly when it began, because it had already reached a certain pitch of intensity when I became aware of it . . .)

All I know is that as I let my eyes roam over the outlines of the picture, I suddenly realized that they *were melting*. They were melting, but in a very special way that I find it difficult to describe. When I tried to distinguish the drawing of the Person of Christ, the lines seemed to be sharply defined. And then, if I relaxed my visual concentration, the whole of Christ's outline, the folds of his robe, the bloom of his skin, merged (though without disappearing) into all the rest.

You might have said that the edge which divided Christ from

the surrounding World was changing into a layer of vibration in which all distinct delimitation was lost.

As I remember it, the change must first have been noticeable in a particular spot on the edge of the picture; it started there, and then ran all round the outline of the figure – it was in that order, at any rate, that I became aware of it. And then, after that, the metamorphosis spread rapidly and included every detail.

First I noticed that the vibrant atmosphere which formed a halo around Christ was not confined to a narrow strip encircling him, but radiated into Infinity. From time to time what seemed to be trails of phosphorescence streamed across it, in which could be seen a continuous pulsing surge which reached out to the furthest spheres of Matter – forming a sort of crimson ganglion, or nervous network, running across every substance.

The whole Universe was vibrating. And yet, when I tried to look at the details one by one, I found them still as sharply drawn, their individual character still intact.

All this movement seemed to emanate from Christ – from his Heart in particular. And it was while I was trying to find my way back to the source of this effluence and determine its rhythm that my attention returned to the portrait itself, and then I saw the vision rapidly mount to its climax.

. . . I see that I have forgotten to tell you how Christ was dressed. His 'raiment was white as the light', as we read in the account of the Transfiguration. But what struck me most was that it was not woven on any loom – unless the hand of the Angels is the hand of Matter. It was from no crudely spun thread that warp and weft were made; but Matter, a florescence of Matter, had spontaneously woven itself, working with the most intimate essence of its substance, to produce a magically textured lawn. And I thought I could see the interlocked fibres running on and on, harmoniously combining to form a natural design which was built into them from their first beginning.

And yet, you must understand, I could not give my full attention to this garment, so marvellously woven by the endless co-operation of all the energies of Matter and its whole order. It was the transfigured Face of the Master that drew me and held me.

At night time, you have often seen some stars that change the quality of their light: at one moment they are blood-red beads, and then they take on the shimmer of purple velvet. Similarly, you have seen the colours of the rainbow float in a transparent bubble.

It was thus that the light and the colours of all the beauties we know shone, with an inexpressible iridescence, over the face of Jesus, itself unmoved. I cannot say whether it was an expression of my own wishes or whether it was the choice of Him who determined and knew my tastes; but one thing I know, that these countless modifications, instinct with majesty, sweetness, and irresistible appeal, followed one another in succession, were transformed, melted into one another in a harmony that was utterly satisfying to me.

And all this time, beneath this surface movement – both supporting it and concentrating it in a higher unity – floated the incommunicable Beauty of Christ . . . Again, I guessed at rather than apprehended that Beauty; for every time I tried to see through the screen of lesser beauties that hid it from me, other particular and fragmentary beauties came to the surface and drew a veil between me and *True Beauty*, even as they allowed me to glimpse it and stimulated my longing.

The whole Face gave out this radiance regulated by this same law. But the centre of radiation and iridescence was hidden in the eyes of the transfigured portrait.

The Reflection – or was it the Creative Form, the Idea? – of all that can charm, of all that has life, overlaid, in a rainbow, the rich depths of those eyes . . . And as I tried to read the secret of the luminous simplicity of their fire, it dissolved into a fathomless complexity in which were united all that the expressive eye has ever held to bring warmth to the heart of man and enthral it. For example, those eyes, which at first were so sweet and tender that I thought it was my mother that I saw, became in the next moment as full of passion and as dominating as those of a sovereign lady – so imperiously pure, at the same time, that it would have been physically impossible for sensibility to be misguided. And then again they were filled with a great and virile majesty, akin to that which can be seen in the eyes of a man who has great courage or great strength – and yet incomparably more lofty and more delightful in its mastery.

This scintillation of beauties was so total, so all-embracing, and at the same time so swift, that it reached down into the very powerhouse of my being, flooding through it in one surge, so that my whole self vibrated to the very core of me, with a full note of explosive bliss that was completely and utterly unique.

Now, while I eagerly concentrated my attention on the very pupils of Christ's eyes, in which I saw an infinite depth of Life, enchanting and glowing, from those same depths I saw a sort of cloud forming, which overlaid and drowned the shifting play of expression that I have been trying to describe. Gradually a look of extraordinary intensity spread over the fluctuating shades of emphasis I could read in the divine glance, first seeping into them and then absorbing them into itself.

I was completely at a loss.

I found it impossible to decipher this final expression, which dominated and summed up all that had gone before. I could not say whether it evidenced an unspeakable agony or, on the contrary, an excess of triumphant joy. All I know is that, since that occasion, I believe I have seen a hint of it once, and that was in the eyes of a dying soldier.

My own eyes were instantly dimmed by tears. But when I was able to look again at the picture of Christ in the church, it had resumed its over-defined outline and the blank immobility of its features.

*   *   *

. . . 'I have always,' my friend went on, 'had a soul that is by

nature pantheist. I used to feel its irrepressible innate aspirations;
but I was afraid to give free rein to them because I did not know
how to reconcile them with my faith. Since these various
experiences (and there were others, too) I can say that I found that
my life held an inexhaustible interest for me and brought me a
peace that nothing could disturb.

I live in the bosom of a unique Element, the Centre and the
individuality of all – personal Love and cosmic Power.

To enable me to reach it and to unite myself to it, I have the
whole Universe before me, with its noble struggles, with its
thrilling explorations, with its countless souls to be restored to
health and brought to perfection. I can fling myself to the point of
exhaustion into the full stream of man's work. The more fully I
play my part, the more I shall rest on the whole surface of the Real,
the more I shall reach Christ and cling to Him.

God, eternal Being-in-himself, is everywhere, we might say, in
process of formation *for us*.

And God is also *the Heart of All*. So true is this that the vast
scene of the Universe may grow dark or arid, or may be taken
from me by death, without diminishing my fundamental joy.
The dust that is animated by an aureole of energy and glory
might be scattered and vanish, but substantial Reality, in which
all perfection is gathered, never to know corruption, would
remain intact. The rays would fold back into their Source: and
there I should still clasp them in my embrace.

That is why even War itself does not disconcert me. In a few
days' time we shall be sent in to recapture Douaumont – a grand
gesture which symbolizes for me an undeniable advance by the
World towards the liberation of souls. Make no mistake. I am
going into this show in a spirit of religion, impelled by a single
driving force in which I cannot determine where human passion
ends and worship begins.

And if I do not come back from up there, I would like my
body to remain, moulded into the clay of the redoubts, like a
living mortar laid by God between the stones of the New City.'

Thus it was, on an October evening, that my dearly loved friend spoke to me – the man whose soul was in instinctive communication with the unique Life of all things – and whose body now rests, as he wished, somewhere in the lonely earth.

Nant-le-Grand (before the attack on Fort Douaumont) 14 October 1916

2. The Spiritual Power of Matter

And as they went on walking and talking together, behold a fiery chariot and fiery horses parted them both asunder; and of a sudden Elijah was caught up by a whirlwind into heaven.

THE BOOK OF KINGS

The man was walking in the desert, followed by his companion, when the Thing swooped down on him.

From afar it had appeared to him, quite small, gliding over the sand, no bigger than the palm of a child's hand – as a pale, fleeting shadow like a wavering flight of quail over the blue sea before sunrise or a cloud of gnats dancing in the sun at evening or a whirlwind of dust at midday sweeping over the plain.

The Thing seemed to take no heed of the two travellers, and was roaming capriciously through the wilderness. Then, suddenly, it assumed a set course and with the speed of an arrow came straight at them.

And then the man perceived that the little pale cloud of vapour was but the centre of an infinitely greater reality moving towards them without restriction, formless, boundless. The Thing as it approached them spread outwards with prodigious rapidity as far as his eye could reach, filling the whole of space, while its feet brushed lightly over the thorny vegetation beside the torrent, its brow rose in the sky like a golden mist with the reddening sun behind it. And all about it the ether had become alive, vibrating palpably beneath the crude substance of rocks and plants as in summer the landscape quivers behind the overheated soil in the foreground.

What was advancing towards them was the *moving heart of an immeasurable pervasive subtlety.*

The man fell prostrate to the ground; and hiding his face in his hands he waited.

A great silence fell around him.

Then, suddenly, a breath of scorching air passed across his forehead, broke through the barrier of his closed eyelids, and penetrated his soul. The man felt that he was ceasing to be merely himself; an irresistible rapture took possession of him as though all the sap of all living things, flowing at one and the same moment into the too narrow confines of his heart, was mightily refashioning the enfeebled fibres of his being. And at the same time the anguish of some superhuman peril oppressed him, a confused feeling that the force which had swept down upon him was equivocal, turbid, the combined essence of all evil and all goodness.

The hurricane was within himself.

And now, in the very depths of the being it had invaded, the tempest of life, infinitely gentle, infinitely brutal, was murmuring to the one secret point in the soul which it had not altogether demolished:

'You called me: here I am. Driven by the Spirit far from humanity's caravan routes, you dared to venture into the untouched wilderness; grown weary of abstractions, of attenuations, of the wordiness of social life, you wanted to pit yourself against Reality entire and untamed.

'You had need of me in order to grow; and I was waiting for you in order to be made holy.

'Always you have, without knowing it, desired me; and always I have been drawing you to me.

'And now I am established on you for life, or for death. You can never go back, never return to commonplace gratifications or untroubled worship. He who has once seen me can never forget me: he must either damn himself with me or save me with himself.

'Are you coming?'

'O you who are divine and mighty, what is your name? Speak.'

'I am the fire that consumes and the water that overthrows; I am the love that initiates and the truth that passes away. All that compels acceptance and all that brings renewal; all that breaks apart and all that binds together; power, experiment, progress – matter: all this am I.

'Because in my violence I sometimes slay my lovers; because he who touches me never knows what power he is unleashing, wise men fear me and curse me. They speak of me with scorn, calling me beggar-woman or witch or harlot; but their words are at variance with life, and the pharisees who condemn me, waste away in the outlook to which they confine themselves; they die of inanition and their disciples desert them because I am the essence of all that is tangible, and men cannot do without me.

'You who have grasped that the world – the world beloved of God – has, even more than individuals, a soul to be redeemed, lay your whole being wide open to my inspiration, and receive the spirit of the earth which is to be saved.

'The supreme key to the enigma, the dazzling utterance which is inscribed on my brow and which henceforth will burn into your eyes even though you close them, is this: *Nothing is precious save what is yourself in others and others in yourself.* In heaven, all things are but one. In heaven all is one.

'Come, do you not feel my breath uprooting you and carrying you away? Up, man of God, and make haste. For according to the way a man surrenders himself to it, the whirlwind will either drag him down into the darkness of its depths or lift him up into the blue skies. Your salvation and mine hang on this first moment.'

'O you who are matter: my heart, as you see, is trembling. Since it is you, tell me: what would you have me do?'

'Take up your arms, O Israel, and do battle boldly against me.'

The wind, having at first penetrated and pervaded him stealthily, like a philtre, had now become aggressive, hostile.

From within its coils it exhaled now the acrid stench of battle.

The musky smell of forests, the feverish atmosphere of cities, the sinister, heady scent that rises up from nations locked in battle: all this writhed within its folds, a vapour gathered from the four corners of the earth.

The man, still prostrate, suddenly started, as though his flesh had felt the spur: he leapt to his feet and stood erect, facing the storm.

It was the soul of his entire race that had shuddered within him: an obscure memory of a first sudden awakening in the midst of beasts stronger, better-armed than he; a sad echo of the long struggle to tame the corn and to master the fire; a rancorous dread of the maleficent forces of nature, a lust for knowledge and possession . . .

A moment ago, in the sweetness of the first contact, he had instinctively longed to lose himself in the warm wind which enfolded him.

Now, this wave of bliss in which he had all but melted away was changed into a ruthless determination towards increased being.

The man had scented the enemy, his hereditary quarry.

He dug his feet into the ground, and began his battle.

He fought first of all in order not to be swept away; but then he began to fight for the joy of fighting, the joy of feeling his own strength. And the longer he fought, the more he felt an increase of strength going out from him to balance the strength of the tempest, and from the tempest there came forth in return a new exhalation which flowed like fire into his veins.

As on certain nights the sea around a swimmer will grow luminous, and its eddies will glisten the more brightly under the sturdy threshing of his limbs, so the dark power wrestling with the man was lit up with a thousand sparkling lights under the impact of his onslaught.

In a reciprocal awakening of their opposed powers, he stirred up his utmost strength to achieve the mastery over it, while it revealed all its treasures in order to surrender them to him.

'Son of earth, steep yourself in the sea of matter, bathe in its fiery waters, for it is the source of your life and your youthfulness.

'You thought you could do without it because the power of thought has been kindled in you? You hoped that the more thoroughly you rejected the tangible, the closer you would be to spirit: that you would be more divine if you lived in the world of pure thought, or at least more angelic if you fled the corporeal? Well, you were like to have perished of hunger.

'You must have oil for your limbs, blood for your veins, water for your soul, the world of reality for your intellect: do you not see that the very law of your own nature makes these a necessity for you?

'Never, if you work to live and to grow, never will you be able to say to matter, "I have seen enough of you; I have surveyed your mysteries and have taken from them enough food for my thought to last me for ever." I tell you: even though, like the Sage of sages, you carried in your memory the image of all the beings that people the earth or swim in the seas, still all that knowledge would be as nothing for your soul, for all abstract knowledge is only a faded reality: this is because to understand the world knowledge is not enough, you must see it, touch it, live in its presence and drink the vital heat of existence in the very heart of reality.

'Never say, then, as some say: "The kingdom of matter is worn out, matter is dead": till the very end of time matter will always remain young, exuberant, sparkling, new-born for those who are willing.

'Never say, "Matter is accursed, matter is evil": for there has come one who said, "You will drink poisonous draughts and they shall not harm you", and again, "Life shall spring forth out of death", and then finally, the words which spell my definitive liberation, "This is my body".

'Purity does not lie in separation from, but in a deeper penetration into the universe. It is to be found in the love of that unique, boundless Essence which penetrates the inmost depths of all things and there, from within those depths, deeper than the mortal zone where individuals and multitudes struggle, works upon them and moulds them. Purity lies in a chaste contact with that which is "the same in all".

'Oh, the beauty of spirit as it rises up adorned with all the riches of the earth!

'Son of man, bathe yourself in the ocean of matter; plunge into it where it is deepest and most violent; struggle in its currents and drink of its waters. For it cradled you long ago in your preconscious existence; and it is that ocean that will raise you up to God.'

Standing amidst the tempest, the man turned his head, looking for his companion.

And in that same moment he perceived a strange metamorphosis: the earth was simultaneously vanishing away yet growing in size.

It was vanishing away, for here, immediately beneath him, the meaningless variations in the terrain were diminshing and dissolving; on the other hand it was growing ever greater, for there in the distance the curve of the horizon was climbing ceaselessly higher.

The man saw himself standing in the centre of an immense cup, the rim of which was closing over him.

And then the frenzy of battle gave place in his heart to an irresistible longing to *submit*: and in a flash he discovered, everywhere present around him, *the one thing necessary*.

Once and for all he understood that, like the atom, man has no value save for that part of himself which passes into the universe. He recognized with absolute certainty the empty fragility of even the noblest theorizings as compared with the definitive plenitude of the smallest *fact* grasped in its total, concrete reality.

He saw before his eyes, revealed with pitiless clarity, the

ridiculous pretentiousness of human claims to order the life of the world, to impose on the world the dogmas, the standards, the conventions of man.

He tasted, sickeningly, the triteness of men's joys and sorrows, the mean egoism of their pursuits, the insipidity of their passions, the attenuation of their power to feel.

He felt pity for those who take fright at the span of a century or whose love is bounded by the frontiers of a nation.

So many things which once had distressed or revolted him – the speeches and pronouncements of the learned, their assertions and their prohibitions, their refusal to allow the universe to move – all seemed to him now merely ridiculous, non-existent, compared with the majestic reality, the flood of energy, which now revealed itself to him: omnipresent, unalterable in its truth, relentless in its development, untouchable in its serenity, maternal and unfailing in its protectiveness,

Thus at long last he had found a *point d'appui*, he had found refuge, *outside* the confines of human society.

A heavy cloak slipped from his shoulders and fell to the ground behind him: the dead weight of all that is false, narrow, tyrannical, all that is *artificially contrived*, all that is merely *human* in humanity.

A wave of triumph freed his soul.

And he felt that henceforth nothing in the world would ever be able to alienate his heart from the greater reality which was now revealing itself to him, nothing at all: neither the intrusiveness and individualist separatism of human beings (for these qualities in them he despised) nor the heavens and the earth in their height and breadth and depth and power (for it was precisely to these that he was now dedicating himself for ever).

A deep process of renewal had taken place within him: now it would never again be possible for him to be human save *on another plane*. Were he to descend again now to the everyday life of earth – even though it were to rejoin his faithful companion, still prostrate over there on the desert sand – he would henceforth be for ever *a stranger*.

Yes, of this he was certain: even for his brothers in God, better men than he, he would inevitably speak henceforth in an incomprehensible tongue, he whom the Lord had drawn to follow the road of fire. Even for those he loved the most his love would be henceforth a burden, for they would sense his compulsion to be for ever seeking something *behind themselves*.

Because matter, throwing off its veil of restless movement and multiplicity, had revealed to him its glorious unity, chaos now divided him from other men. Because it had for ever withdrawn his heart from all that is merely local or individual, all that is fragmentary, henceforth for him it alone in its totality would be his father and mother, his family, his race, his unique, consuming passion.

And not a soul in the world could do anything to change this.

Turning his eyes resolutely away from what was receding from him, he surrendered himself, in superabounding faith, to the wind which was sweeping the universe onwards.

And now in the heart of the whirling cloud a light was growing, a light in which there was the tenderness and the mobility of a human glance; and from it there spread a warmth which was not now like the harsh heat radiating from a furnace but like the opulent warmth which emanates from a human body. What had been a blind and feral immensity was now becoming expressive and personal; and its hitherto amorphous expanses were being moulded into features of an ineffable face.

A Being was taking form in the totality of space; a Being with the attractive power of a soul, palpable like a body, vast as the sky; a Being which mingled with things yet remained distinct from them; a Being of a higher order than the substance of things with which it was adorned, yet taking shape within them.

The rising Sun was being born in the heart of the world.

God was shining forth from the summit of that world of matter whose waves were carrying up to him the world of spirit.

The man fell to his knees in the fiery chariot which was bearing him away.

And he spoke these words:

HYMN TO MATTER

'Blessed be you, harsh matter, barren soil, stubborn rock: you who yield only to violence, you who force us to work if we would eat.

'Blessed be you, perilous matter, violent sea, untameable passion: you who unless we fetter you will devour us.

'Blessed be you, mighty matter, irresistible march of evolution, reality ever new-born; you who, by constantly shattering our mental categories, force us to go ever further and further in our pursuit of the truth.

'Blessed be you, universal matter, immeasurable time, boundless ether, triple abyss of stars and atoms and generations: you who by overflowing and dissolving our narrow standards or measurement reveal to us the dimensions of God.

'Blessed be you, impenetrable matter: you who, interposed between our minds and the world of essences, cause us to languish with the desire to pierce through the seamless veil of phenomena.

'Blessed be you, mortal matter: you who one day will undergo the process of dissolution within us and will thereby take us forcibly into the very heart of that which exists.

'Without you, without your onslaughts, without your up-rootings of us, we should remain all our lives inert, stagnant, puerile, ignorant both of ourselves and of God. You who batter us and then dress our wounds, you who resist us and yield to us, you who wreck and build, you who shackle and liberate, the sap of our souls, the hand of God, the flesh of Christ: it is you, matter, that I bless.

'I bless you, matter, and you I acclaim: not as the pontiffs of science or the moralizing preachers depict you, debased, disfigured – a mass of brute forces and base appetites – but as you reveal yourself to me today, *in your totality and your true nature.*

'You I acclaim as the inexhaustible potentiality for existence and transformation wherein the predestined substance germinates and grows.

'I acclaim you as the universal power which brings together and unites, through which the multitudinous monads are bound together and in which they all converge on the way of the Spirit.

'I acclaim you as the melodious fountain[25] of water whence spring the souls of men and as the limpid crystal whereof is fashioned the new Jerusalem.

'I acclaim you as the divine *milieu*, charged with creative power, as the ocean stirred by the Spirit, as the clay moulded and infused with life by the incarnate Word.

'Sometimes, thinking they are responding to your irresistible appeal, men will hurl themselves for love of you into the exterior abyss of selfish pleasure-seeking: they are deceived by a reflection or by an echo.

'This I now understand.

'If we are ever to reach you, matter, we must, having first established contact with the totality of all that lives and moves here below, come little by little to feel that the individual shapes of all we have laid hold on are melting away in our hands, until finally we are at grips with the *single essence* of all consistencies and all unions.

'If we are ever to possess you, having taken you rapturously in our arms, we must then go on to sublimate you through sorrow.

'Your realm comprises those serene heights where saints think to avoid you – but where your flesh is so transparent and so agile as to be no longer distinguishable from spirit.

'Raise me up then, matter, to those heights, through struggle and separation and death; raise me up until, at long last, it becomes possible for me in perfect chastity to embrace the universe.'

Down below on the desert sands, now tranquil again, someone was weeping and calling out: 'My Father, my Father! What wild wind can this be that has borne him away?'

And on the ground there lay a cloak.

Jersey, 8 August 1919

1. 'Incidentally, the Graham Greene title (*The Heart of the Matter*) would be wonderful for me (although with a quite different meaning) for an essay I am dreaming to write since some time under a name which occurs to my mind in English (untranslatable into French): "The Golden Glow" (meaning the appearance of God from and in the "Heart of Matter").'

'... the whole thing (the essay, 'The Heart of Matter') has to be woven with four (and not only three) threads, namely: *Le Cosmique, L'Humain, Le Christique* and *Le Féminin*'. (Letters (in English) of 10 October 1948 and 12 August 1950, in *Letters to Two Friends*, London, 1970, pp. 190, 212. (Ed.'s note.)

2. This is what I wrote as early as 1917 in one of my first essays (called 'My Universe', written in the thick of the fighting) about the same subject:

'Ever since my childhood, the need wholly to possess some 'absolute' was the axis of my entire inner life. I can now remember quite clearly that amid all my youthful pleasures I found happiness only *in relation to* a fundamental joy: and that mostly consisted in the possession (or the thought) of some more precious object, more permanent, less corruptible. Sometimes it would be a piece of metal – and another time I would jump to the other extreme and take delight in the thought of God-Spirit (at that age the Flesh of Christ seemed to me to be something too fragile and subject to corruption).

'This predilection will seem curious, but I can assure you that it was with me *continuously*. From those very first days I had an irresistible (and at the same time vitalizing and soothing) need to rest *continuously* in Some Thing that was tangible and definite; and I looked everywhere for this beatifying Object.

'The story of my inner life is the story of this search, directed towards ever more universal and more perfect realities. Fundamentally, my natural underlying purpose has been unwavering, ever since I can remember what I was like.'

3. 'I am doing my best, just now, to recapture and to express my feelings, as a child, toward what I have called, later on, *la sainte Matière*. A rather delicate and critical point, since it is unquestionably out of these early contacts with the "essence" of the World that my whole internal life has sprung and grown. In this case, at least, nobody can say that I am intruding on the grounds of philosophy or theology – a personal psychological experience: nothing more, but also nothing less.' (Letter (in English) of 18 August 1950, in *Letters to Two Friends*, London, 1970, p. 214.). 'Yes, on the whole I was glad to revisit Sarcenat yesterday. But the two main things I brought back from this driving in the past were (a) the confirmation that the psychological analysis (such as I have sketched it these days in my essay) of my mystical trends (when I was a child) is correct; and (b) the final evidence that an entire previous circle of myself is completely dead (because the wave is by now much deeper inside).' (Letter (in English) of 22 August 1950, *ibid.*, p. 215) (Ed.'s note.)

4. If nothing better were available, I preferred Coleoptera to butterflies: the latter were too delicate – and the more robust the former and the hornier, the more attractive I found them.

5. Moreover, since this lacked 'convergence' (cf. above, Section II) this did not give me what I wanted.

6. And here (I mean in the idiom I use) we meet again my irrepressible urge to *universalize* whatever I love.

7. Not until 1935 does the word *Man* appear in the brief *Credo* I used as an Epigraph to 'How I Believe', even though that essay itself rests its argument explicitly on the Phenomenon of Man. Today I would say:
'. . . I believe that Evolution proceeds towards Spirit.
I believe that *in Man*, Spirit is fully realized in Person.' It is only an added touch, but it allows us to emerge unequivocally from metaphysics and move into the historical, the biological – the planetary.

8. I can still see myself – 'experience' myself – (I might have been about five or six) by some fireplace, noticing, with a dismay that had repercussions on my devotion to *le petit Jésus*, the nasty smell of burning as a lock of hair fell into the flames.

9. Edouard Le Roy was so good as to devote considerable time in his lectures at the *Collège de France* ('The idealist demand and the fact of evolution') to this first essay of mine on the Phenomenon of Man – thus lending his authority to the word 'Noosphere', which has since gained wide acceptance.
(The reference is to 'Hominization', an essay written in Paris in May 1925. It is included in *The Vision of the Past*, 1966, pp. 51–79.) (Ed's note.)

10. On the scale of the cell, the body of the metazoon ceases to be perceptible; and so the molecule on the scale of the atom.

11. Though I am quite sure that, like the cosmic sense and simultaneously with it, it will rapidly become general in the make-up of future generations.

12. This awakening is unmistakably apparent in a rather over-free fantasy, entitled 'La Grande Monade', which was written in the trenches, about 1917: the full moon emerging over the barbed wire – symbol and image of the thinking Earth: and more clearly still in the last paragraph (omitted by the editors) of 'La Nostalgie du Front', in *Etudes*, 20 November 1917. See below, pp. 167–95.

13. From below to above – even though under the active influence of 'above'.

14. Somewhat as, in atomic physics, no micro-molecule can be conceived as at rest and without its wave (the greater the mass of the molecule, the greater is its penetrative power) – so, we might say in terms of physical biology, no mega-molecule can exist without a psychism (and the more complex the molecule in question, the higher is the psychism).

15. 'Union (*biological* union) does not identify; but it differentiates the simple living organism, and personalizes the Reflective upon itself.' It is therefore an organic heresy to consider the totalized Reflective as forming a single 'soul'. It is not a single soul, but a soul that super-animates all the assembled souls.

16. More or less stimulated and fed by the influence of the Feminine (cf. Conclusion, above).

17. I tried to express this in the first of my 'Three stories in the style of Benson', written in 1916, between two attacks at Verdun. (See above, pp. 61–7.)

18. And more generally, I am convinced, in the inmost depths of *every* modern soul.

19. This was the well-known Père Paul Troussard – see Robert Speaight, *Teilhard de Chardin*, p. 31. (Translator's note.)

20. On this spiritual 'power' and 'stimulus' to be found in Matter, see *Le Milieu Divin* – and also the characteristic essay (on 'the cloak of Elijah') which was written in Jersey, in 1919, just after the war. (Cf. 'The Spiritual Power of Matter', in *Hymn of the Universe*, pp. 59–71; also above pp. 67–76.)

21. The censors who were asked in 1948 to give their views on this essay by Père Teilhard, held that this passage was incompatible with orthodoxy. Père Teilhard agreed to replace the words *complétion* and *achèvement* (translated here as 'completion' and 'fulfilment') by *satisfaction*. Shortly afterwards, however, when he was turning this over in his

mind, he told us: 'All the same, the Universe is, for God, much more than a satisfying product (*un produit de satisfaction*).'

A passage by Cardinal de Bérulle, which we read after Teilhard's death, should make it clear that it was the latter who was in the right. This is what de Bérulle, called by Urban VIII 'the Apostle of the Incarnate Word' has to say:

'(God) the Father, who is the fontal source of the Godhead . . . produces two divine Persons in himself. And the Son, who is the second producing Person in the Godhead, concludes his productiveness in a single divine Person. And this third Person, who does not produce anything eternal and uncreated, produces the incarnate Word. And this incarnate Word . . . produces the order of grace and of glory which ends . . . in making us Gods by anticipation . . . This completes God's communication in himself and outside himself.' (*Les Grandeurs de Jésus*, 1623.)

Thus, since the God-Man represents the fecundity of the Holy Spirit, and since the incarnation of the Word is linked to the creation of an evolutive universe, we may legitimately conclude that the universe is indeed 'a mysterious product of completion and fulfilment for the Absolute Being himself'. (Ed.'s note.)

22. 'Finally, I think that the *Féminin* will be presented and discussed as a kind of Conclusion or *Envoi*: not so much as an element by itself, than as a kind of light illuminating the process of universal concentration: *vraiment*, in fact, as I wrote you, "the spirit of Union".' (Letter in English from Père Teilhard, 14 August 1950, in *Letters to Two Friends*, p. 213.) (Ed.'s note.)

23. That Père Teilhard himself added as an appendix to his autobiography the story of his first mystical experiences, shows that he wished the illumination he had then attained to extend to what he had written.

If we are to understand the *The Feminine* at the high level at which he had been living since 1919, we must appreciate the full force of the following passage from *The Spiritual Power of Matter*:

'A profound re-formation had just been effected in him, of such a nature that it was now no longer possible for him to be Man except *on another plane*.

'His affection would be a burden, even for those he loved most, for they would feel that he was always, with invincible determination, looking *for something behind them*.'

With the 'conclusion' printed here, we should compare 'The Eternal Feminine' (*Writings in Time of War*, pp. 191–202).

At the end of his life, Père Teilhard assured us again of his unshakeable fidelity to the solemn vow of chastity he took when he was professed as a religious in 1918. 'I do not remember,' he added, 'that this fidelity cost me any struggles. It is only Christ whom I can love.' It is, then, the 'spiritual power' of the Feminine, and the spiritual power alone, of which he is writing here. (Ed.'s note.)

24. *Hymn of the Universe*, pp. 41–55.

25. When Père Teilhard re-read the 'Hymn to Matter' in my presence, he told me, after some thought, that he preferred *source* (translated here and in *Hymn of the Universe*, p. 68, as 'fountain') to *somme*. (Note by J.M.)

THE CHRISTIC

Even before Père Teilhard had finished *The Heart of Matter*, he was turning over in his mind his last work. Of this he wrote (in a letter to J. Mortier, 19 August 1950): '. . . this extraordinary Christic – I want to live long enough to have time to express it more or less as I now see it taking shape, with an ever-increasing sense of wonder.'

And we read, in his Retreat Notes dated the 29 September of the same year, 'Jesus my God, once again the same prayer, the most ardent, the most humble prayer: Make me end *well* . . . end well – that is, let me have had time and opportunity to express my Essential Message, the Essence of my Message.'

During the Spring of the second year of his exile in New York, Père Teilhard writes: 'The first thing I shall write "for myself" (and for close friends) will perhaps be a study of "the Christosphere" – or the Christic (the Christic Point, Milieu and Energy), which brings me back more or less to the "Divine Milieu".' (To J.M., 30 April 1952.)

He returns to his project in 1954: 'Meanwhile I am thinking more and more about writing something "confidential" about the Christic: a sort of quintessence of *Le Milieu Divin*, "The Mass on the World" and "The Heart of Matter". An evocation of the massive psychological "integration" (to use the modern term) that can be effected (and is even now inevitably being effected) by the coming together of the pleromizing-

Christ of Revelation and the convergent Evolutive of Science. The whole Universe which is being amorized, from the infinitesimal to the immense over all Duration . . .' (To J.M., 22 September 1954).

Finally, two months before his death, he began to put on paper the essay which had been maturing for five years: 'I am really getting down to the Christic, though I am not quite sure what the general tone of the piece will be or how it will work out (between *Le Milieu Divin*, 'The Mass on the World' and 'The Heart of Matter'). Pray that I may make as good a job of it as possible – that his "kingdom" may come'. (To J.M., 9 February 1955.)

INTRODUCTION: THE AMORIZATION OF THE UNIVERSE

What follows is not a mere speculative dissertation in which the main lines of some long-matured and cleverly constructed system are set out.

It constitutes the evidence brought to bear, with complete objectivity, upon a particular interior event, upon a particular personal experience, in which I cannot but distinguish the track followed by a general drift of the Human as it folds in upon itself.

During the course of my life there has gradually been aroused in me, until it has become habitual, the capacity to see two fundamental psychic movements or currents in which we all share, without, however, being sufficiently aware of what they mean.

On one side, there has been the irresistible convergence of my individual thought with every other thinking being on the Earth – and in consequence with everything that is going through a gradual process of 'arrangement', wherever it be, and to whatever degree, in the immensities of Time and Space.

And on the other side, there has been the persistent individualization, at the centre of my own small *ego*, of an ultra-Centre of Thought and Action: in the depths of my consciousness, the rise, which nothing can stop, of a sort of Other who could be even more I than I am myself.

On one side there was a flux, at once physical and psychic, which made the Totality of the Stuff of Things fold in on itself, by giving it complexity: carrying this to the point where that Stuff is made to co-reflect itself.

And on the other side, under the species of an incarnate divine being, a Presence so intimate that it could not satisfy itself or satisfy me, without being by nature universal.

This was the double perception, intellectual and emotional, of a *Cosmic Convergence* and a *Christic Emergence* which, each in its own way, filled my whole horizon.

Although they both made themselves felt in the very core of my being, it is conceivable that these two new tides of consciousness might have had no effect upon one another – for they reached me from different angles.

But it was not so; and it is precisely this contrary experience that I hope to describe in this essay, for the delight of my life and all that gives it strength will have been my discovery that when these two spiritual ingredients were brought together, they reacted endlessly upon one another in a flash of extraordinary brilliance, releasing by their implosion a light so intense that it transfigured (or even 'transubstantiated') for me the very depths of the World.

I saw how the joint coming of age of Revelation and Science had suddenly opened a door for twentieth-century Man into a sort of ultra-dimension of Things, in which all differences between Action, Passion [in the sense of being acted upon] and Communion vanish – not by being neutralized but by reaching an explosive climax: and this at the high temperatures of the Centre and on the scale of the Whole.

I saw the Universe becoming amorized and personalized in the very dynamism of its own evolution.

It is already a long time since, in response to these new ways of seeing things, still barely defined in my mind, I tried, in *The Mass on the World* and *Le Milieu Divin*, to give distinct expression to my sense of wonder and amazement.

Today, after forty years of continuous thought,[1] it is still exactly the same fundamental vision that I feel I must present, and enable others to share in its matured form – for the last time.

It may not be expressed with the same freshness and exuberance as resulted from my first meeting with it – but the wonder and the passion will still be there, undimmed.

A. THE CONVERGENCE OF THE UNIVERSE

Whether we admit it or not, we have today no choice: we have all become 'evolutionists'. Through the narrow Darwinian crack opened a century ago in zoology, the feeling of Duration has now so completely and permanently coloured the whole of our experience that we have to make an effort, for example, to get back to those not so distant days (about 1900!) when the formation of species was still a matter for bitter argument, and we had not the vaguest suspicion that fifty years later the whole economy of mankind would be based on the birth of the Atom.

Today, of course, we all inevitably think and act as if the World were in a state of continual formation and transformation.

This is far from meaning, however, that this general frame of mind has yet reached its final and complete expression in our thought.

At a first stage, and that the vaguest, to *evolve* can mean to *change*, irrespective of the nature and modalities of the changing: they may be irregular or methodical, continuous or periodical, additive or dispersive and so on.

At this elementary level, we may say that so far as Physics and Biology are concerned there is no longer any uncertainty. The movement that animates the Stuff of the Universe in and around us, is no mere agitation and no mere drifting into the homogeneous.

It presents itself to our experience as a distinctly recognizable process – or, more correctly, as the product of two processes – which is by nature *subject to direction*.

1. First there is the process of 'arrangement' which, through the gradual 'corpusculizing' of cosmic Energy, produces the infinite variety (ever more complex and ever more 'psychized') of atoms, molecules, living cells, etc.

2. Secondly, there is the process of 'dis-arrangement' (Entropy), which is constantly bringing arranged Energy back to its most probable, and therefore most simple, forms.

84

We may say that competent observers today are in agreement about the general picture of an Evolution which may be compared, broadly speaking, to a river made up of amorphous streams (Entropy) within which countless eddies are individualized by a counter-current. 'Phenomenally' speaking, we see the World not merely as a system that is simply in movement, but as one that is in a state of *genesis* – a very different matter. Across the metamorphoses of Matter something is being made (and at the same time being unmade) in accordance with a particular global orientation – and this irreversibly and cumulatively.

Once we understand that, a further problem – not to say the final problem – presents itself.

In the case of the river we have just used as a comparison, what is most permanent and most important is, of course, the main stream – and not the eddies that come and go in the general mass of moving water. In Cosmogenesis, on the other hand, how are we to decide the relative value of the two confronting terms? Is (as might well at first appear) that majestic and inflexible Entropy really 'what counts' in Evolution? In other words, is it Entropy that has the last word cosmically? Or (in spite of certain apparent indications of fragility) is it rather the ever more complex and ever more centred nuclei that are successively formed in the course of planetary ages? To put it in another way, does the Universe ultimately come to rest upon itself in equilibrium in the direction of the non-arranged-unconscious (which is the materialist solution), or in the direction of the Arranged-conscious (which is the spiritual solution)?

Vital though this problem is for us – for it bears on real values and our real future – Science as yet refuses to make up its mind, opinions are divided. We are constantly being told that it is a matter which cannot be solved experimentally: the answer must be left to the philosophers or dictated by personal feeling.

I cannot emphasize too strongly that the problem is, on the contrary, soluble by the techniques we command provided our eyes are opened to the bio-cosmic significance of a phenomenon which is at the same time so enormous and so close to us that in the end we are completely swamped by it and entirely fail to see it. And the Phenomenon I refer to is that of human *co-reflection*.

Because we are born and live in the very heart of this thing that is happening, we still find it quite natural not only to think with ourselves but also, inevitably, to think with all other persons at the same time: in other words, we cannot move a finger without finding ourselves involved in the construction of a total human act that includes what we see and what we make.

We must try a different approach, first retracing our steps sufficiently, and so re-introduce into our general picture of the World the process of 'co-conscientizing' in which we share.

Once we do that, a perfectly clear (and strangely emancipating) indication emerges from the facts: that beneath the apparent commonplace superficiality of the Earth's technico-social disposition, it is Evolution itself – in that aspect of it which is orientated towards the Improbable – that is extending itself with increasing speed beyond our own insignificant individual centres in the direction of a Complexity-Consciousness of planetary dimensions.

The discovery of this simple fact is of decisive importance for both our understanding and our will.

Among those who theorize about Biogenesis, there are still many who speak as though the cosmic (anti-entropic) drift into Arrangement ultimately found expression in a *diversifying and dispersing expansion* of living forms. If the fact of terrestrial co-reflection is correctly interpreted, however, we see that when this drift has fully developed it inevitably takes on the form of a *centration* of the hominized portion of the Stuff of Things, which at the same time *differentiates* and fosters a common unanimous mind and spirit.

Experientially, if the *Universe* is examined in its most advanced areas, in the direction of the Improbable, it is seen that it *converges upon itself*.

To my mind, it is impossible to be fully an evolutionist in the true sense of the word without seeing and admitting this 'psycho-genic' concentration of the World upon itself.

And it is equally impossible, I may add, to arrive at an understanding of such a 'centripetal' form of cosmogenesis without being obliged to recognize and accept as a fact (for a number of reasons, as much physical as psychological[2]) that the Universe simultaneously takes on consistence and value in the direction, inevitably, in which it folds in upon itself – and not in the opposite direction. It is thus that a universal Flux, both *unifying and irreversifying*, appears and asserts its power; it transfigures the World that it illuminates, warms and consolidates – and we, too, are swept along in that Flux.

This is the higher dynamism, that controls and superanimates all the other dynamisms from within.

It provides, in fact, the neo-milieu of vision and action, for lack of which we might well fear that Anthropogenesis will lose its vigour and so wither: but within which, on the other hand, we can see that there is no further forward limit to the forces of ultra-hominization.

B. THE EMERGENCE OF CHRIST

I have tried in the preceding section to bring home how completely the shape of the World is transformed as soon as we make up our minds to allow the *Human Phenomenon of Co-Reflection* to find in it its full expression and its true place.

If we now look in an apparently completely different direction, if, that is, we move from the physical grounding of knowledge to its mystical plane, we may well consider a further point: let us see whether, perhaps, a metamorphosis of the same order (symmetrical – or even complementary) is not found to be operative in our intellectual and emotional outlook on the Universe, if we examine more attentively the *Christian Phenomenon* of Worship.

The Christian Phenomenon . . .

As a result of the progressive extension of the realm of Science by the study of comparative religion, this great event (which for nearly two thousand years has been universally regarded in the West as unique in world-history) might at first appear to be now passing through an eclipse, in the same way as did Man's appearance in Nature during the Quaternary age, when Darwinism first came on the scene. 'Christianity: a remarkable sort of religion, of course: but only one among many, and for only a particular period of time.' That is what the vast majority of 'intelligent' persons say to themselves, and openly proclaim, more or less explicitly.

In the case of Man, all that was needed to restore the Human to its primacy – no longer at the centre, but now at the head of things – was the gradual entry into our world-view of the place and evolutive function of Reflection. In just the same way, it seems to me, Christianity is far from losing its primacy in the vast religious medley let loose by the totalization of the modern world; on the contrary it is regaining and consolidating its axial, directive, place as the spear-head of human psychic energies – so long, that is, as we allow sufficient weight to its extraordinary and effectively significant power of 'pan-amorization'.

Christian love – Christian charity.

I know very well, from my experience, the reaction – sometimes kindly, and sometimes of ill-natured incredulity – that is generally aroused when those terms are used in front of non-Christians. 'Surely,' is the objection we hear, 'there is a psychological absurdity in loving God and loving the World? How, in fact, can we love the Intangible and the Universal? Further, in so far as a love of all and of the All can, more or less metaphorically, be said to be possible, is not that inner gesture already familiar to the Hindu Bakti, to the Persian Babis – and to any number of others. No, it is far from being specifically Christian.'

And yet, are not the facts there, staring us in the face, to prove to us the contrary, to prove it concretely, almost brutally?

On the one hand, whatever may be said, a love (a *true* love) of

God is perfectly possible; for, if it were not, all the monasteries and churches in the world would be emptied overnight, and Christianity, in spite of its framework of ritual and teaching and hierarchical order, would inevitably collapse into nothingness.

And on the other hand, this love has in Christianity something stronger than it has anywhere else. Were this not so, all the virtues and all the charms of the tenderness we find in the gospels could not have prevented the teaching of the Beatitudes and of the Cross from long ago having made way for some more assertive Creed – and more particularly for some humanism or 'terrenism'.

Whatever may be the merits of other religions, and whatever the explanation that may be given, it is indisputable that the most ardent collective focus of love ever to appear in the World is glowing *hic et nunc* at the heart of the Church of God.

The *facts* tell us that no religious Faith releases – or ever has released at any moment in History – a higher degree of warmth, a more intense dynamism of unification than the Christianity of our own day – and the more Catholic it is, the truer my words. And *logic* tells us that it is perfectly natural that that should be so; for in no other Creed, present or past, can be found so miraculously and effectively associated in their power to attract and captivate us, the three following characteristics of the incarnate Christian God:

1. Tangibility in the experiential order, as the result of Christ Jesus's historical entry (by his birth) into the very process of Evolution.

2. Expansibility in the cosmic order, conferred on the Christic Centre by the operative power of 'resurrection'.

3. And finally, assimilative power, in the organic order, potentially integrating the totality of the human race in the unity of a single 'body'.

It is easy enough to bring abstract criticisms against this apparently illogical mixture of primitive 'anthropomorphism', mythical marvel and gnostic extravagance. But the remarkable fact remains – let me emphasize this – that, however strange the combination of the three factors may appear, it *holds good* – *it works* – and that you have only to diminish the reality (or even the realism) of a single one of the three confronting components for the flame of Christianity to be immediately extinguished.

When all is said and done, what constitutes the impregnable superiority of Christianity over all other types of Faith, is that it is ever more consciously identified with a *Christogenesis*, in other words with an awareness of the rise *of a certain universal Presence* which is at once *immortalizing* and *unifying*.

Here we have the exact counterpart of what was earlier disclosed to us (but in terms of 'Flux') by a full analysis of the Phenomenon of Man.

In the second case, the Christian, we reach an expanding Centre which is trying to find itself a sphere.

In the former, the Human, we reach a sphere that is extending deeper and deeper, and needs a centre.

Could so remarkable a complementarity be no more than a coincidence – or an illusion?

C. THE CHRISTIFIED UNIVERSE

First, we are aware of being contained in a World whose two halves (the physical and the mystical) are slowly closing in with planetary force upon a Mankind that is born of their approach to one another. And then we realize that we are moving into a hyper-milieu of Life, produced by the coincidence of an emergent Christ and a convergent Universe.

Here we touch the very heart of the experience I am trying to describe, from what I know myself, in this essay.

My description will be more forceful if I can put things in their proper order. Let us, then, look in turn at the following:

First, the way in which, as the process develops, the Universe and Christ – one on one side and the other on the other side – find fulfilment in their conjunction.

And secondly, how from that very conjunction a third Thing

appears (a universal Element, a universal Milieu, and a universal Countenance: all three at the same time). And how in that third Thing the most familiar categories of our activity and our understanding cease to conflict with one another and yet at the same time attain their fullest expression.

1. The Consummation of the Universe by Christ

Writing with full sincerity, I have already (in Section 1) noted and extolled the reality and spiritualizing value of the new form of 'cosmic sense' aroused in modern Man by the evidence that Science provides of his belonging to a convergent-type Universe.

I know as well as anyone, from my own experience, to what a degree this 'sense of evolution' (or 'sense of man') can simultaneously fill one's mind, strengthen and exalt one. And I am therefore completely convinced that the great spiritual edifices of tomorrow can be constructed (and will in fact be constructed) only if we start from this new element and use it as our foundation.

For a number of important reasons, however, I am still doubtful whether, left to itself, our consciousness (however intense it may be in each one of us) of sharing in a planetary Flux of co-reflection is capable of building up the sort of religion that has been foretold with such warmth and brilliance by my friend Julian Huxley: to which he has given the name of 'evolutionary humanism'.

Let me explain why I say this: either of two things may convince us that a higher Pole of completion and consolidation (which we may call Omega) awaits us at the higher term of Hominization; those two are the specific curve followed by the cosmic milieu in which we are involved, and the absolute necessity of being irreversible which is inherent in our reflective Action. Nevertheless, however strongly convinced we may be of the existence of this Omega Pole, we can never in the end reach it except by extrapolation: it remains by nature conjectural, it remains a postulate.

There is the further reason that even if Omega is accepted as 'guaranteed in its future existence', our hopes can envisage its features only in a vague and misty way; in our picture of it the Collective and Potential are dangerously mixed up with the Personal and Real.

What, on the other hand, do we find if our minds can embrace simultaneously both contemporary neo-Christianity and contemporary neo-Humanism, and so first suspect and then accept as proved that the *Christ of Revelation* is none other than the *Omega of Evolution*?

Forthwith, we both see with our minds and feel with our hearts that the experiential Universe is once and for all activized and plenified.

On the one hand, we can indeed begin to distinguish above us the positive gleam of a way out at the highest point of the future. There is no longer any danger of our suffocating, for we are in a World whose peak certainly opens out *in Christo Jesu.*

And on the other, what comes down to us from those heights is not merely air for our lungs; it is the radiance of a love. The World, therefore, is not simply a place in which a Life can breathe because its power to look into the future has been aroused; we can now see its evolutive summit and so feel its absorbing magnetic attraction.

Speaking in terms of energy, we have to recognize that Christ intervenes today at exactly the right moment not only to save Man from revolt against Life, justifiably prompted by the mere threat, the mere suspicion, of a total death – but also to give him that most forceful stimulus without which, it would appear, Thought cannot attain the planetary term of its Reflection.

It is Christ, in very truth, who saves,

– but should we not immediately add that at the same time it is Christ who is saved by

Evolution?

2. The Consummation of Christ by the Universe

Christian tradition is unanimous that there is more in the total Christ than Man and God. There is also He who, in his 'theandric' being, gathers up the whole of Creation: *in quo omnia constant.*

Hitherto, and in spite of the dominant position accorded to it by St Paul in his view of the World, this third aspect or function – we might even say, in a true sense of the words, this third 'nature' of Christ (neither human nor divine, but cosmic) – has not noticeably attracted the explicit attention of the faithful or of theologians.

Things have changed today: we now see how the Universe, along all the lines known to us experientially, is beginning to grow to fantastic dimensions, so that the time has come for Christianity to develop a precise consciousness of all the hopes stimulated by the dogma of the Universality of Christ when it is enlarged to this new scale, and of all the difficulties, too, that it raises.

Hopes, of course: because, if the World is becoming so dauntingly vast and powerful, it must follow that Christ is very much greater even than we used to think.

But difficulties, too: because, in a word, how can we conceive that Christ 'is immensified' to meet the demands of our new Space-Time, without thereby losing his personality – that side of him that calls for our worship – and without in some way evaporating?

It is precisely here that in a flash there comes into the picture the astounding, emancipating, harmony between a religion that is Christic, and an Evolution that is convergent, in type.

Were the World a static Cosmos – or if, again, it formed a divergent system – the only relations we could invoke as a basis for Christ's Primacy over Creation would be (make no mistake about this) by nature conceptual and juridical. He would be Christ the king of all things because he has been *proclaimed* to be such – and not because any organic relationship of dependence exists (or could even conceivably exist) between Him and a Multiplicity that is fundamentally *irreducible*.

From such an *'extrinsical'* point of view, one could hardly, with any honesty, speak of a Christic 'cosmicity'.

But if, on the other hand, and as the facts make certain, the Universe – our Universe[3] – does indeed form a sort of biological 'vortex' dynamically centred upon itself, then we cannot fail to see the emergence at the system's temporo-spatial peak, of a unique and unparalleled position, where Christ, effortlessly and without distortion, becomes literally and with unprecedented realism, the *Pantocrator*.

Starting from an evolutive Omega at which we assume Christ to stand, not only does it become possible to conceive Christ as radiating *physically* over the terrifying totality of things but, what is more, that radiation must inevitably work up to a maximum of penetrative and activating power.

Once he has been raised to the position of Prime Mover of the evolutive movement of complexity-consciousness, the cosmic-Christ becomes cosmically possible. And at the same time, *ipso facto*, he acquires and develops in complete plenitude, a veritable *omnipresence of transformation*. For each one of us, every energy and everything that happens, is superanimated by his influence and his magnetic power. To sum up, Cosmogenesis reveals itself, along the line of its main axis, first as Biogenesis and then Noogenesis, and finally culminates in the Christogenesis which every Christian venerates.

And then there appears to the dazzled eyes of the believer the eucharistic mystery itself, extended infinitely into a veritable universal transubstantiation, in which the words of the Consecration are applied not only to the sacrificial bread and wine but, mark you, to the whole mass of joys and sufferings produced by the Convergence of the World as it progresses.[4]

And it is then, too, that there follow in consequence the possibilities of a universal Communion.

94

3. The Divine Milieu

Hitherto Man had tried only two roads in his efforts to unite himself to the Divine. The first was to escape from the World into the 'beyond'. The second, on the other hand, was to allow himself to dissolve into things and so be united with them monistically. What else, in fact, could man try in a cosmic economy if he wished to escape from the internal and external multiplicity that was tormenting him?

By contrast, from the moment when the Universe, through Cosmogenesis directed upon a Christic Omega, assumes for us the shape of a truly convergent whole, a third and completely new road opens up by which the 'mystic' may arrive at total unity. And (since the whole Sphere of the World is precisely a Centre in process of centration upon itself) that road is to give all one's strength and all one's heart to coinciding with the Focus of universal unification, as yet diffuse but nevertheless already in existence.

With the Christified Universe (or, which comes to the same thing, with the universalized Christ) an evolutive super-milieu appears – which I have called 'the Divine Milieu' – and it is now essential that every man should fully understand the specific properties (or 'charter') of that milieu, which are themselves linked with the emergence of completely new psychic dimensions.

All that I have just been saying leads up to this, that what basically characterizes the Divine Milieu is that it constitutes a dynamic reality in which all opposition between Universal and Personal is being wiped out, but not by any confusion of the two: the multiple 'reflected' elements of the World attaining their fulfilment, each one still within its own infinitesimal *ego*, by integrant accession to the Christic *Ego*, towards which the totality of Participated Being gravitates; and in so doing, the Participated, in consummating itself, consummates that *Ego* too.

By virtue of this total inter-linking of convergence, no elementary *ego* can move closer to the Christic Centre without causing the entire global sphere to be compressed more tightly; similarly, the Christic Centre cannot even begin to communicate itself more fully to the least of the World's elements, without causing itself to be contained more strictly within the entire integument of concrete realities.

Whether rising or descending, every operation (because of the very curvature of the particular 'space' within which it finds completion) is ultimately pan-humanizing and pan-Christifying at the same time.

So true is this, that to the 'informed eye' all opposition is blurred between attachment and detachment, between action and prayer, between centration upon self and excentration upon the Other.

And this because God can in future be experienced and apprehended (and can even, in a true sense, be completed) by the whole ambient totality of what we call Evolution – *in Christo Jesu* . . .

This is still, of course, Christianity and always will be, but a Christianity re-incarnated for the second time (Christianity, we might say, squared) in the spiritual energies of Matter. It is precisely the 'ultra-Christianity' we need here and now to meet the ever more urgent demands of the 'ultra-human'.

D. THE RELIGION OF TOMORROW

Although we are not as alive to it as we should be, the key question that is beginning to present itself to Mankind in process of planetary arrangement is a problem of spiritual *activation*. In our recent mastery of the Atomic we have reached the primordial sources of the *Energy of Evolution*. This decisive victory cannot be carried to its conclusion unless, to match it at the other pole of things, we find a way to increase the *Drive of Evolution* to an equal degree within the Noosphere. New powers call for new aspirations. If Mankind is to use its new access of physical power with balanced control, it cannot do without a rebound of intensity in its eagerness to act, to seek, to create.

For a reflective being, such an eagerness for self-fulfilment can fundamentally be found only in the expectation of a supreme Summit of consciousness which can be attained, and so provide a permanent home.

And such a hope-inspired faith in some future consummation cannot, in turn, take any form but that of a 'religion' in the truest, and most psychologically apt, meaning of the word.

A Religion of Evolution: that, when all is said and done, is what Man needs ever more explicitly if he is to survive and 'super-live', as soon as he becomes conscious of his power to ultra-hominize himself and of his duty to do so.

'*In a system of cosmo-noo-genesis, the comparative value of religious creeds may be measured by their respective power of evolutive activation.*'

If we use this criterion, where, among the various currents of modern thought, can we hope to find, if not the fullness at least the germ, of what (judging by its power to ultra-hominize) may be regarded as the Religion of tomorrow?

In this order of ideas, we immediately meet a fact which it is impossible to reject. It is this: the sort of Faith that is needed, in terms of energy, for the correct functioning of a totalized human world has not yet been satisfactorily formulated in any quarter at all – neither among the *religions of the Ahead* (Marxist and other Humanisms) nor among the *religions of the Above* (the various theisms and pantheisms).

When I say '*neither among the religions of the Ahead*', I speak advisedly. It may be because they are nervous of admitting the reality of a biological convergence of Mankind upon itself and the consequences that this entails; or it may be because they persist in seeing in the evolutive rise of the Psychic no more than an ephemeral epi-phenomenon: whatever the reason, all the existing forms of Humanism (even the least materialist) are demonstrably equally incapable of giving Man the stimulus of confidence that is

indispensable to his advance towards a supremely desirable and –
what is even more important – indestructible goal, lying at
the term of his activities. Whether the reason be the depersonal-
izing socializing of individuals or the unexorcized threat of a
total death, there is not a single one of the 'religions' as yet
produced by Science in which the Universe does not become
hopelessly icy, hopelessly closed (and that ultimately means
uninhabitable) ahead, in its 'polar' zones. There you have the
truth!

Nor, let me add, *among the religions of the Above*. For (and in this
direction we may confine ourselves to the most significant and
the most promising instance, by which I mean 'classical'
Christianity) it is becoming every day more obvious that our
generation finds something lacking in an *Evangelism* infected
with a *near-Manichaeanism*, in which the advances of Knowledge
and Technology are presented not as a primary accompanying
condition of human spiritualization, but simply as an added
extra; in which failure is regarded as on the same level with
success, endowed with just as much, if not more, sanctifying
value; in which the Cross is constantly held up before us to
remind us of our world's initial miscarriage; in which the
Parousia floats on the horizon in an atmosphere of coming
catastrophe rather than of fulfilment.

We must admit that if the neo-humanisms of the twentieth
century de-humanize us under their uninspired skies, yet on the
other hand the still-living forms of theism – starting with the
Christian – tend to under-humanize us in the rarified atmosphere
of too lofty skies. These religions are still systematically closed
to the wide horizons and great winds of Cosmogenesis, and can
no longer truly be said to feel with the Earth – an Earth whose
internal frictions they can still lubricate like a soothing oil, but
whose driving energies they cannot animate as they should.

It is here that the power of the 'Christic' bursts into view – in
the form in which it has emerged from what we have been
saying, engendered by the progressive coming together, in our

consciousness, of the cosmic demands of an incarnate Word and the spiritual potentialities of a convergent Universe. We have already seen how a strictly governed amalgam is effected, in the Divine Milieu, between the forces of Heaven and the forces of Earth. An exact conjunction is produced between the old God of the Above and the new God of the Ahead.

Indeed, once we cease to isolate Christianity and to oppose it to the moving, once we resolutely connect it up to the World in movement, then, however obsolete it may appear to our modern Gentiles, it instantly and completely regains its original power to activate and attract.

And this is because, once that 'coupling' has been effected, it is only Christianity, of all the forms of worship born in the course of human history, that can display the astonishing power of energizing to the full, by 'amorizing' them, both the powers of growth and life and the powers of diminishment and death, at the heart of, and in the process of, the Noogenesis in which we are involved.

As I said before, it is still, and will always be, Christianity: but a 're-born' Christianity, as assured of victory tomorrow as it was in its infancy – because it alone (through the double power, *at last fully understood*, of its Cross and Resurrection) is capable of becoming the Religion whose specific property it is to provide the driving force in Evolution.

CONCLUSION: THE PROMISED LAND[5]

Energy, then, becomes Presence.

And so the possibility is disclosed for, opens out for, Man, not only of believing and hoping but (what is much more unexpected and much more valuable) *of loving*, co-extensively and co-organically with all the past, the present and the future of a Universe which is in process of concentration upon itself.

It would seem that a single ray of such a light falling like a spark, no matter where, on the Noosphere, would be bound to produce an explosion of such violence that it would almost instantaneously set the face of the Earth ablaze and make it completely new.

How is it, then, that as I look around me, still dazzled by what I have seen, I find that I am almost the only person of my kind, the only one to have *seen*? And so I cannot, when asked, quote a single writer, a single work, that gives a clearly expressed description of the wonderful 'Diaphany' that has transfigured everything for me?

How, most of all, can it be that 'when I come down from the mountain' and in spite of the glorious vision I still retain, I find that I am so little a better man, so little at peace, so incapable of expressing in my actions, and thus adequately communicating to others, the wonderful unity that I feel encompassing me?

Is there, in fact, a Universal Christ, is there a Divine Milieu?

Or am I, after all, simply the dupe of a mirage in my own mind?

I often ask myself that question.

Every time, however, that I begin to doubt, three successive waves of evidence rise up from the deep within me to counter that doubt, sweeping away from my mind the mistaken fear that my 'Christic' may be no more than an illusion.

First, there is the evidence provided by the *coherence* that this ineffable element (or Milieu) introduces into the underlying depths of my mind and heart. As, of course, I know only too well, in spite of the ambitious grandeur of my ideas, I am still, in practice, imperfect to a disturbing degree. For all the claims implicit in its expression, my faith does not produce in me as much real charity, as much calm trust, as the catechism still taught to children produces in the humble worshipper kneeling beside me. Nevertheless I know, too, that this sophisticated faith, of which I make such poor use, is the only faith I can tolerate, the only faith that can satisfy me – and even (of this I am certain) the only faith that can meet the needs of the simple souls, the good folk, of tomorrow.

Next there is the evidence provided by the *contagious power* of a form of Charity in which it becomes possible to love God 'not only with all one's body and all one's soul' but with the whole Universe-in-evolution. It would be impossible for me, as I admitted earlier, to quote a single 'authority' (religious or lay) in which I could claim fully to recognize myself, whether in relation to my 'cosmic' or my 'Christic' vision. On the other hand, I cannot fail to feel around me – if only from the way in which 'my ideas' are becoming more widely accepted – the pulsation of countless people who are all – ranging from the border-line of unbelief to the depths of the cloister – thinking and feeling, or at least beginning vaguely to feel, just as I do. It is indeed heartening to know that I am not a lone discoverer, but that I am, quite simply, responding to the vibration that (given a particular condition of Christianity and of the world) is necessarily active in all the souls around me. It is, in consequence, exhilarating to feel that I am not just myself or all alone, that my name is legion, that I am 'all men', and that this is true even in as much as the single-mindedness of tomorrow can be recognized as throbbing into life in the depths of my being.

Finally, there is the evidence contained in the *superiority* of my vision compared with what I had been taught – even though there is at the same time an *identity* with it. Because of their very function, neither the God who draws us to himself, nor the world whose evolution we share, can afford to be, the former less perfect a Being, the latter less powerful a stimulant, than our concepts and needs demand. In either case – unless we are going to accept a positive discord in the very stuff of things – it is in the direction of the fullest that the truth lies. Now, as we saw earlier, it is in the 'Christic' that, in the century in which we are living, the Divine reaches the summit of adorability, and the evolutionary the extreme limit of activation. This can mean only one thing, that it is in that direction that the human must inevitably incline; there, sooner or later, to find unity.

Once that is understood, I immediately find a perfectly natural explanation for my isolation and apparent idiosyncrasy.

Everywhere on Earth, at this moment, in the new spiritual atmosphere created by the appearance of the idea of evolution, there float, in a state of extreme mutual sensitivity, love of God and faith in the world: the two essential components of the Ultra-human. These two components are everywhere 'in the air'; generally, however, they are not strong enough, *both at the same time*, to combine with one another *in one and the same subject*. In me, it happens by pure chance (temperament, upbringing, background) that the proportion of the one to the other is correct, and the fusion of the two has been effected spontaneously – not as yet with sufficient force to spread explosively – but strong enough nevertheless to make it clear that the process is possible – and that *sooner or later there will be a chain-reaction.*

This is one more proof that Truth has to appear only once, in one single mind, for it to be impossible for anything ever to prevent it from spreading universally and setting everything ablaze.

New York, March 1955

1. In *The Heart of Matter* (above) I have tried to describe, more or less autobiographically, the general process and the principal stages of this 'apparition'.

2. The physical reasons are structural: it is the nature of union to consolidate – so long as the unification continues. And the psychological reasons are based on logical necessity: if the biological unification of the World could be conceived as being bound sooner or later to come to a halt, the anticipation of such an ending (see below) would be sufficient to produce in us an abhorrence of super-living and so kill our evolutive effort of co-reflection.

3. And probably (in so far as to create is to unify) *every* possible Universe.

4. Cf. *The Priest* in *Writings in Time of War*, pp. 203-24. (Ed.'s note)

5. Soon after the end of the World War I, Père Teilhard had discerned, from the summit his thoughts had reached, the emergence of the other Earth:

'I shall advance into the future with the new strength of my twofold faith as man and as Christian: for, from the mountain peak, I have seen *the Promised Land.*' Goldscheuer (Baden) February 1919. In *Writings in Time of War*, p. 288. (Ed.'s note)

THE LAST PAGE OF
PIERRE TEILHARD DE CHARDIN'S DIARY

Maundy Thursday, 7 April 1955

Three days before his death, Pierre Teilhard de Chardin wrote the notes that are printed overleaf; with the last page of his diary, they represent his supreme testimony as thinker and religious. The text has been deciphered and annotated by Claude Cuénot, and published by him in *Ce que Teilhard a vraiment dit* (Paris 1973).

4 April 1955 (. . .)

distinguish Man $\begin{cases} \text{1) } \textit{fully developed} \text{ (Cosmos-humanism)} \\ \text{2) } \textit{fully evolved} \text{ (= the planetary-phyletic} \end{cases}$
$\qquad\qquad\qquad\qquad\qquad\qquad$ the planetary Human

Humanism of Cosmogenesis

7 April[1]
(Maundy Thursday) → *What I believe*
$\qquad\qquad\qquad$ *Syntheses* (theological confirmation! . . .
$\qquad\qquad\qquad\qquad$ Revelation ultra-satisfied!)

$\begin{cases} \text{1) St Paul } \dots \text{ the 3 verses:}[2] \ \epsilon\nu \ \pi\alpha\sigma\iota \ \pi\alpha\nu\tau\alpha \ \theta\epsilon os[3] \\ \text{2) } Cosmos = Cosmogenesis - biogenesis - noogenesis - Christogenesis \\ \quad cosmos = cosmogenesis \rightarrow biogenesis \rightarrow noogenesis \end{cases}$

$\qquad\qquad\qquad$ (The Phenomenon of Man)

The 2 articles
of my Credo
$\left\{\begin{array}{l} \text{3) The Universe is centred (Evolutively, Above} \\ \qquad\qquad\qquad\qquad\qquad\qquad\qquad\qquad \text{Ahead} \\ \text{Christ is its centre} \\ \qquad\qquad \text{(Christian Phenomenon)} \\ \qquad\qquad noogenesis = Christogenesis \end{array}\right\}$

$\begin{cases} (\equiv \text{St Paul, loco citato!}) \\ \text{The } consistencel \text{ of 'Spirit'} \end{cases}$
$\qquad\qquad$ (radial)

? *Plan* 'What I believe'
$\begin{cases} \text{1) Centred Cosmos – in } \textit{the 3rd infinite} \text{ – } neo\text{-}humanism \text{ (ultra-Human)} \\ \text{2) Christ is the centre of the Cosmos (noogenesis = Christogenesis)} \end{cases}$
$\qquad\qquad\qquad$ → neo–Christianity (Neo-Nicaea)
$\qquad$ → saves noogenesis $\Big\}$ $\qquad\qquad$ ($\equiv$ Paul . . .)
$\qquad\quad$ is saved by it

1. The text is wrongly dated 6 April: but Easter Sunday fell on 10 April 1955. (Note by C.C.)
2. 1 Cor. xv. 26, 27, 28. (Note by C.C.)
3. En pàsi panta theos = God all in all (Note by C.C.)

PART II

NOTE ON THE ESSENCE
OF TRANSFORMISM

The *Note on the Essence of Transformism* (not dated by the author) has been published in Volume 2 of *Études teilhardiennes*, with the approval of the Teilhard de Chardin Foundation. When the editor of that review, Dr J. P. Demoulin, was trying to determine as closely as possible the date when the Note was written, he drew our attention to Père Teilhard's war-time *Diary*. There, under the date 21 November 1919, we find a page headed *The Essence of Transformism (L'Essentiel du Transformisme)*. A careful reading of what is written there, combined with a re-reading of 'How the Transformist Question Presents itself today' (of which the third section is entitled 'The Essence of Transformism') in *The Vision of the Past*, pp. 7–25, suggests that the Note printed here is intermediate between the other two.

A further reason for dating it in the middle of 1920 is provided by what we read in the third paragraph, 'The aim of the first note, etc.' The only second note Père Teilhard could have had in mind is the 'Note on Progress', which is dated 10 August 1920.

This latter note, in fact, supports transformism (in the sense of organic connection in the succession of living beings) by emphasizing the movement which ensures that connection – continuous and directed Progress: in one word, Evolution.

The lyrical ending of this second Note admirably summarizes the two essays:

'... the man whose eyes have been opened will make his way back into the sealed depths of Nature. There he will peer down into the vast tangle of branches that supports him and disappears into the far distance below him, lost in the heart of the dim Past; and once again he will fill his soul to overflowing as he contemplates and vibrates in sympathy with a single-minded and determined movement which is written into the series of dead layers and the present distribution of all living beings. If he then looks upwards, to the wide areas that wait for new creations, he will consecrate himself, body and soul, with newly strengthened faith, to a Progress which draws or sweeps along even those who reject it.' Cf. *The Future of Man*, p. 24. The second volume of the *Diary*, which includes this passage, is to be published by *Editions Fayard*, edited by Dr Karl Schmitz-Moormann.

It is often difficult for a scientist not to be irritated when he has occasion to read a paper that deals with problems of evolution. Nine times out of ten, if the writer is an opponent of transformism, his blows are wide of the mark, or he is flogging a dead horse. Nine times out of ten, again, if he is a supporter of Darwin or Lamarck, his arguments in favour of biological evolution leave intact the essential position of those who believe in fixed species, or do no more than offend them to no good purpose.

Discussions about Transformism are generally fruitless because there is no common meeting ground.

The aim of the first *Note* is to discover the exact point to which the fundamental opposition between fixists and transformists can be narrowed down. It is a point, I believe, that is not explicitly recognized by all; but all feel it instinctively and unmistakably; and fundamentally, while questions that are at times of very minor importance and relevance are being discussed, it is in the end the acceptance or rejection of this single point that is the occasion of such passionate argument.

If we wish to be certain of not missing this most important spot at which the basic divergence first makes itself felt, we have only to take up our position first in an area where, as all are agreed, there is as yet no cleavage between our minds; we can then advance progressively towards those areas where opinions are disputed.

Let us start, then, in this analysis from the fact, eminently clear to everyone, that there is a certain unity of forms in Nature. We did not have to wait for Darwin to note that there is a resemblance between Man and the monkey, between the crab and the crayfish, between the cat and the leopard. Living creatures are grouped in categories; they form families, genera, species. A child needs no help to discover that fact.

The immediate consequence, universally recognized, of the existence of a morphological continuity in Nature is that since living beings form an 'arranged' whole, they are not scattered objects completely detached from one another. Something connects them, in their forms and in their order of appearance. *They hold together by something.* Here again, everyone is of the same mind.

Already, however, we find that we have to take a further step, and that a decisive one. At its most generalized level, what is the nature of this 'something' in virtue of which living beings are constituted of elements, in which we see kinship and gradation, of one and the same whole? What sort of 'cement' is it that is distributed among the pieces added to the Universe in succession? Is the *stuff* of this element *intellectual* or *physical*? It is here that we come close to the great rift where, if we are not careful, the transformist question becomes a tangle of misunderstandings.

A first, and theoretically possible, answer to the question we have asked is as follows: 'Living beings are distributed in the Universe according to a purely intellectual plan. There is no determinism to bridge their various forms, no connection that is physical in nature; there is only an artificial continuity. The law which governs the succession of living forms, the reason for their resemblances, is not to be sought within things: it is entirely concentrated in a creative idea, which develops the design it has, in its wisdom, conceived, in successive points established in a given series. The Universe is a concatenation of beings, germinating independently of one another. If the motion of its curve is to be understood, it must be broken down into a series of individual terms, each one established as a distinct new whole. If, for example, the product of the term $N+1$ is governed by the term N, it is solely in virtue of its numerical order in the creative plan, and not as the result of an influence exerted upon it organically by N. Living forms constitute a chain, they lead on from one to another, by reason of a *logical take-over sequence* that exists in the mind of God.

This theory might be called 'logicalism'.

The second answer, again expressed in very general terms, to the crucial question: 'What is the nature of the mechanism that governs the form of successive living beings and the order in which they appear?' is as follows. 'Living beings are disposed in their various categories, they control one another in their successive appearances, through the influence of that factor which, in its reality and immediacy, is *physical, organic, and cosmic.* The Universe is so constituted that living beings, regarded as in the order of secondary causes, gradually encourage one another's development as an effect of their biological condition. Thus, if the Horse followed *Mesohippus*, if Man was born after certain Primates, this was through the *operation* of a *specific physical agent.* It was physically impossible for the first Horse, the first Man or the first Moneron to appear either earlier or later than they did. Without as yet pre-judging in any way the particular physical nature of this connection, and without even asserting that there is a line of descent, properly so called, linking organic beings, we hold firmly to the belief that the various terms of life appear as a physical response to one another. Each one of them has already been formed by the whole past of the Universe, and when its own turn comes it is introduced, like a ripe fruit, at its appointed place in the development of the whole.'

That sums up the position of the advocates of the physical theory.

When once these two basic attitudes, the logical and the physical, have been properly understood, it will be evident that the roots of the transformist controversy do not lie where we thought they did; it is not a matter of Darwinism or Lamarckism (that is quite clear) nor of Mono- or Poly-phyletism (which is not so widely appreciated), nor is it even quite the problem of the line of descent (which may well come as a surprise to many persons). The only real issue is, should we be logicalists or physicalists?

An experiment will illustrate my point.

Suppose that you are a fixist and that you concede to the transformist a fluctuation, as extensive as you please, within animal forms. Grant his assertion that all the Mammals, all the Fishes, all the Insects are descended each from the same stock. But hold fast to your view that the first Mammal, the first Fish, the first Insect, appeared arbitrarily and artificially at the moment chosen by the Creator, and not in response to the Universe's physical need to accept them – not, that is to say, to meet the Universe's fully developed power to produce them – then the Transformist will turn a deaf ear to your arguments.

On the other hand, prove to this same Transformist by good solid facts that the animal Kingdom is essentially poly-phyletic and that there are as many different stocks as there are systematic genera or species: then he will accept your discoveries without turning a hair, he will be grateful to you and will believe that he has no need to change in any respect his fundamental transformist attitude – even though the shape of his vision of the World has been completely modified. Why is this? It is because these countless phyla you have pointed out to him will still seem to him to be successive bursts that obey a single law. They will be to him the surface shoots produced in succession by an invisible, but physically present, rhizome.

We see, then, that we might imagine a transformist who believed in the original multiplicity of species, and a fixist who would accept only a single one! They would have reversed their apparent positions without modifying their fundamental point of view.

If you reduce a transformist to the simplest terms, you will be left with a physicalist. It is 'faith' in one organic physical inter-relation of living beings, it is that and *nothing else* which constitutes the necessary and sufficient disposition for an evolutionist mind.

Biologists are apt to argue about the limits of heredity or about the nature of some particular primitive characteristics, or they may reject this or that line of descent. Some writers conclude from this that the idea of transformism is losing ground. This is pure *naïveté*. When it comes to the existence of an organic connection between all living forms, there is not a single natural scientist worthy of the name who does not feel his fundamental conviction grow stronger every day with every new detail. He may hesitate about the precise nature of the physical agent shared by the successive forms of life; but the belief that such an agent exists, whether it be confused with the generative function or not, the dream that one day we shall be able to put a name to it and define its behaviour, it is there we find his most precious conviction and his grandest hope.

So much for the transformists. And now it will be no injustice to the fixists, I am sure, to say that the very adoption of their fixist position shows that it is they who are logicalists. Nor, indeed, can they logically be anything else. They will, I know, take exception to this judgement, and deny the attribution. They will maintain that, in their view, the divine plan can and must be expressed in a property conferred on secondary causes of being able progressively to stimulate the development of living forms. Yet, in so doing, the fixists are contradicting themselves and are already, strictly speaking, transformist. For the transformist retains the right, as much as anyone else, to believe that a creative act is necessary to set the world in motion. What he postulates is quite simply that this perennial and indispensable act on the part of the first cause, comes to us in the order of history and experience *in the form of an organically established movement.* And that is precisely what you fixists are now conceding.

We have to make a choice: there is either evolution or intrusion. Living forms, in the order of their appearance, either physically pave the way for one another and introduce one another: and this is true transformism, with all its historical and biological consequences. Or, the various living forms arise in isolation (without, that is, any created being to introduce them), there are no offshoots and no phyla, and we are therefore obliged *immediately* to fall back on the intervention of an extra-cosmic intelligence in order to explain the resemblances we find among organic beings. If that alternative is accepted, we have pure logicalism, with all its improbabilities.

If the fixists push their view home, they are left with no hypothesis but that of a divine plan which is effected *with no created intermediary*. Only so can they interpret the glaring fact of the morphological unity of living forms. They are either unreservedly logicalists, or they are transformists, or they can give us no explanation at all.

Nevertheless, we are obliged to find an explanation of the inter-connection of living beings. And this not to satisfy an unworthy whim nor for the mere pleasure of argument, but under the irresistible impulse of what is most sacred in Man, the need to know and feel a sense of direction.

The three simple considerations I have outlined above seem to me to merit attention. The fact is that to recognize that trans-formists are in reality physicalists, and fixists are logicalists – and so reduce to a single profound divergence the thousand and one superficial controversies that so uselessly surround discussion of biological evolution – finally, to replace the secondary problems of heredity and generation by the great question of the 'universal cement' in things: to do this would really place the philosophic question of transformism on solid ground. It is on this exact point of Physicalism and Logicalism, and nowhere else, that those who hold opposing views can make contact and meet face to face – if indeed any discussion be still possible when the terms of the problem are expressed in so simple and crude a form.

For we must admit that when the transformist question is reduced to its essentials it seems almost to disappear; and this because it becomes so clear, first, that nobody is inflexibly fixist unless he takes refuge in the abstract domain of the First Cause; and secondly, that in the domain of concrete realities, everyone is, if not avowedly at least substantially, transformist.

1920. Earlier than the *Note on Progress* of 10 August 1920.

ON MY ATTITUDE TO
THE OFFICIAL CHURCH

As early as 1921, Père Teilhard, with characteristic insight and foresight, was discerning the danger of a breach between a Christianity folded back upon its own past, and a world that was being drawn ahead at breakneck speed by science. Caught between the consequent stalemate on the one side and the irresistible pressure on the other of the Holy Spirit whose function it is to lead the mystical body of Christ to its final term, his life was torn between two loyalties to which he wished at all costs to be true: loyalty to the ecclesiastical hierarchy, and loyalty to the Spirit of God. It was in this state of mind, which was to last until his death, that Père Teilhard wrote the following statement, addressed to a non-Catholic friend who accused him of bad faith in his submission. It need hardly be pointed out that he deliberately confined his reasons for loyalty to such as would be acceptable to an unbeliever.

For inclusion in this volume, we have detached the statement itself from the accompanying letter. The latter will be published in its entirety in one of the volumes of correspondence.

If there is one thing I fear less than everything else, it is, I believe, persecution for my opinions. There are a good many points about which I may be diffident, but when it comes to questions of Truth and intellectual independence there is no holding me – I can envisage no finer end than to sacrifice oneself for a conviction. That is precisely how Christ died. Still, there is rather more involved: the more I become aware of certain failures on the part of the Church to adapt herself, of a loss of her vitality (to which I shall return later), the more I recognize how incompetent I am and how ill-qualified to take it upon myself to give a definitive appreciation of her in her general or, if you prefer the word, her axial character. The Church represents so powerful a channelling of what constitutes the moral and 'sublimating' life-blood of souls, a conduit dug so deep into the whole of man's past – in spite of certain accidental and ephemeral lapses from generosity, she has to so marked a degree the faculty of encouraging human nature to develop itself fully and harmoniously, that I would feel guilty of disloyalty to Life if I tried to free myself from so organic a current as the Church provides. In spite of the unvoiced and instinctive wish I have at certain times experienced, the wish to find a positive reason for 'dropping everything', I cannot shut my eyes to the fact that 'It would be a biological blunder for me to leave the religious current of Catholicism'.

Everything in that current is not equally to my taste; but everything in it has a certain flexibility, and I can see nothing outside it that sorts better with the tendencies and hopes that I feel. Even if we were to suppose that this form of religion is even further from Truth than we think, the fact would still remain that it is the most perfect approximation to that Truth – and that, if we are to mount higher, *we have to outdistance it by growing with it*; we must not abandon it to seek our road by ourselves. – If there is a Being who is the Centre of the convergence of all, then that Being is in some way *implicated* in the Church's moral success, and it is impossible that he should hold it against us that we have subordinated our personal preferences to her on many obscure points where our intellectual loyalty is not involved.

Granted that, and since I do not consider that I have the right to break with the Church (it would be suicide), how can I reconcile this communion with her, that I have to maintain, with the divergences that, on certain points, divide me from the *form* commonly accepted *today* in which certain of her beliefs are expressed? Simply by allowing full weight to this essentially orthodox truth, that the Church possesses and transmits from century to century a view of Christ – an experience of Christ, a way of living Christ – whose *definitive form, and whose richness,* she is unable at any given moment *to express completely*. All theologians are obliged to admit this: the Pope and all the assembled Bishops are *powerless* to tell us exactly all that there is in Christ. Christ (his life, knowledge of him) has been part of the deposit of the whole Church (priests and laity) of *all* ages. For Christ to be finally understood calls for the energy of all the Christians that will ever exist until the end of time; and no Council can hasten this long period of maturing. – I am well aware that the evolution of Dogma (a phenomenon which is becoming the over-riding organic law of the Church for all who examine her from outside or experience her from within), I am also well aware that it is still explained by some theologians in terms of a narrowing, naïvely intellectualist theory. In their view Dogma evolves simply by rational analysis of the formulas in which it is expressed. Such a view is untenable. Were that true, it would call only for a sufficiently penetrating intelligence to unravel Dogma and exhaust its meaning, just as one does with a geometric proposition. No, as I have just pointed out, Dogma evolves in accordance with a much more complex logic, much slower, much richer, than that of concepts. It evolves as a man does: he is *the same* at the age of forty as he was at the age of ten but his shape at forty cannot be *deduced* from what it was at ten. The Church changes in the same way: she has a certain identity, but it is the identity of a person, of an organism; and it does not exclude – on the contrary it presupposes – a framework of truths that can be expressed in formulas. (They can practically all be reduced to this single one: Christ is the physical centre of the gathering together of souls in God.) These formulas, however, express an invariable basis of truth *which will necessarily assume a continually new aspect* according as man becomes more conscious of his past and of his environment. In a sense, Christ is in the Church in the same way as the sun is before our eyes. We see the same sun as our fathers saw, and yet we understand it in a much more magnificent way. I believe that the Church is still a

117

child. Christ, by whom she lives, is immeasurably greater than she imagines. And yet, when thousands of years have gone by and Christ's true countenance is a little more plainly seen, the Christians of those days will still, without any reservations, recite the Apostles' Creed.

5 January 1921

THE MASS ON THE WORLD

Père Teilhard had written a first version of *The Mass on the World* (then called *The Priest*) in July 1918, in the Forest of Laigue (*Writings in Time of War*, pp. 203-24). He had just taken, when on leave in Lyons, his solemn vows in the Jesuit house there.

This is the final version. Until his death, however, Père Teilhard was to continue to live his Mass on the World in an ever more intense light. (Cf. *The Christic*, above, p. 80.)

From the desert of Ordos he wrote as follows: 'When for days on end I am travelling by mule I repeat, as I used to – for lack of any other Mass – the "Mass on the World" which you know, and I believe I say it with even more clarity and conviction than before'. (*Letters to Léontine Zanta*, p. 52, 7 August 1923: beside the Shara-osso-gol, eastern Ordos.)

In the same month he was writing to the Abbé Breuil: 'I keep developing, and slightly improving, with the help of prayer, my "Mass upon things". It seems to me that in a sense the true substance to be consecrated each day is the world's development during that day – the bread symbolizing appropriately what creation succeeds in producing, the wine (blood) what creation causes to be lost in exhaustion and suffering in the course of its effort.' (*Letters from a Traveller*, p. 86, 26 August 1923.)

THE OFFERING

Since once again, Lord – though this time not in the forests of the Aisne but in the steppes of Asia – I have neither bread, nor wine, nor altar, I will raise myself beyond these symbols, up to the pure majesty of the real itself; I, your priest, will make the whole earth my altar and on it will offer you all the labours and sufferings of the world.

Over there, on the horizon, the sun has just touched with light the outermost fringe of the eastern sky. Once again, beneath this moving sheet of fire, the living surface of the earth wakes and trembles, and once again begins its fearful travail. I will place on my paten, O God, the harvest to be won by this renewal of labour. Into my chalice I shall pour all the sap which is to be pressed out this day from the earth's fruits.

My paten and my chalice are the depths of a soul laid widely open to all the forces which in a moment will rise up from every corner of the earth and converge upon the Spirit. Grant me the remembrance and the mystic presence of all those whom the light is now awakening to the new day.

One by one, Lord, I see and I love all those whom you have given me to sustain and charm my life. One by one also I number all those who make up that other beloved family which has gradually surrounded me, its unity fashioned out of the most disparate elements, with affinities of the heart, of scientific research and of thought. And again one by one – more vaguely it is true, yet all-inclusively – I call before me the whole vast anonymous army of living humanity; those who surround me and support me though I do not know them; those who come, and those who go; above all, those who in office, laboratory and factory, through their vision of truth or despite their error, truly believe in the progress of earthly reality and who today will take up again their impassioned pursuit of the light.

This restless multitude, confused or orderly, the immensity of which terrifies us; this ocean of humanity whose slow, monotonous wave-flows trouble the hearts even of those whose faith is most firm: it is to this deep that I thus desire all the fibres of my being should respond. All the things in the world to which this day will bring increase; all those that will diminish; all those too that will die: all of them, Lord, I try to gather into my arms, so as to hold them out to you in offering. This is the material of my sacrifice; the only material you desire.

Once upon a time men took into your temple the first fruits of their harvests, the flower of their flocks. But the offering you really want, the offering you mysteriously need every day to appease your hunger, to slake your thirst is nothing less than the growth of the world borne ever onwards in the stream of universal becoming.

Receive, O Lord, this all-embracing host which your whole creation, moved by your magnetism, offers you at this dawn of a new day.

This bread, our toil, is of itself, I know, but an immense fragmentation; this wine, our pain, is no more, I know, than a draught that dissolves. Yet in the very depths of this formless mass you have implanted – and this I am sure of, for I sense it – a desire, irresistible, hallowing, which makes us cry out, believer and unbeliever alike: 'Lord, make us *one*.'

Because, my God, though I lack the soul-zeal and the sublime integrity of your saints, I yet have received from you an overwhelming sympathy for all that stirs within the dark mass of matter; because I know myself to be irremediably less a child of heaven than a son of earth; therefore I will this morning climb up in spirit to the high places, bearing with me the hopes and the miseries of my mother; and there – empowered by that priesthood which you alone (as I firmly believe) have bestowed on me – upon all that in the world of human flesh is now about to be born or to die beneath the rising sun I will call down the Fire.

FIRE OVER THE EARTH

Fire, the source of being: we cling so tenaciously to the illusion that fire comes forth from the depths of the earth and that its flames grow progressively brighter as it pours along the radiant furrows of life's tillage. Lord, in your mercy you gave me to see that this idea is false, and that I must overthrow it if I were ever to have sight of you.

In the beginning was *Power*, intelligent, loving, energizing. In the beginning was the *Word*, supremely capable of mastering and moulding whatever might come into being in the world of matter. In the beginning there were not coldness and darkness: there was the *Fire*. This is the truth.

So, far from light emerging gradually out of the womb of our darkness, it is the Light, existing before all else was made which, patiently, surely, eliminates our darkness. As for us creatures, of ourselves we are but emptiness and obscurity. But you, my God, are the inmost depths, the stability of that eternal *milieu*, without duration or space, in which our cosmos emerges gradually into being and grows gradually to its final completeness, as it loses those boundaries which to our eyes seem so immense. Everything is being; everywhere there is being and nothing but being, save in the fragmentation of creatures and the clash of their atoms.

Blazing Spirit, Fire, personal, supersubstantial, the consummation of a union so immeasurably more lovely and more desirable than that destructive fusion of which all the pantheists dream: be pleased yet once again to come down and breathe a soul into the newly formed, fragile film of matter with which this day the world is to be freshly clothed.

I know we cannot forestall, still less dictate to you, even the smallest of your actions; from you alone comes all initiative – and this applies in the first place to my prayer.

Radiant Word, blazing Power, you who mould the multiple so as to breathe your life into it; I pray you, lay on us those your hands – powerful, considerate, omnipresent, those hands which do not (like our human hands) touch now here, now there, but which plunge into the depths and the totality, present and past, of things so as to reach us simultaneously through all that is most immense and most inward within us and around us.

May the might of those invincible hands direct and transfigure for the great world you have in mind that earthly travail which I have gathered into my heart and now offer you in its entirety. Remould it, rectify it, recast it down to the depths from whence it springs. You know how your creatures can come into being only, like shoot from stem, as part of an endlessly renewed process of evolution.

Do you now therefore, speaking through my lips, pronounce

over this earthly travail your twofold efficacious word: the word without which all that our wisdom and our experience have built up must totter and crumble – the word through which all our most far-reaching speculations and our encounter with the universe are come together into a unity. Over every living thing which is to spring up, to grow, to flower, to ripen during this day say again the words: This is my Body. And over every death-force which waits in readiness to corrode, to wither, to cut down, speak again your commanding words which express the supreme mystery of faith: This is my Blood.[1]

FIRE IN THE EARTH

It is done.

Once again the Fire has penetrated the earth.

Not with sudden crash of thunderbolt, riving the mountain-tops: does the Master break down doors to enter his own home? Without earthquake, or thunderclap: the flame has lit up the whole world from within. All things individually and collectively are penetrated and flooded by it, from the inmost core of the tiniest atom to the mighty sweep of the most universal laws of being: so naturally has it flooded every element, every energy, every connecting-link in the unity of our cosmos; that one might suppose the cosmos to have burst spontaneously into flame.

In the new humanity which is begotten today the Word prolongs the unending act of his own birth; and by virtue of his immersion in the world's womb the great waters of the kingdom of matter have, without even a ripple, been endued with life. No visible tremor marks this inexpressible transformation; and yet, mysteriously and in very truth, at the touch of the supersubstantial Word the immense host which is the universe is made flesh. Through your own incarnation, my God, all matter is henceforth incarnate.

Through our thoughts and our human experiences, we long ago became aware of the strange properties which make the universe so like our flesh:

like the flesh it attracts us by the charm which lies in the mystery of its curves and folds and in the depths of its eyes;

like the flesh it disintegrates and eludes us when submitted to our analyses or to our fallings away and in the process of its own perdurance;

as with the flesh, it can only be embraced in the endless reaching out to attain what lies beyond the confines of what has been given to us.

All of us, Lord, from the moment we are born feel within us this disturbing mixture of remoteness and nearness; and in our heritage of sorrow and hope, passed down to us through the ages, there is no yearning more desolate than that which makes us weep with vexation and desire as we stand in the midst of the Presence which hovers about us nameless and impalpable and is indwelling in all things. *Si forte attrectent eum.*[2]

Now, Lord, through the consecration of the world the luminosity and fragrance which suffuse the universe take on for me the lineaments of a body and a face – in you. What my mind glimpsed through its hesitant explorations, what my heart craved with so little expectation of fulfilment, you now magnificently unfold for me: the fact that your creatures are not merely so linked together in solidarity that none can exist unless all the rest surround it, but that all are so dependent on a single central reality that a true life, borne in common by them all, gives them ultimately their consistence and their unity.

Shatter, my God, through the daring of your revelation the childishly timid outlook that can conceive of nothing greater or more vital in the world than the pitiable perfection of our human organism. On the road to a bolder comprehension of the universe the children of this world day by day outdistance the masters of Israel; but do you, Lord Jesus, 'in whom all things subsist', show yourself to those who love you as the higher Soul and the physical centre of your creation? Are you not well aware that for us this is a question of life or death? As for me, if I could not believe that your real Presence animates and makes tractable and enkindles even the very least of the energies which invade me or brush past me, would I not die of cold?

I thank you, my God, for having in a thousand different ways led my eyes to discover the immense simplicity of things. Little by little, through the irresistible development of those yearnings you implanted in me as a child, through the influence of gifted friends who entered my life at certain moments to bring light and strength to my mind, and through the awakenings of spirit I owe to the successive initiations, gentle and terrible, which you caused me to undergo: through all these I have been brought to the point where I can no longer see anything, nor any longer breathe, outside that *milieu* in which all is made one.

At this moment when your life has just poured with super-abundant vigour into the sacrament of the world, I shall savour with heightened consciousness the intense yet tranquil rapture of a vision whose coherence and harmonies I can never exhaust.

What I experience as I stand in face of – and in the very depths of – this world which your flesh has assimilated, this world which has become your flesh, my God, is not the absorption of the monist who yearns to be dissolved into the unity of things, nor the emotion felt by the pagan as he lies prostrate before a tangible divinity, nor yet the passive self-abandonment of the quietist tossed hither and thither at the mercy of mystical impulsions. From each of these modes of thought I take something of their motive force while avoiding their pitfalls: the approach deter-mined for me by your omnipresence is a wonderful synthesis wherein three of the most formidable passions that can unlock the human heart rectify each other as they mingle: like the monist I plunge into the all-inclusive One; but the One is so perfect that as it receives me and I lose myself in it I can find in it the ultimate perfection of my own individuality;

like the pagan I worship a God who can be touched; and I do indeed touch him – this God – over the whole surface and in the depths of that world of matter which confines me: but to take hold of him as I would wish (simply in order not to stop touching him), I must go always on and on through and beyond each undertaking, unable to rest in anything, borne onwards at each moment by creatures and at each moment going beyond them, in a continuing welcoming of them and a continuing detachment from them;

like the quietist I allow myself with delight to be cradled in the divine fantasy: but at the same time I know that the divine will, will only be revealed to me at each moment if I exert myself to the utmost: I shall only touch God in the world of matter, when, like Jacob, I have been vanquished by him.

Thus, because the ultimate objective, the totality to which my nature is attuned has been made manifest to me, the powers of my being begin spontaneously to vibrate in accord with a single note of incredible richness wherein I can distinguish the most discordant tendencies effortlessly resolved: the excitement of action and the delight of passivity: the joy of possessing and the thrill of reaching out beyond what one possesses; the pride in growing and the happiness of being lost in what is greater than oneself.

Rich with the sap of the world, I rise up towards the Spirit whose vesture is the magnificence of the material universe but who smiles at me from far beyond all victories; and, lost in the mystery of the flesh of God, I cannot tell which is the more radiant bliss: to have found the Word and so be able to achieve the mastery of matter, or to have mastered matter and so be able to attain and submit to the light of God.

Grant, Lord, that your descent into the universal Species may not be for me just something loved and cherished, like the fruit of some philosophical speculation, but may become for me truly a real Presence. Whether we like it or not by power and by right you are incarnate in the world and we are all of us dependent upon you. But in fact you are far, and how far, from being equally close to us all. We are all of us together carried in the one world-womb; yet each of us is our own little microcosm in which the

Incarnation is wrought independently with degrees of intensity, and shades that are incommunicable. And that is why, in our prayer at the altar, we ask that the consecration may be brought about *for us: Ut nobis Corpus et Sanguis fiat* . . .[3] If I firmly believe that everything around me is the body and blood of the Word,[4] then for me (and in one sense for me alone) is brought about that marvellous 'diaphany' which causes the luminous warmth of a single life to be objectively discernible in and to shine forth from the depths of every event, every element: whereas if, unhappily, my faith should flag, at once the light is quenched and everything becomes darkened, everything disintegrates.

You have come down, Lord, into this day which is now beginning. But alas, how infinitely different in degree is your presence for one and another of us in the events which are now preparing and which all of us together will experience! In the very same circumstances which are soon to surround me and my fellow-men you may be present in small measure, in great measure, more and more or not at all.

Therefore, Lord, that no poison may harm me this day, no death destroy me, no wine befuddle me, that in every creature I may discover and sense you, I beg you: give me faith.

COMMUNION

If the Fire has come down into the heart of the world it is, in the last resort, to lay hold on me and to absorb me. Henceforth I cannot be content simply to contemplate it or, by my steadfast faith, to intensify its ardency more and more in the world around me. What I must do, when I have taken part with all my energies in the consecration which causes its flames to leap forth, is to consent to the communion which will enable it to find in me the food it has come in the last resort to seek.

So, my God, I prostrate myself before your presence in the universe which has now become living flame: beneath the lineaments of all that I shall encounter this day, all that happens to me, all that I achieve, it is you I desire, you I await.

It is a terrifying thing to have been born: I mean, to find one-self, without having willed it, swept irrevocably along on a torrent of fearful energy which seems as though it wished to destroy everything it carries with it.

What I want, my God, is that by a reversal of forces which you alone can bring about, my terror in face of the nameless changes destined to renew my being may be turned into an overflowing joy at being transformed into you.

First of all I shall stretch out my hand unhesitatingly towards the fiery bread which you set before me. This bread, in which you have planted the seed of all that is to develop in the future, I recognize as containing the source and the secret of that destiny you have chosen for me. To take it is, I know, to surrender myself to forces which will tear me away painfully from myself in order to drive me into danger, into laborious undertakings, into a constant renewal of ideas, into an austere detachment where my affections are concerned. To eat it is to acquire a taste and an affinity for that which in everything is above everything – a taste and an affinity which will henceforward make impossible for me all the joys by which my life has been warmed. Lord Jesus, I am willing to be possessed by you, to be bound to your body and led by its inexpressible power towards those solitary heights which by myself I should never dare to climb. Instinctively, like all mankind, I would rather set up my tent here below on some hill-top of my own choosing. I am afraid, too, like all my fellow-men, of the future too heavy with mystery and too wholly new, towards which time is driving me. Then like these men I wonder anxiously where life is leading me . . . May this communion of bread with the Christ clothed in the powers which dilate the world free me from my timidities and my heedlessness! In the whirlpool of conflicts and energies out of which must develop my power to apprehend and experience your holy presence, I throw myself, my God, on your word. The man who is filled with an impassioned love of Jesus hidden in the forces which bring increase to the earth, him the earth will lift up, like a mother, in the immensity of her arms, and will enable him to contemplate the face of God.

If your kingdom, my God, were of this world, I could possess you simply by surrendering myself to the forces which cause us, through suffering and dying, to grow visibly in stature – us or that which is dearer to us than ourselves. But because the term towards which the earth is moving lies not merely beyond each individual thing but beyond the totality of things; because the world travails, not to bring forth from within itself some supreme reality, but to find its consummation through a union with a pre-existent Being; it follows that man can never reach the blazing centre of the universe simply by living more and more for himself nor even by spending his life in the service of some earthly cause however great. The world can never be definitively united with you, Lord, save by a sort of reversal, a turning about, an *excentration*, which must involve the temporary collapse not merely of all individual achievements but even of everything that looks like an advancement for humanity. If my being is ever to be decisively attached to yours, there must first die in me not merely the monad ego but also the world: in other words I must first pass through an agonizing phase of diminution for which no tangible compensation will be given me. That is why, pouring into my chalice the bitterness of all separations, of all limitations, and of all sterile fallings away, you then hold it out to me, 'Drink ye all of this.'

How could I refuse this chalice, Lord, now that through the bread you have given me there has crept into the marrow of my being an inextinguishable longing to be united with you beyond life; through death? The consecration of the world would have remained incomplete, a moment ago, had you not with special love vitalized for those who believe, not only the life-bringing forces, but also those which bring death. My communion would be incomplete – would, quite simply, not be christian – if, together with the gains which this new day brings me, I did not also accept, in my own name and in the name of the world, as the most immediate sharing in your own being, those processes, hidden or manifest, of enfeeblement, of ageing, of death, which unceasingly consume the universe, to its salvation or its condemnation. My God, I deliver myself up with utter abandon to those fearful forces of dissolution which, I blindly believe, will this day cause my narrow ego to be replaced by your divine presence. The man who is filled with an impassioned love for Jesus hidden in the forces which bring death to the earth, him the earth will clasp in the immensity of her arms as her strength fails, and with her he will awaken in the bosom of God.

PRAYER

Lord Jesus, now that beneath those world-forces you have become truly and physically everything for me, everything about me, everything within me, I shall gather into a single prayer both my delight in what I have and my thirst for what I lack; and following the lead of your great servant I shall repeat those enflamed words in which, I firmly believe, the christianity of tomorrow will find its increasingly clear portrayal:

'Lord, lock me up in the deepest depths of your heart; and then, holding me there, burn me, purify me, set me on fire, sublimate me, till I become utterly what you would have me be, through the utter annihilation of my ego.'

Tu autem, Domine mi, include me in imis visceribus Cordis tui. Atque ibi me detine, excoque, expurga, accende, ignifac, sublima, ad purissimum Cordis tui gustum atque placitum, ad puram annihilationem meam.

'Lord.' Yes, at last, through the twofold mystery of this universal consecration and communion I have found one to whom I can wholeheartedly give this name. As long as I could see – or dared to see – in you, Lord Jesus, only the man who lived two thousand years ago, the sublime moral teacher, the Friend, the Brother, my love remained timid and constrained. Friends, brothers, wise men: have we not many of these around us, great souls, chosen souls, and much closer to us? And then can man ever give himself utterly to a nature which is purely human? Always from the very first it was the world, greater than all the elements which make up the world, that I was in love with; and never before was there anyone before whom I could in honesty bow down. And so for a long time, even though I believed, I strayed, not knowing what it was I loved. But now, Master, today, when through the manifestation of those superhuman powers with which your resurrection endowed you you shine forth from within all the forces of the earth and so become visible to me, now I recognize you as my Sovereign, and with delight I surrender myself to you.

How strange, my God, are the processes your Spirit initiates! When, two centuries ago, your Church began to feel the particular power of your heart, it might have seemed that what was captivating men's souls was the fact of their finding in you an element even more determinate, more circumscribed, than your humanity as a whole. But now on the contrary a swift reversal is making us aware that your main purpose in this revealing to us of your heart was to enable our love to escape from the constrictions of the too narrow, too precise, too limited image of you which we had fashioned for ourselves. What I discern in your breast is simply a furnace of fire; and the more I fix my gaze on its ardency the more it seems to me that all around it the contours of your body melt away and become enlarged beyond all measure, till the only features I can distinguish in you are those of the face of a world which has burst into flame.

Glorious Lord Christ: the divine influence secretly diffused and active in the depths of matter, and the dazzling centre where all the innumerable fibres of the multiple meet; power as implacable as the world and as warm as life; you whose forehead is of the whiteness of snow, whose eyes are of fire, and whose feet are brighter than molten gold; you whose hands imprison the stars; you who are the first and the last, the living and the dead and the risen again; you who gather into your exuberant unity every beauty, every affinity, every energy, every mode of existence; it is you to whom my being cried out with a desire as vast as the universe, 'In truth you are my Lord and my God.'

'Lord, lock me up within you': yes indeed I believe – and this belief is so strong that it has become one of the supports of my inner life – that an 'exterior darkness' which was wholly outside you would be pure nothingness. Nothing, Lord Jesus, can subsist outside of your flesh; so that even those who have been cast out from your love are still, unhappily for them, the beneficiaries of your presence upholding them in existence. All of us, inescapably, exist in you, the universal *milieu* in which and through which all things live and have their being. But precisely because we are not self-contained ready-made entities which can be conceived equally well as being near to you or remote from you; precisely because in us the self-subsistent individual who is united to you grows only in so far as the union itself grows, that union whereby we are given more and more completely to you: I beg you, Lord, in the name of all that is most vital in my being, to hearken to the desire of this thing that I dare to call *my* soul even though I realize more and more every day how much greater it is than myself, and, to slake my thirst for life, draw me – through the successive zones of your deepest substance – into the secret recesses of your inmost heart.

The deeper the level at which one encounters you, Master, the more one realizes the universality of your influence. This is the criterion by which I can judge at each moment how far I have progressed within you. When all the things around me, while preserving their own individual contours, their own special savours, nevertheless appear to me as animated by a single secret spirit and therefore as diffused and intermingled within a single element, infinitely close, infinitely remote; and when, locked within the jealous intimacy of a divine sanctuary, I yet feel myself to be wandering at large in the empyrean of all created beings: then I shall know that I am approaching that central point where the heart of the world is caught in the descending radiance of the heart of God.

And then, Lord, at that point where all things are set ablaze, do you act upon me through the united flames of all those internal and external influences which, were I less close to you, would be neutral or ambivalent or hostile, but which when animated by an Energy *quae possit sibi omnia subjicere*[5] become, in the physical depths of your heart, the angels of your triumphant activity. Through a marvellous combination of your divine magnetism with the charm and the inadequacy of creatures, with their sweetness and their malice, their disappointing weakness and their terrifying power, do you fill my heart alternately with exaltation and with distaste; teach it the true meaning of purity: not a debilitating separation from all created reality but an impulse carrying one through all forms of created beauty; show it the true nature of charity: not a sterile fear of doing wrong but a vigorous determination that all of us together shall break open the doors of life; and give it finally – give it above all – through an ever-increasing awareness of your omnipresence, a blessed desire to go on advancing, discovering, fashioning and experiencing the world so as to penetrate ever further and further into yourself.

For me, my God, all joy and all achievement, the very purpose of my being and all my love of life, all depend on this one basic ᵧision of the union between yourself and the universe. Let others, fulfilling a function more august than mine, proclaim your splendours as pure Spirit; as for me, dominated as I am by a vocation which springs from the inmost fibres of my being, I have no desire, I have no ability, to proclaim anything except the innumerable prolongations of your incarnate Being in the world of matter; I can preach only the mystery of your flesh, you the Soul shining forth through all that surrounds us.

It is to your body in this its fullest extension – that is, to the world become through your power and my faith the glorious living crucible in which everything melts away in order to be born anew; it is to this that I dedicate myself with all the resources which your creative magnetism has brought forth in me: with the all too feeble resources of my scientific knowledge, with my religious vows, with my priesthood, and (most dear to me) with my deepest human convictions. It is in this dedication, Lord Jesus, I desire to live, in this I desire to die.

Ordos, 1923

1. There is no confusion here between transubstantiation in the strict sense and the universal presence of the Word: as the author states explicitly in *The Priest*, 'The transubstantiation is encircled by a halo of divinization – real, even though less intense – that extends to the whole universe'. From the cosmic element into which he has entered through his incarnation and in which he dwells eucharistically 'the Word is active to master and assimilate to himself all that still remains'. (*Writings in Time of War*, p. 207).

2. 'That they [all mankind] should seek God, if haply they may feel after him or find him . . .' (Acts 17.27.)

3. 'That it may become for us the Body and Blood of your dearly loved Son, our Lord Jesus Christ.'

4. Through the 'physical and overmastering' contact of him whose appanage it is to be able *omnia sibi subicere* ['to subdue all things unto himself.' Phil. 3.21]. (*Le Milieu Divin*, p. 114.)

5. 'Which is able to subdue all things unto itself.'

TWO WEDDING ADDRESSES

At the Wedding of Odette Bacot and Jean Teilhard d'Eyry

Mademoiselle, my dear Jean,

When I look at you both here, united for all time, my old professional habits reassert themselves, and I cannot help glancing back at the two roads – your two roads – which for so long seemed to be independent of one another, but which have suddenly converged and here and now, in a moment, are about to run as one. And you will not be surprised that, presented with a meeting so unexpected and yet prepared for so long, I am filled with wonder and joy, as though I were witnessing another of life's triumphs.

Your road, Jean, began far from here, under the heavy clouds of the tropics, in the flat paddy-fields enclosed by the blue silhouette of Cape Saint-Jacques. It called for nothing less than this vigorous mixture of cold Auvergne and the Far East worthily to continue in you a fearless, far-ranging mother, and that legendary 'Uncle Georges' too. When I was only a child, I used occasionally to gaze with admiration at his face, beside the already white-haired grandmother, in that rather dark, and half-Chinese, drawing-room in the Rue Savaron.

By tradition, and by birth, you are of Asia; and that is why, from time to time, you have gone back to Asia to breathe in its quality.

But what are these journeyings of the heart and mind? Only you could draw up that itinerary, the stages and detours through which your being had to travel before the emergence in the end, of the man you are today. At home, as a young cadet, everywhere what influences were at work, what meetings came about, what attractions were felt, what choices made! . . . How slender the fibres in the web from which our lives are suspended!

Finally, having found your way through the shifting labyrinth of external and internal forces, you have succeeded in finding your

135

soul. In this inner domain (for it is within you much more than outside you) to which life has brought you, are you not going to find yourself alone and lost? Men are crowded together and have to force their way along our roads, metalled or earthen; even in the skies they are already beginning to find themselves cramped. But in the thousand times vaster and more complex domain of the mind, each one of us, the more he is human (and therefore unique), the more he is condemned by his very success to wander, endlessly lost. You might well have feared, Jean, that where such a succession of chances had driven your ship no other vessel, except by some even greater chance, would be found.

And it was then, Mademoiselle, in that very habitation of souls in which it seemed impossible that two beings should find one another, that you, like the princess in a fairy story, quite naturally appeared. That, among some thousands of human beings, the eyes of two individuals should meet is in itself a remarkable and precious coincidence: what, then, can we say when it is two minds that meet?

While you, Jean, were engaged in the long circumnavigation during which the real core of every living creature – its power to love – was maturing within you, you, Mademoiselle, were following a different curve, the rhythm of whose approach was nevertheless wonderfully harmonized; and so the two of you were passing through those successive cycles whose culmination we are witnessing here today.

Through your family origins you, too, blossomed on a stem whose roots lie deep in one of France's ancient provinces – Touraine instead of Auvergne – which has about it something warmer and gentler; and, to crown this, you had that finishing touch which only the atmosphere of Paris can give. From your childhood you, too, learnt to revere that same historic academy and the exact science of honourable warfare. In a circle of three children – which included yet another Jacqueline – with an exceptional mother, you, too, received that generously liberal up-bringing, firmly based on Christian principles, which has given so wonderfully harmonious a balance to your development. And so it was – with how astonishing a symmetry in your destinies – that, without realizing it, you were gradually moving towards your meeting with the man who, in equal ignorance, was moving towards you.

I referred, a moment ago, to fairy tales. Who was the fairy who, without ever breaking her thread, worked alone to weave today into one perfect whole the double web of your two lives?

Was it only chance that blindly worked this miracle? Must we really resign ourselves to believing that the value of the loveliest things around us depends simply on what is unpredictable, unusual, and in consequence impermanent, in the confluence of the elements from which they seem to us to have emerged?

True enough, there are days when the world appears to be one vast chaos. Great, indeed, is the confusion; so great that if we look at ourselves we may very well reel with dizziness at the prospect of our very existence. With such heavy odds against us, is it not most improbable that we should find ourselves whole and entire, and living – as single individuals, let alone as two? We wonder, then, whether true wisdom may not consist in holding on to every chance that comes our way, and immediately drawing all we can from it. It would be madness, surely, to take any further risk with the future and to strive after a life that is even more improbable because even more elevated.

For years now, Jean, my work has been such that every day of my life has necessarily been lived under the shadow of the improbability of life's successes. And once again it is this improbability which I meet today when I look at the happiness of both of you together.

So: since you have asked me to speak today, allow me to tell you what, after a long confrontation with the splendid reality of the world, is my dearest and most profound conviction. I began, like everyone else, by being impressed by the superior importance, among events, that must be accorded to what comes lower down the scale, and to the past. Then, unless I was to cease to understand anything that goes on within me or around me, I was obliged to shift my point of view and accord absolute supremacy to the future and the greater.

No, I believe what gives the universe around us its consistence is not the apparent solidity of the ephemeral materials from which bodies are made. Rather is it the flame of organic development which has been running through the world since the beginning of time, constantly building itself up. With all its weight behind it, the world is being impelled upon a centre which lies ahead of it. Far from being impermanent and accidental, it is souls, and alliances of souls, it is the energies of souls, that alone progress infallibly, and it is they alone that will endure.

What is imponderable in the world is greater than what we can handle.

What radiates from living beings is more valuable than their caresses.

What has not yet come is more precious than what is already born.

That is why what I want to say to you now, Jean – what I want to say to both of you – is this:

'If you want, if both of you want, to answer the summons (or respond to the grace, for that is the better word) which comes to you today from God-animated life, then take your stand confidently and unhesitatingly on tangible matter; take that as an indispensable bulwark – but, through and above that matter, put your faith in the bulwark of the intangible.'

Put your faith in the spirit that lies behind you; by that I mean the long series of unions similar to your own which throughout the ages have accumulated, to pass on to you, a great store of healthy vigour, of wisdom and of freedom. Today this treasure is entrusted to your keeping. Remember that you are responsible for it to God and the universe.

Put your faith, then, in the spirit that lies ahead of you. Creation never comes to a halt. It is through you two that life seeks to prolong itself. Your union, therefore, must not be a self-enclosed embrace; let it express itself in that deliberate act, infinitely more unifying than any inactivity, which consists in an effort directed towards one and the same, ever-greater, passionately loved, goal.

And finally, in a phrase that sums up all the rest, put your faith in the spirit which dwells between the two of you. You have each offered yourself to the other as a boundless field of understanding, of enrichment, of mutually increased sensibility. You will meet above all by entering into and constantly sharing one another's thoughts, affections, dreams and prayer. There alone, as you know, in spirit which is arrived at through the flesh, you will find no surfeit, no disappointments, no limits. There alone the skies are ever open for your love; there alone lies the great road ahead.

At this very moment can you not feel this spirit, to which I am urging you, concentrating upon you; can you not feel its mantle spread over you?

The united love of so many kinsfolk and friends gathered together, the warmth and purity of wishes transmitted, through some subtle medium, from Auvergne, from Touraine or Poitou, and from the Côte d'Argent, too; the blessings sent by those whom we no longer see; and above all the infinite tenderness of Him who sees in you two, forming one, the welding of one more precious link in his great work of creative union.

In very truth, grander than the external, material ceremonial which surrounds and honours you, it is the accumulated forces of an invisible loving-kindness which fill this church.

I pray that this spiritual ardour may come down upon your nascent love, and preserve it for eternal life. Amen.

14 June 1928

At the Wedding of M. and Mme de la Goublaye de Ménorval

Mademoiselle, Monsieur,

At this moment, when your two lives are being made one in this chapel, I can think of nothing more appropriate nor more valuable to offer you than a few words in praise of unity.

Unity: an abstract term, maybe, in which philosophers delight; and yet it is primarily a very concrete quality with which we all dream of endowing our works and the world around us. To the apparent fragmentation of material elements, to nature's capricious movements, to the irregularity of colour and sound, to the busy confusion of the masses of mankind, and the undisciplined vacillations of our aspirations and thoughts – what is it that, through all that is best in our activities, we are trying to do, if not constantly to introduce a little more unity? Science, art, politics, ethics, thought, mysticism: these are so many different forms of one and the same impulse towards the creation of some harmony; and in that impulse is expressed, through the medium of our human activities, the destiny and, I would even say, the very essence of the universe. Happiness, power, wealth, wisdom, holiness: these are all synonyms for a victory over the many. At the heart of every being lies creation's dream of a principle which will one day give organic form to its fragmented treasures. God is unity.

What conscious line of action, then, will enable us to pursue and attain this divine unity?

Will it, perhaps, be attained by each one of us setting himself up at the heart of his own little world as an exclusive centre of domination and enjoyment? Does our happiness lie in relating to ourselves, to the greatest possible degree, all that lies outside us? Shall we be happy only if we each become our own little god?

That you two should be here today, bride and bridegroom, shows how completely you have been untouched by this illusion of the self as centre. One of the most pernicious hallucinations that life meets as it awakes to intelligence is the closed concentration of the element on itself; and by this you have not been misled. You have seen that the being in each one of us does not contain its own final pole; it represents a particle which is destined to be incorporated in higher syntheses. Your example shows us not the unity of isolation – but the unity of union.

It is the unity of union that you have chosen; and you have

chosen well. But this higher unity which is promised to the elements which seek for one another in a common principle that brings them together – how precisely can that unity reach its perfection in you two? How, being two, will you be more truly one? The question brings me to the very point I want to deal with in these few words; and my answer is: 'By never relaxing your effort to become more yourselves by the giving of yourselves.'

Because union brings fulfilment, it can appear to be a final term, a resting-place. In fact, nothing has a greater share of life's incessantly progressive nature. If the elements are to be able to coalesce, they must spend a long time in first developing in themselves those complementary values which can combine with one another. And when at last the elements meet, they still cannot link up with one another except by advancing continually further along the line of their own fulfilment. True union, as it brings together, so, and precisely so, it differentiates. It is a continual discovery and a continual conquest.

Perhaps my language is a little ponderous, but it is in those terms that I look for an explanation of your past, and of the promise that the future holds for you.

Your past . . . When we look at you, Mademoiselle, in this festive setting – we, your friends, who have so often seen you deep in the study of rocks or maps, we who have followed you in our thoughts through distant and dangerous expeditions – we might well have a vague feeling that your life has gone off at a tangent, and that you have become a different woman. 'What was the good of conquering *this*, in order finally to choose *that*?' And the right answer to our question is, 'What is the good of *this* except as a preparation for *that*?' Never, Mademoiselle, never – should you, impossible thought it be, ever be so tempted – regret those long hours in the laboratory, all the careful work that went into those lengthy reports, those strenuous journeys through the forests of Madagascar. During these adventures of mind and body, were you not developing in yourself the perfect companion for a man who himself – for this is true of you, the bridegroom, too, is it not? – belongs to the race of those who work for the earth and explore its secrets? It took life millions of years to mould, in the work of creation, the heart and mind that your mother passed on to you, Mademoiselle. And it still called for all the work and all the hazards of your early youth to perfect in you a being with the capacity to give its self.

And now that same law of which I was speaking, which required that each of you should, alone, make ready for union, is again waiting for you to complete one another, each through the other, in union. What will be the never-ended story of your mutual conquest? This is known to God alone, who is about to bless you. But for my part, I can, on the authority of all human experience, assure you of this: that your happiness will depend on the width of the field you allow to your hopes. An affection that is narrowly closed in one itself stifles body and soul. If you are to ensure the uninterrupted progress that is essential to the fruitfulness of your union, you must extend still further the horizons that have bounded the years of your development.

You will be happy, happy as our prayers and wishes would have you be, only if your two lives come together and extend each other, boldly launching themselves upon the future in a passionate drive towards one greater than yourselves.

15 June 1935

MY INTELLECTUAL POSITION

When Père Teilhard sent me a copy of this statement, he wrote as follows: 'I enclose a copy of a sheet I have just sent to a colleague in Namur, who asked me to let him have (for a book he is bringing out) a statement of my point of view.' (J.M.)

In its essence, the thought of Père Teilhard de Chardin is expressed not in a metaphysics but in a sort of phenomenology.

A certain law of recurrence, underlying and dominating all experience, he thinks, forces itself on our attention. It is the law of complexity-consciousness, by which, within life, the stuff of the cosmos folds in upon itself continually more closely, following a process of organization whose measure is a corresponding increase of tension (or psychic temperature). In the field of our observation, *reflective* man represents the highest term attained by an element in this process of organization.

Above individual man, however, this involution is carried further, in mankind, by the social phenomenon, at the term of which can be discerned a higher critical point of collective reflection.

From this point of view 'hominization' (including socialization) is a convergent phenomenon: in other words it displays an upper limit or internal point of maturity. At the same time this *convergent* phenomenon is also, in virtue of its structure, *irreversible* in nature: in this sense, that Evolution having become reflective and free, in man, it can no longer continue its ascent towards complexity-consciousness unless it realizes two things about 'vital involution' – that, looking ahead, it escapes annihilation or total death, and, what is more, that it gathers together all that can be permanently saved of the essence of what life will have engendered in the course of its progress. This demand for irreversibility has a structural implication, the existence, at the upper term of cosmic convergence, of a transcendent centre of unification, 'Omega Point'. Unless this focus-point, which gathers things together and ensures their irreversibility, does in fact exist, the law of evolutionary recurrence cannot hold good to the very end.

It is upon this 'Physics' that, in a 'second phase', Père Teilhard builds first an apologetics: under the illuminating influence of Grace, our minds recognize in the unifying properties of the Christian phenomenon a manifestation (or a reflection) of Omega upon human consciousness, and so identify the Omega of reason with the Universal Christ of revelation.

It is upon this Physics that Père Teilhard simultaneously builds up, secondly, a Mysticism:

The whole of Evolution being reduced to a process of union (communion) with God, it becomes, in its totality, loving and lovable in the innermost and most ultimate of its developments.

Taken together the three branches of the system (physics, apologetics and mysticism) suggest and readily lend themselves to forming an outline of a Metaphysics of Union, dominated by love, in which even the Problem of Evil is given an acceptable intellectual solution (the statistical necessity of disorders within a multitude in process of organization).

This 'philosophy' has been criticized as being no more than a generalized Concordism. To this Père Teilhard answers that concordism and coherence should not be confused. Religion and science obviously represent two different meridians on the mental sphere, and it would be wrong not to keep them separate (that is the concordist mistake); but these meridians must necessarily meet somewhere at a pole of common vision (that is, coherence). Otherwise all that is ours in the domain of thought and knowledge collapses.

New York, April, 1948

NOTE ON THE TEACHING
OF PREHISTORY

There is no serious lack of instruction in Prehistory in France.[1] We have the *Institut de Paléontologie Humaine* (which provides the fullest courses); the Sorbonne's *Institut d'Ethnologie* (now, I understand, being re-organized), and the *Institut de l'Homme* (particularly for Ethnology and Linguistics). On the whole, however, instruction in this subject is still 'peripheral'. There are no examinations and courses are designed to produce amateurs rather than real scientists; there are no professional chairs, and no certificates that count for much. Things are better in England (Cambridge, in particular) and America (Harvard, Columbia . . .)

Simply from this point of view the creation of a chair of Prehistory in the Collège de France would certainly be of special value, for it would raise the importance and standing of this branch of knowledge.

But there is a further, and quite different, consideration.

Even abroad, and in the best equipped Universities, we still find in the teaching of Prehistory a tendency to study human problems piecemeal, 'scrappily': a series of scattered details (stratigraphic, osteological, archaeological, ethnographic . . .) in which the main lines of the phenomenon lose their sharpness. – So far as I know, there are no courses offered anywhere in which the *background*, the *structure*, and the *full expansion* (followed by *compression* upon itself) of the human zoological group, considered as one whole, are taken as subjects for technical study: starting, of course, from precise facts, but examining also the main features of their general disposition and development.

It is, I believe, in this still new direction that it would be gratifying to see the Collège de France make an experiment that I would be disposed to try out: starting with human palaeontology and palaeo-sociology – using them as a foundation or platform – to sketch out the first outlines of a science of Anthropogenesis – the higher reaches, as yet imperfectly charted, of Biology.

Paris, 23 September 1948

1. This note, addressed to Monsieur Paul Fallot, Professor of Mediterranean Geology at the Collège de France, was written by Père Teilhard when he was invited to fill the chair just vacated by the Abbé Breuil on reaching the age for retirement.

THE BASIS OF MY ATTITUDE

1. For the last forty years my attitude and my activities have been based on the threefold, ever stronger, conviction:[1]

a. First, that (for many irresistible reasons) we have just entered historically a period of neo-humanism (characterized by the surmise, or even the acceptance as proved, that Man is far from having completed the biological curve of his growth – which means that he has not only a future in time, but also 'a future' to look forward to).

b. Secondly, that the conflict – only an apparent conflict – between this neo-humanism and the 'classic' formulation of Christianity is the underlying source of all today's religious disquiet.

c. Finally, that the synthesis 'in Christo Jesu' between the ascensional force of traditional Christianity and the propulsive force of modern neo-humanism is what our world, albeit confusedly, looks to for its salvation (and the Society of Jesus, incidentally, has once again exactly the same role in this situation, but at a higher stage, as it had 400 years ago when it was confronted by the Humanism of the Renaissance).

2. Neither in my book (*The Phenomenon of Man*), nor, should occasion arise, in my lectures (at the Collège de France, or in America) do I explicitly treat of (or propose to treat of) this fundamental religious problem. Both in writing and teaching, my aim is simply and solely to present objectively (without reference to philosophy or theology) the experiential foundations and prospects of what I have just referred to as contemporary neo-humanism. In such a presentation I see the following advantages: I can

a. Show, by example, that a Christian (and even a religious) can (or even, logically, must) be as fully 'human' as a Marxist. 'Plus et ego...'

b. Establish on rational grounds (apart from any *a priori* assumptions), that the neo-humanist point of view – seen against its historical background – must accept the primacy of Spirit if there is to be a 'biological' justification for Mankind's further progress ahead.

c. Support and disseminate a 'phenomenal' view of the Universe which seems to me not only true, but vital to Modern Man's spiritual progress: by which I mean that it is in the context and scale of a World in process of convergence that (to my mind) Christianity can find the best psychological and intellectual climate for its future developments.

Nobody dreams of blaming Canon Lemaître for speaking of an 'expanding Universe' (spatially). For my part, I am doing no more than putting forward the complementary picture of a Universe 'that folds in (organically, that is physico-chemically and psychically) upon itself'. Neither of us introduces philosophy or theology. But what we have here, as Péguy would have said, is a 'porch' which for many of our contemporaries, I believe, provides a way into the Church.[2]

Rome, 7 October 1948

1. Written for Reverend Father Janssens, General of the Society of Jesus. (Ed's note.)
2. See the popularity, both in Europe and America, of Leconte de Noüy's book, *La Destinée humaine*, sketchy though it is.

MY *PHENOMENON OF MAN*:
AN ESSENTIAL OBSERVATION[1]

For a correct understanding of what is said, and what is not said, in *The Phenomenon of Man*, it should be noted that the book represents only the beginnings of a pendulum-like 'dialectic' whose stages may be defined as follows:

1. *Observation of the Phenomenal World.* Perception, purely experiential, of an infolding movement ('evolution') which causes the successive emergence of beings that are progressively more complicated organically and more centred psychically. – With Reflection (Man) the appearance of the need for irreversibility (for 'immortality') which postulates, if Evolution is to continue, the existence of a centre (super-personal and partially transcendent) of consistence: 'Omega'.

2. *Re-descent, starting from Omega.* Once the existence of Omega is accepted, our minds have to accept two consequences:
  a. First, that Evolution must be interpreted as a pull from above (and not merely as an immanent push).
  b. Secondly, that an influence, by nature personal and free, emanating from Omega (Revelation) is not only possible but to be expected. – In the light of this, the significant value of the Christian Fact (or phenomenon).

3. Perception (recognition), under the sensitizing influence of grace, of a Revelation in the Christian fact.

4. In the light of Revelation, definitive vision of the World and of Evolution in terms of Incarnation and Redemption.

It will be seen that my book covers only stages 1-2 of the dialectical process; that is, it confines itself strictly to the first phase of the Vatican Council (rational demonstration of the existence of God). – As concerns the dialectic itself, it will be noted that it is precisely classical apologetics – but (in conformity with modern views) transposed from a static Universe to a Universe in movement – from a Cosmos to a Cosmogenesis.

Rome, 17 October 1948

1. Addressed to Reverend Father Janssens, General of the Society of Jesus, when Père Teilhard was in Rome, to ask for permission to publish *The Phenomenon of Man*.

WEDDING ADDRESS

At the Wedding of Christine Dresch and Claude-Marie Haardt

My dear Christine, my dear Claude,

Life is indeed, full of strange coincidences and, perhaps, strange designs. As Christmas was approaching in the year 1932, when I was accompanying Georges-Marie Haardt on a journey across the deserts of Central Asia, who would have guessed that sixteen years later it would fall to me to address these words to you, as you in your turn are about to set out on another great adventure, that of your two combined lives? And since the coincidence probably disguises a secret design of destiny, may not this plan contained in material things (or worked out by Providence) be that I should pass on to you both – and more particularly to you, my dear Claude, in the presence of the mother to whom you owe so much – the admonition, the watchword, that your father, that great inspirer and great traveller, continually offered us by his example, mile after mile over the tracks of Asia, as he urged us to press on and keep our eyes fixed on the peaks that towered ahead of us?

He crossed the Sahara, he crossed Africa and China; and these undertakings, each with its different problems, were all (as is every living reality) built upon a solid material structure. Each was carefully worked out with an eye to a precise end. And yet, beyond any economic goal, it was always towards some sort of distantly envisaged dream that the fleet of trucks and half-tracks followed him as their leader across the sand. For those who were privileged to take part, these expeditions were always to some extent, and will always remain in their memories, the following of a guiding star . . .

My dear Christine, my dear Claude, now that your turn has come, do you too, imitating you father's grand demeanour in a different sphere, enter into life with your feet firmly on the ground but your eyes fixed on what is greater and finer than you. The temptation which besets love, you know, and makes it barren, is to rest upon what is possessed – it is a shared selfishness. To find one another, and to be truly made one, you must seek no other road but that of a strong passion for a common ideal. Between the two of you (and here the very structure of the world forces upon you a law that cannot be broken) – between the two of you, remember, no unblemished union can exist except in some higher centre which brings you together.

May that centre soon be the child!

And, come what may, may that centre be the excitement and joy of each discovering and completing the other, ever more fully, in heart and mind!

And, above all, may that centre in one way or another (depending on what is your own particular way) be the God before whom and in whom you are on the point of uniting your two lives for ever: God, the only definitive centre of the universe; not the distant God of common formulas, but God in the form in which he must, and strives to, show himself incommunicably to you if only you surrender unconditionally to the inner force which is at this moment operating to bring you together.

21 December 1948

THE SCIENTIFIC CAREER
OF PIERRE TEILHARD DE CHARDIN

On the occasion of his election to the *Académie des Sciences* Père Teilhard was asked by the editor of *Etudes* to let him have a *curriculum vitae* for publication in his review. The following is what Père Teilhard wrote.

Père Teilhard, who has just been elected to the *Académie des Sciences,* is an old and faithful contributor to this review. Readers of *Etudes* will accordingly like to know the main lines of the new Academician's scientific career.

Like every true natural scientist, the young Pierre felt himself drawn even as a small child to the things of Life and Earth. The hereditary effect of genes, or the influence of the mountains of Auvergne? – who could say? – but so strong was it that his classical teacher, the future Academician Henri Bremond had occasion in one of his books to deplore his pupil's blindness to the charms of literature. Later, Bremond's disciple was to show that he could write. Meanwhile, his mind was elsewhere, – with the rocks. And this was probably the result of some deep-rooted instinct; for, oddly enough, it was precisely from a starting point in the Mineral that Père Teilhard, following a clearly defined psychological spiral, was one day to emerge decisively and permanently into ardent study of the Human – nay, of the ultra-Human ...

In spite of the passionate tenacity of his scientific appetites, and notwithstanding a series of lucky finds (first in the eruptive rocks of Jersey, then in the calcareous rocks of the Mokattam Hills – when he was in Cairo – and later in the Wealden clays of Sussex) there was for a long time nothing to suggest that the young geologist was one day to emerge from the ranks of the 'amateurs'. But then there came a series of unexpected events: first a two-year spell at the Palaeontological Laboratory of the Natural History Museum in Paris, where the great Marcellin Boule was at that very time engaged in studying the celebrated La Chapelle-aux-Saints Man; then, after the war, appointment to a lectureship in Geology at the Institut Catholique de Paris. It was these that finally decided Père Teilhard to complete his academic training, and they had the further permanent effect of introducing him into the more elevated circle of professional Geologists.

It was only then (1923) that the event occurred which was to decide his fate. Out of the blue came an invitation from China, suggesting that he join Père Emile Licent in his bold explorations of the basin of the Yellow River. Until that time, Teilhard had been profoundly conscious of the attraction of the Earth and its phenomena, but he had not fully realized their size. This was to be revealed to him by Asia. During the first ten years of his 'Chinese life' – sometimes at the quiet jog-trot of the mules of Shansi – or at the majestic rumble of the Citroën half-tracks (the 'Yellow Expedition') – or speeding in the American Dodges (Roy Chapman Andrews's Central Asiatic Expedition) – from Shantung to the Pamir, and from the Khingan mountains to Indo-China – during all this time it was the mind-compelling history of an entire Continent that was gradually to be unfolded before the eyes of the traveller: a history written initially in the foldings and granitization of the ancient continental mass, but to be read with equal clarity in the formation of the astonishing sheet of red and yellow earths spread, during the Tertiary, over the vast undulations of the ancient peneplains. But also, and above all, a history laid bare in the existence of vast faunal complexes, whose establishment and evolution can be followed in one single line at one and the same place, to a depth of several millions of years, from the Miocene to the present day.

Nothing could have fitted in more aptly for our geologist-palaeontologist, now in his fiftieth year, than this awakening;

it helped him to meet the most decisive event of his career – by which we mean his share (in his capacity of adviser to the Geological Survey of China) in the quite unexpected discovery of the famous Peking Man (Sinanthropus). Correct dating and interpretation of this sensationally new fossil Man called for a thorough and up-to-date stratigraphic, physiographic and palaeontological examination of the whole Quaternary age in the Far East. It was to this central problem that Père Teilhard decided to devote the full maturity of his experience for the last fifteen years of his time in the Far East; and (with the massive help of various American Foundations and Universities) its ramifications were to take him in turn to India, to Burma and Java: these far-ranging researches (conducted in close co-operation with those of a team of Chinese, American, English and Dutch friends) leading him to suspect the individuality (both morphological and geographic) of a 'pithecanthropic' branch that appeared during the Pleistocene on the eastern extremity of the main body of Mankind.

Slowly, then, his intimate contact with facts brought about a gradual combination of the two linked notions of the genetic structure of fauna and the genetic structure of continents; this ultimately forced the geologist to accept a third notion, that of the genetic structure of Mankind, this latter being envisaged as a biological unit *sui generis*, of planetary dimensions. Here there was a move into an area that is still obscure and only now being opened up to tentative exploration: but a fascinating area on which, in a final phase, the whole scientific effort of the new Academician will no doubt in future be concentrated.

Etudes, July–August 1950

THE PHENOMENON OF MAN

(How can one go beyond a philosophico-juridico-literary 'anthropology' and establish a true Science of Man: an Anthropo-dynamics and an Anthropogenesis?)

An initial double observation:

1. Man (the Human) is coming to be seen experientially as, ever more clearly, the extreme, and in consequence the supremely characteristic, state of the 'Weltstoff' in the direction of the Arranged.

2. But he is still treated as a sort of world apart, in juxtaposition with, but not as an extension of, the Universe of Science.

We must therefore:

a. attach the Human (Man-as-element *and* social Man) to a *general process* that covers all the experiential Arrangement of the Universe.

b. determine the possible *extensions* of the process in the direction of some 'ultra-human'.

c. discover and define the *energetical conditions* of this movement – which involves a scientific re-thinking of the series:

Quantity (measurable) of energy absorbed by Hominization.

Arrangement of the Energy of Hominization.

Activation (of the arrangement) of the Energy of Hominization.

In short, we need a generalized Physics or Energetics, capable of integrating into itself both an Anthropo-dynamics and an Anthropogenesis.

N.B. American moves (John Stewart, P. Bridgman) to construct a *Sociometry* (by mathematical research into statistical constants in the Phenomenon of Man).

This experiment should be completed by an attempt to establish a *Sociodynamics* investigating the conditions under which human energies are activated and function.

In practical terms: advantage of a symposium, with restricted membership, composed exclusively of physicists, astrophysicists, chemists, biologists and geo-palaeontologists *interested in the Phenomenon of Man.*

Note written for Jacques Rueff, June 1954.

QUALIFICATIONS, CAREER, FIELD-WORK
AND WRITINGS OF
PIERRE TEILHARD DE CHARDIN

This document was written by Père Teilhard in September 1948, for the attention of the Director of the Collège de France, when he was offered the chair of Palaeontology, left vacant by the Abbé Breuil's retirement on reaching the age limit. In deference to his religious superiors, Teilhard was obliged to decline the offer. He was elected a resident Member of the Institute (Académie des Sciences) in May 1950.*

Docteur-ès-Sciences, 1922
President of the Société Géologique de France, 1922–3
Professor of Geology at the Institut Catholique de Paris, 1922–8
Adviser to the National Geological Survey of China, since 1929
Director of the Laboratoire de Géologie appliquée à l'Homme (Hautes-Etudes), since 1938
Director of Research at the Recherche Nationale scientifique, since 1947
Corresponding Member of the Institut (Académie des Sciences), since 1947
Officier of the Légion d'Honneur – Médaille militaire.

I. SCIENTIFIC CAREER

In a life during which unexpected events have constantly obliged me to shuttle between East and West, the three following phases may be distinguished:

* For the bibliography, drawn up by Teilhard in September 1948, to which the numbers in the document refer, see below, pp. 253–61.

a. *Phase of Preliminary Field-work*
In the Channel Islands (Jersey, 1901–5); Egypt (Cairo, 1905–8); England (Sussex Weald, 1908–12). Apart from some Notes (not mentioned in the Bibliography) published by the *Société Jersiaise* (on the Mineralogy of the Island of Jersey) or in the Bulletin of the Scientific Society of Cairo (on the Eocene in Upper Egypt) the chief result of these first researches was to provide specimens and observations (numerous new species) for eminent geologists or palaeontologists, such as René Fourtou, Sir Arthur Smith-Woodward, Professor Seward, etc.

b. *Phase of Palaeontological Researches in Europe (1912–23)*
During this second period, spent mainly (except for the war years) at the National Museum's Palaeontological Laboratory (Paris), my work was particularly directed to the palaeontology of Mammals of the Middle and Lower Tertiary in Europe: first making use of older material, not as yet studied, relating to the Phosphorites of Le Quercy, the Sparnacian of Epernay, and the Palaeocene of Rheims; then, later, describing completely new (microfaunal) material collected in the Sparnacian of Belgium (Orsmaël) under the direction of Professor Louis Dollo. At the same time, daily and particularly friendly contact with Marcellin Boule gradually initiated me into the study of human palaeontology.

c. *Phase of Exploration in Eastern Asia (1923–45)*
From 1923 onwards almost the whole of my time and activities was taken up by work in the Far East: either in association with Père Emile Licent; or as adviser to the Geological Survey of China; or as a member of various expeditions: the Central Asiatic Expedition (Roy Chapman Andrews Expedition) of the American Museum of Natural History (1930); the Haardt-Citroën Expedition (1931–2); the Yale-Cambridge Expedition in northern and central India (1935–6); the Harvard-Carnegie Expedition in Burma (1937–8). During these numerous journeys –

to which should be added a scientific mission in French Somaliland and the Harrar (1928–9) – my researches were divided, as might be expected, over a large number of different subjects, ranging from tectonics and physiography to Palaeontology and Prehistory – always, however, as I shall be showing, with a more clearly marked tendency to concentrate on the scientific study of human problems.

II. LIST OF MOST NOTABLE INVESTIGATIONS OR RESULTS

In listing the most notable results obtained from the researches, European and extra-European, mentioned above, a distinction should be made between scientific contributions relating (1) to general Geology; (2) to the Palaeontology of Mammals; and finally (3) to human Palaeontology and Prehistory.

1. General Geology

Thanks to the many expeditions I have had the honour of joining in the Far East, I have been accorded the unusual opportunity of being enabled to carry out, step by step (and following a number of different lines) (a) a complete geological section running East-West, from the edge of Shantung to the borders of Pamir; and (b) another North-South section, almost as complete, running down from Manchuria (Harbin) to the frontier of Indo-China. In these two general directions, most of the geological routes I noted concerned areas that were until then completely unknown to Science (Wei-Chang, the Great Khingan Mountains, Ordos, Western Gobi, the Tsinling range, Pei-Shan etc.; cf. Bibliography 15, 24, 61, 69, 80, 95). This, of course, provided a considerable number of new facts for geologists (chain of Quaternary volcanoes at the Dalai-Nor, Oligocene of the Ordos, sunken Eocene basins of the Tsinling range, etc.); at the same time, so far as I was personally concerned, they made it possible for me to develop certain very general views on the NW-SE migration of granites and conglomerates inside the area studied; and that enabled me finally to put forward certain views relating to the flexured structure of Eastern Asia, with possible consequences supporting the idea of an expansion of Continents by granitization. (84, 101, 107, 112, 124.)

In a less ambitious and purely stratigraphic field, the most important part of my geological work in China will no doubt prove to have been the analysis of the massive sheet of terrigenous deposits (silts and loess) in which the Cenozoic ends in the basin of the Hwang-ho. As a result of close scrutiny of certain lithological characteristics (rubefaction and concretion) of the fossil soils; and also by establishing the stratigraphic succession of the Mole Rats or Siphnaea (see below), a whole series of new stratigraphic terms, intercalated between the Red Earths (Pontian) and the Yellows (Upper Pleistocene) of Richthofen – each, moreover, with its corresponding lacustrine *facies* – have gradually been identified by me, or through my influence, in Northern China. (34, 36, 50, 72.) And it was from this solid foundation that I was able later to attempt (73, 108) a general synchronism of the Pontian and post-Pontian formations of Northern China with those of Central and Southern China – and even, further afield, with those of Northern India, Burma and Malaysia (see below).

2. *Palaeontology of Mammals*

To return to my first studies in Palaeontology, pursued in Europe on European material, I have hopes that these may have contributed to (a) a better arrangement of the whole of our knowledge of the Sparnacian fauna and the Palaeocene of France, Belgium and England (4, 31); (b) clarification of the particularly intricate complex of the Eocene and Oligocene Carnivores in the Phosphorites of Le Quercy (3); (c) finally, to bringing out the individuality and importance of certain little-known zoological groups, such as that of the curious Chiromyids (4, 31).

Circumstances, however, were such that my initial taste for the archaic or primitive forms of the Lower Tertiary gradually gave way to the increasing necessity (and desire) to study ever more closely and exclusively the relatively recent fossil species from which the modern fauna of Eastern Asia are directly derived. Apart, in fact, from one paper (26) on the Oligocene of the Ordos, it can be said that all my palaeontological work from 1923 onwards has been devoted to gradually reconstructing the post-Pontian history of the Mammals of Northern China: fauna of the Middle Pliocene (Yushe basin, in Shan-si – 96, 97, 100); Villafranchian fauna (Nihowan beds in Hopei – 53, 106 . . .); fauna of the Lower Pleistocene Choukoutien fissures – 89, 109 . . .); fauna of the Upper Pleistocene (Shara-osso-gol beds – 43); a 'resurrection' which is not only faunal but also ecological, climatic and physiographical, since the collection of fossil forms and their distribution according to age were necessarily closely associated with the study of sedimentary cycles and the analysis of the *facies* in each newly explored basin.

Thus there was gradually built up a stratigraphic and faunal framework that was indispensable to the progress of the far-reaching investigations carried out at precisely the same time, as we shall see, by the Geological Survey of China, in human Palaeontology. Simultaneously, moreover, a certain number of quite general biological laws or characteristics were emerging from the reconstructed evolution of Chinese fauna – and these threw a new light on the existence and the rhythms of change of collective organic movements within the Biosphere:

a. Initial proliferation of Pontian Mustelids – oddly reminiscent of that of the Oligocene *Cynodictis* and *Cynodon* in the Phosphorites of Le Quercy (119).

b. Development in Northern China, during the Pliocene, of a fauna of strepsiceral antelopes, exactly parallel to and yet *not* directly attachable to, that of the antelopes of Africa (100).

c. Remarkable orthogenesis of the Siphnaea (Mole Rats),

allowing continuous observation, from the Pontian to our own day, of one and the same perfectly defined series of osteological and dental modifications (fusion of the cervical vertebrae, loss of roots in the molariform teeth, increase in size . . .), which occur simultaneously in the various exceptionally well-defined branches of the same strictly limited zoological group (111).

And so on.

Thanks to the richness and the continuity of the fauna thus dug up, it becomes possible (as I have shown, in collaboration with my colleague Pierre Leroy in the case of the felids and mustelids) to follow, down from the Pontian, the introduction, adaptation and modifications on the spot, of a large part of the present-day fauna of China: one of the first attempts ever made, if I am not mistaken, to construct a zoology which no longer proposes to differentiate between living and extinct forms in the same region.

3. *Human Palaeontology*

Prolonged contact with eruptive and sedimentary formations, all adding to the importance for me of a stratigraphy of soils and of a geology of Continents – opportunities before long of studying certain particularly ancient and particularly well preserved Primate fossils (3, 4, 31) – the initial atmosphere of a Laboratory in which every day I could watch the preparation and examination of the La Chapelle-aux-Saints and La Feyrassie skeletons – all these factors, not to mention the intrinsic fascination of the subject itself, converged from the beginning to direct me gradually and increasingly towards the problems of fossil Man and the search for him.

My first stroke of good fortune in this field of human palaeontological excavation came in 1923, when, with Emile Licent, I was able to establish the hitherto contested existence of a Palaeolithic Man in Northern China (43). But the second, and the most decisive, was certainly my being enabled for nearly ten years (1929–37) to collaborate very closely in the great excavations at Choukoutien, near Peking, and the discovery of *Sinanthropus*.

In this collective work, which was conducted by the combined resources of the Rockefeller Foundation and the Geological Survey of China, my function was primarily to direct the stratigraphic, palaeontological and archaeological study of the site (45, 65, 73, 108): a task of some difficulty, since six different types of fissures, corresponding to as many distinct periods of filling (from the Miocene to the Upper Pleistocene), were to be found together in the same calcareous massif. But on the other hand it was a most rewarding study, for the abundance of fossils collected was so great that it was possible to carry out a cross-check between 'two geologies', that of basins and terraces, and that of fissures – both independently built up under my direction or by my own work, and whose adjustment was effected without the least difficulty.

In fact, from 1933 onwards, it was in connection with and starting from the problems raised by *Sinanthropus* that my researches mostly developed: a journey to Kwang-si, establishing the synchronism of the *Sinanthropus beds* of Northern China with the *Orang beds* of Southern China (82); expeditions to India (89, 93), then to Burma (98) with Helmut de Terra, both leading to the discovery of a rich Palaeolithic of great age in the then at last classified terraces of the three basins of the Indus, the Narbada and the Irrawaddy; a visit to, and examination of the *Pithecanthropus* sites of Java, on two occasions, under the guidance of Dr von Koenigswald . . .

In 1939 a remarkable network of research, centred on Peking, Singapore and Bandoeng and strongly supported by the American scientific institutions, was set up in Eastern Asia, systematically covering the various problems raised one after another by the search for fossil Man in the Far East. This 'model network', in which I had the privilege of sharing, was temporarily interrupted by the war, but not before a consistent series of results had been obtained. As a result of these we can now say that it is on the

Pacific fringe of the Old World that, in the last fifty years, Palaeontology has made most progress into the mystery of human origins.

As an offshoot of these primarily geological and palaeontological investigations, I have had the opportunity, on two occasions in particular, to broach subjects whose nature is more strictly archaeological. First in East Africa, where, after studying the Early Palaeolithic industries of the terraces at Obock (105), I discovered and quickly excavated a cave near Dire-Dawa (Harrar) with a rich industry of the Upper Palaeolithic type. Then in China itself, where, after having recognized with my friend W. G. Pei, the existence of a Mesolithic industry in the caves of Kwang-si, 1 decided to sum up in a short paper the essence of my observations and ideas concerning the Mesolithic and Neolithic of China – or even, in a more general way, on the peopling of China (114).

And now, to be absolutely complete and sincere, I must surely conclude by this admission: from the junction slowly effected in my mind by contact with the facts, between the two allied notions of the genetic structure of fauna and the genetic structure of continents, a third notion has gradually emerged for me: that of the genetic structure of Mankind, regarding Mankind as a special biological unit of planetary extension; and that third notion is now coming to take precedence for me over every other object of research, and will continue so to do. It is to the tentative exploration of this as yet undefined and nameless discipline, which tomorrow, maybe, will become a *Science of Anthropogenesis*, that I have (for lack of a better medium) recently devoted a series of essays (49, 123, 124, 125 . . .): popular articles, to all appearances, yet into them I feel that I have distilled all that is most valuable in my experience and the essence of my vision.

PART III

NOSTALGIA FOR THE FRONT

On 14 August 1917, Père Teilhard wrote to his cousin from Beaulieu-les-Fontaines (Oise), where he had just finished writing *The Mystical Milieu*, as follows: 'I'm experiencing a certain pleasure in feeling free now to start on some fresh subject, if any should suggest itself'; and in the same letter he continues, 'As always after a long rest, I feel overcome again by nostalgia for the front'. (*The Making of a Mind*, pp. 200, 201.) Such, in fact, was to be the subject of his new essay. Only a few weeks later, on 23 September, we find him, in a letter from Muret-et-Crouttes, outlining his theme:

'I would rather like to be able to analyse and account for, briefly, this feeling of a plenitude of being and of something more than human that I've often experienced at the front and that I fear I'll miss after the war. I think that one could show that the front isn't simply the firing-line, the exposed area corroded by the conflict of nations, but the "front of the wave" carrying the world of man towards its new destiny. When you look at it during the night, lit up by flares, after a day of more than usual activity, you seem to feel that you're at the final boundary between what has already been achieved and what is striving to emerge. It is not only that activity culminates in a sort of intense but completely calm paroxysm, dilating to the scale of the vast work in which it is playing its part – but the mind, too, gets something like an overall view of the whole forward march of the human mass, and feels not quite so lost in it. It's at such moments, above all, that one lives what I might call "cosmically" – aroused intellectually as much as emotionally . . .

'I don't yet know,' he continues, 'whether I could really do justice to this theme in a few pages.' (pp. 203–4). Two days later, however, he finds that the idea is taking shape; he has decided on his title, and is proposing to describe what is meant by 'nostalgia for the front' and explain the reasons that lie behind the feeling:

'The reasons, I believe, come down to this; the front cannot but attract us, because it is, in one way, the *extreme boundary* between what

167

one is already aware of, and what is still in process of formation. Not only does one see there things that you experience nowhere else, but one also sees emerge from within one an underlying stream of clarity, energy, and freedom that is to be found hardly anywhere else in ordinary life – and the new form that the soul then takes on is that of the individual living the quasi-collective life of all men, fulfilling a function far higher than that of the individual, and becoming fully conscious of this new state. It goes without saying that at the front you no longer look on things in the same way as you do in the rear: if you did, the sights you see and the life you lead would be more than you could bear. This exaltation is accompanied by a certain pain. Nevertheless, it is indeed an exaltation. And that's why one likes the front in spite of everything, and misses it.' (pp. 205–6)

At that time, Père Teilhard was still wondering whether he would be able to achieve 'the clarity of ideas and language' without which he would be unable to express his meaning; but on 4 October he tells us (p. 206) that he had already posted his 'paper' two or three days earlier to Père de Grandmaison in Paris. On 7 October he had an encouraging acknowledgement. Père de Grandmaison found 'the little article most original and interesting' (p. 209), and it was in fact printed in the issue of *Etudes* dated 20 November, but with the final paragraph cut out.

It was twilight, and I had walked up to the top of the hill from which there was a general view of the sector we had just left and to which we would shortly, no doubt, be returning. Stretched out before me lay rough meadow-lands wreathed in the mist that was now forming, and in these the elbow-bends of the Aisne curved into milk-white splashes; and beyond, the bare ridge of the Chemin des Dames stood out, sharp as a knife-edge, against the golden sunset, dotted with *drachen* [kite-balloons]. At intervals a mine sent up a plume of smoke into the silence.

Why, I wondered to myself, am I standing at just this place on just this evening?

When I am in the front-line, I am frightened of the shelling, just as everyone else is. Like everyone else, I count the days until our relief, and I watch carefully for the signs that announce its arrival. When we 'go down the line', no one is more delighted than I am. Every time this happens I feel that this time I have at last had enough, and more than enough, of the trenches and war. As recently as this afternoon, I was still drinking in the joy of living again, with no nagging at the back of my mind, in the warm embrace of innocent nature. I was savouring the bliss of stretching out beneath the trees and of allowing their foliage to be reflected in a completely relaxed and carefree mind.

And now, as always, I find myself turning back instinctively towards the Front and the fighting!

Is it not ridiculous to be so drawn into the magnetic field of the war as to be unable to spend a week in the rear without scanning the horizon, as one scans a well-loved sea-strand, for the motionless line of 'sausage balloons'? To be so polarized as to be unable suddenly to glimpse at night the silvery spark of a swooping flare, or even its reflection in the clouds, without feeling my heart beat faster, without a sense of regret, without hearing a summons?

More than ever, on this particular evening, in this wonderfully calm and stimulating setting – in which I am sheltered from the violent emotions and intolerable strain of the trenches and can feel the impressions that three years of war have sunk deep into my being emerge with a new vigour – more than ever the Front casts its spell over me.

Earnestly I question that sacred line of banked-up earth, that line of shell-craters, that line of balloons sinking regretfully to rest one after another like misshapen burnt-out stars, that line of flares now beginning to streak upwards.

What, then, when you consider it closely, are the properties peculiar to this fascinating and deadly line? By what hidden power does it attach itself to all that is most alive in my being – and so irresistibly draws it to itself?

Since, at this particular moment, I can look around me with greater calm and a more penetrating eye, I must try to analyse myself more clearly than I have done before. I must know.

The first 'classified' feeling to which I can compare my present emotion is the passion for the unknown and the new.

If I half-close my eyes and allow my consciousness to relax without restraint, if I give free rein to my imagination and let it sink back into its early patterns and allow it to recall the past, then I feel a resurgence of vague memories of long journeys that date back to the time when I was a child. I can once more see that time in railway stations when the multicoloured lights blaze out, to guide the great trains hurrying towards a wonderful and enchanted dawn. In my mind, the flare-lit trenches gradually dissolve into a vast transcontinental track, stretching out to an unimaginable distance . . . into some place beyond everything.

And then my dream becomes more sharply defined.

The devastated ridge whose outline is becoming a deeper and deeper purple as it disappears in the lightening yellow of the sky, has suddenly turned into the desert plateau where, in the East, I so often nursed my dreams – seen as though in a mirage – of what I might do as a discoverer and scientist. The water that shows white in the valley is no longer the Aisne: it is the Nile, whose distant mirror, in the days gone by, used to haunt me like a constant summons to the Tropics. I feel now that I am sitting, at twilight, near the mosque of El-Giyûshi, on the Mokattam Hills, looking south.

And so the answer comes: I have read my own secret.

In the enigmatic and importunate 'I' that loves the Front so obstinately I recognize the 'I' of venture and search, the man who is always longing to travel to the furthest limits of the world in order to enjoy new and uncommon visions and to be able to say that he is 'in the van'.[1]

I admit it: when, the greater part of three years ago, it came to the point where I had to go into the trenches for the first time, it was indeed in that spirit that I went – as a man who was full of curiosity, a jealous curiosity, anxious to see everything, to see more in them than other men could see. And even now the men who are stuck in the rear areas constitute for me an ever-living problem. How can those transport and ambulance-drivers, signallers and so on, how can they spend weeks close to the front lines and not be eaten up by their longing to go and see what is happening up there . . . neighbours as they are to the Front and believing, perhaps, that they are in the Front, but in fact further from it than a man living on the outskirts of Timbuktu! No doubt they have never known the passion for new horizons: but does not that mean that they are not completely men?

In spite of having become used to the Front, in spite of my own fatigue, in spite, too, of having found in it attractions that go deeper than mere novelty, it is still for me that Continent, filled with mysteries and hazards, which has appeared inside our tattered, meretricious Universe. I see it always as the frontier of the known World, the 'promised Land' open to the bold, the edge of 'no-man's-land'.[2]

Men who have suffered, even to the verge of death, from thirst or cold, can never again forget the deserts or the pack-ice where they enjoyed the intoxication of being the first and only men.

It is, in the first place, for that reason and in that way that I can no longer bid a permanent farewell to the Front.

And so I am beginning to read the secret of my nostalgia. I need the Front because I am, as every human being must be, an explorer, an extrovert. But is this first explanation any more than an approximate answer to my disquiet; is it, even, no more than a metaphor? Geographical or spatial exoticism is simply a particular and lower form of the passionate drive to extend ourselves to new and larger dimensions. The airman, who masters the skies – the thinker, whose mind rises up to difficult and unusual ways of looking at things – the opium-smoker who puts out into the sea of his dreams – all these are extroverts in their own way. Each of them is a *conquistador* landing on new shores.

What is it, then, that I myself have seen at the Front, and

what is it that I wish so ardently to find again, in spite of my fear of suffering and evil?

Is it new deserts, new volcanoes? Is it a new harmony of rioting lights and sounds?

Is it the vast dumb expanse of Flanders, on which the confronting armies seem to be sleeping among the stagnant waters?

Is it the dismal tops of the coal-tips scattered around the mining villages?

Is it the burnt-out gorge of the Hauts-de-Meuse, where the thundering explosions make the whole terrain smoke as though it were alive with sulphurous springs?

It is all those, no doubt. But it is above all something more, something more subtle and more substantial, of which all this great scenic setting is no more than the outer skin, the bait to hold the eye of the onlooker. It is something else which I can define for myself only as a unique atmosphere, dense and penetrating, in which all this riot of violence and majesty is contained; or again, I might define it as a superhuman state to which the soul is borne in a uniform, linear, progression, in spite of the diversity of the sectors and the vicissitudes of the battle.[3]

To my mind, the unforgettable experience of the Front is one of a vast freedom.

*

As soon as the man who is going up the line enters the first communication trench, he drops the burden of social conventions. From the very moment when civilian life ends there is no longer any difference between night and day. Instead of the commonplace alternation of getting up and going to bed, the man in the trenches can see before him nothing but a huge slice of duration, full of unforeseen events, in which sleep and meals occur simply as circumstances and opportunities allow, with no well-defined relation to light or dark. In the trenches, you wash when you can, and often you sleep no matter where. All the enslavements and hard and fast divisions of ordinary life collapse like a house of cards. It is interesting to note in one's own self how great a sense of satisfaction can be produced in the mind by this release from day-to-day slavery: a satisfaction that verges, perhaps, on the irresponsible, but, when properly understood, is right and noble.

Let there be no mistake about this: the *poilu*'s somewhat ironic goodnight to the comfortable rear-details is not merely a dismissal of regular routine: it symbolizes and heralds a much more intimate enfranchisement, a release from a wrong concern for self and one's own narrow personality.

Nobody will contradict me when I say that to go up into the trenches is to rise into peace.

As the rear fades into a more final distance, so the irksome and nagging envelope of small and great worries, of health, of one's family, of success, of the future . . . slides off the soul by itself, like an old coat. The heart grows a new skin. A reality of a higher or more urgent order chases away and scatters the whirling cloud of individual servitudes and cares. When we come down the line again we shall perhaps meet their importunate troop again; for the moment they are a mere vague mist, left behind us. And I despair of making anyone understand the serenity of the zone in which the soul finds herself when, secure from a danger whose threat is altogether too great, she has time to consider what light that danger kindles within her.

I can see myself again just as I was, in that peace, a fortnight ago.

It was night, a clear and calm night, in a sector very much broken up by ridges and marshy ground. The smell from the last gas attacks still lingered in the hollows under the poplars. At intervals you could hear more clearly a rustling noise in the wood like that of a startled woodcock taking flight – the falling of a mortar-bomb, which then exploded into the sudden ripping open of a flash-spangled cloud. And even so the crickets did not stop their chirping.

I was free, and I felt that I was free.

I was able to walk about just as I pleased in the moonlight, stroll on straight ahead, knock down some apples if I found any, and then go to sleep in the first shell-hole I came across. I still loved everything in the rear that matters to me or causes me anxiety, but I did so in a rather distant, controlled, way. My life seemed to me more precious than ever; and yet I would have abandoned it at that moment without regret, for I no longer belonged to myself. I was freed and relieved from even my own self. And I felt possessed of an inexplicable lightness.

Precious though this emancipation was, it was still no more than the negative part, or the outer shell, of a higher freedom which I shall call a positive freedom. The air I breathed was not merely pure and fine: it was full and nourishing – full and nourishing (a paradoxical phenomenon which I can nevertheless vouch for) even through the medium of those poisonous and ambiguous odours that were lingering in the tall grasses among the wild mint, full and nourishing through those brutal concussions that periodically shattered the calm of the night, full and nourishing through all the manifestations, dormant at that hour, of the immense human Presence with which the Front is charged.

Ah! I knew then – knew as a personal experience – that by being granted a favour grudgingly doled out to men by the centuries I was enabled unconstrainedly to direct my vital powers upon a *tangible* object. I could at last plunge into the real without the risk of dashing myself against the bottom, I could fill my lungs with terrestrial life and have no fear of having to gasp for air!

How heart-rending it is to find oneself so seldom presented with a task to be accomplished, one to which the soul *feels* that it can commit itself unreservedly! The eye of faith and the will guided by the supernatural, which give a boundless extension and value to the most humble actions – these are a great source of consolation and strength; but for all that they cannot normally, by themselves, replace *experience* in its function of arousing and sensitizing our faculties. That is why many things remain inactive in the setting of a flat, commonplace, life and exist in us as a dull feeling of suffering.

At the Front, the unleashed power of matter, the spiritual grandeur of the battle that is being fought, the triumphant domination of the moral energies released, combine their appeal with that of a noble pride and the imperative need to live, and they offer the heart a passion-charged draught of mixed elements. Up there, there reigns supreme a victorious conviction that one can 'go through with it' on the double plane of terrestrial and celestial action, with all one's strength and all one's soul. All the driving forces of one's being can be released; no boldness is ruled out; for once, man's task is seen to be greater than his desires.

Of this I am certain: in this discharge of energy, carried to the point of self-exhaustion, lies supreme freedom, freedom from all our dormant mass of unrecognized aspirations and uneasy powers, which we are often unable to develop for lack of matter and space – and how wearisome it must be for us to die without having allowed them free play.

No, nothing but the Front will give me back the intoxicating freedom I knew on that September night. It is not only that today I seem to be coming back from far, far, away; but also I have the feeling of having lost a Soul, a Soul greater than my own, which lives in the trenches and which I have left behind.

*

A man must turn in the end to these almost mystical considerations if he wishes fully to explain the emptiness and disenchantment of his returns to the rear, even when they have been most longed for.

The Front is not only the broiling expanse on which the opposing energies piled up in the hostile masses are revealed and neutralize one another. It is also a bond of a special Life which only those share who accept even its risks, and only for as long as they remain in it. When the individual has been admitted at some spot on that Sublime Surface, he has a positive impression that a new existence is enveloping him and taking possession of him.

He retains, it is true, his own individuality. He is not aware of any conscious centre distinct from his own soul. Nevertheless, as soon as he takes up his place on the sacred circumference of the truly active World, a personality of another order is disclosed, which masks and effaces the everyday man. The man of the Front acts as a function of the whole Nation and of all that lies hidden behind the Nations. His individual activity and passivity are directly employed in the service of an entity that is higher in richness, in duration, and in its future, than his own. He is himself only secondarily. Primarily he is part of the tool that bores ahead, an element in the prow that cuts through the waves. This is what he is, and he is conscious of it.

In this new and hazardous part he has to play, the man whom his country has dedicated to the flames receives also a consciousness that nothing can destroy and that brings him peace. Such a man has concrete evidence to prove that he no longer lives for himself – that he is freed from himself – that another Thing lives in him and dominates him. I do not hesitate to say that this special dis-individuation which enables the fighting man to attain some human essence higher than himself is the ultimate secret of the incomparable feeling of freedom that he experiences and that he will never forget.

Let every man observe himself, when he is going up to the firing line, or, again, when he is in billets and sees the next attack coming upon him, like a tunnel in which his life will be swallowed up.[4] He feels the continuous dull pain of a process that is going on in his affective domain, a sort of detachment, operated inexorably by the increasing imminence of D-day or zero hour. What is enveloping things is not precisely melancholy. It is rather a sort of indifference, which makes the details of individual life appear distant and colourless, while the fundamental ardour for action that is to be 'for all time' becomes more intense. – In the Citadel at Verdun, during those days of unforgettable confusion – with clouds of dust everywhere and with all the shouting – when rations, flares and hand-grenades were being chaotically distributed to those who were streaming up for the great offensive: – and again some hours later, during the interminable night march above Belleville and Froideterre, I noticed in myself this forcible and irresistible detachment, to be followed in turn by peace and exaltation in the superhuman atmosphere to which the soul had again become acclimatized.

It was the Soul of the Front being re-born in me.

– And then there is the man who picks himself up, covered in dust but unharmed, after a five-nine has exploded uncomfortably close to him: whence comes this joyful expansion of the heart, this alacrity of the will, this new savour in life – things that we do not experience if we have just missed being run over by a train or shot by a bullet from a carelessly handled revolver? Is it solely the joy of 'staying alive' that so fills the soul of survivors in war-time and gives new youth to their world? For my part, I believe that the completely fresh flavour added to living after a narrow escape derives above all from this deep-seated intuition that the existence we have found again, consecrated by danger, is a new existence. The physical well-being which at that moment spreads over the soul is a sign of the higher Life into which the survivor has just been baptized. The man who has passed through the fire is another species of man among men.

Not long ago, as I was cutting across the fields on my way back to the trenches (I was going towards Hurtebize, which could be seen smoking five kilometres away) I was suddenly stopped by a peasant, who reproached me for walking across his ploughland. The fellow was perfectly justified. But as I listened to him, I felt an inner shock, a dizziness, as though I were falling from a great height... To all appearances we were similar beings, he and I. We used the same words; but he was imprisoned in what concerned him as an individualistic 'man of the soil' – and I was living with the life of the Front. Who has not experienced, when he has been on leave and found himself again among persons and things that greeted him *just as before*, that melancholy feeling of being a stranger, someone out of scale, as though between the others and himself a deep rift had been opened, visible from only one side – and that side not theirs.

It is true to say that without this new and superhuman soul which takes over from our own at the Front, there would be things to endure and see up there that would be intolerable – and which nevertheless seem perfectly ordinary – and even leave (this is a fact) a permanent effect of fuller and wider being.

For my own part I can say that without war there would be a world of feelings that I would never otherwise have known or suspected. Nobody except those who were there will ever have the wonder-laden memory that a man can retain of the plain of Ypres in April 1915, when the air of Flanders stank of chlorine and the shells were tearing down the poplars along by l'Yperlé Canal – or, again, of the charred hillsides of Souville, in July 1916, when they held the odour of death. – Those more than human hours impregnate life with a clinging, ineradicable flavour of exaltation and initiation, as though they had been transferred into the absolute. When I look back, all the magic of the East, all the spiritual warmth of Paris are not worth the mud of Douaumont.[5]

When, therefore, that peace comes which the nations long for (as I do myself, more than anyone) something that I can only compare to a burning light will suddenly be extinguished on Earth. The effect of the war was to break through the crust of the commonplace and conventional. A window was opened onto the hidden mechanisms and deep strata of what man is becoming. A region was created in which it was possible for men to breathe a heaven-laden atmosphere. – When peace comes, everything will once more be overlaid by the veil of the former melancholy and trivialities. Thus it is that around Lassigny, for example, the areas from which the enemy has retreated already seem dreary, empty and spiritless, for the life of the Front has moved on further ahead.

Happy, perhaps, will those be whom death has taken in the very drama and atmosphere of war, when they were invested with, animated by, a responsibility for and a consciousness of a freedom greater than their own – when they were elevated to the very frontier of the World – close to God.[6]

The others, the survivors from the Front, will always have a void in their heart, so large that nothing we can see will ever be able to fill it. Then let them say to themselves, if they are to overcome their nostalgia, that in spite of appearances it is still possible for them to feel something of the life of the Front entering into them. Let them understand that the superhuman reality, which was disclosed to them in the shell-holes and barbed wire, will never completely withdraw from the pacified world. There it will always remain alive, more difficult to detect though it may be. And that man will be able to recognize it, and once more unite himself to it, who devotes himself to the tasks of everyday existence, not in a spirit of selfishness, as before, but *religiously*, with the consciousness of forwarding, in God and for God, the great task of creating and sanctifying a Mankind that is born above all in hours of crisis but can reach its fulfilment only in peace.[7]

. . . The fullness of night was now falling over the Chemin des Dames. I rose to walk down again to our billets. And as I turned to take a last look at that sacred line, the warm, living line of the Front, it was then that in the flash of a nascent intuition I half-saw that the line was taking on the shape of a higher Thing, of great nobility, which I could feel was forming itself even as I watched, but which it would have called for a mind more perfect than my own to dominate and understand. I thought then of those gigantic cataclysms that, long ago, were witnessed only by animals. – And at that moment it seemed to me that as I was confronted by this Thing in process of formation I was like an animal whose soul is awakening and that can see groups of connected realities but cannot understand the unitive principle of what they represent.[8]

On active service, with the *Tirailleurs.*

September 1917

1. Here we already see the emergence of the idea that was often to be expressed in later writings, notably in 'Human Energy' (1937): 'At present the majority of men do not understand Force (the key and symbol of greater-being) except in its most primitive and savage form of war. This is perhaps why it is necessary for us to continue for some time still to manufacture ever greater and more destructive weapons. For we still, alas, need these machines to translate the vital sense of attack and victory into concrete experience. But may the moment come (and it will come) when the masses realize that the true human victories are those over the mysteries of matter and life. May the moment come when the man in the street understands that there is more poetry in a mighty machine for splitting the atom than in any artillery. A decisive hour will strike for man, when the spirit of discovery absorbs the whole vital force contained in the spirit of war . . .' (*Human Energy,* 1969, pp. 135–6), Cf. 'Faith in Peace' (1947) in *The Future of Man,* pp. 149–54.

2. 'The Promised Land': this was to be the title of a later essay, in February 1919. But the last paragraph of 'Nostalgia for the Front' is essential to an understanding of the full significance of the symbol in this context.

3. Later, on 30 December 1929, he expressed a similar but more personal feeling in a letter written to Père Auguste Valensin from Tientsin: 'Always the same dominating impression of impassioned indifference or serenity. It is as though I were breathing a sort of vast freedom . . .'

On 12 October 1921 he wrote from Paris to his colleague Père Licent who was exploring Mongolia: 'You are, in relation to me, what I was during the war in relation to "the rear". I noticed that at that time, because I was *above convention and the pseudo-enslavements of conventional life,* my vision was wider and more true.'

4. In this simile there is perhaps an allusion to the Tavannes tunnel, through which passed units on their way to the trenches east of Verdun, and which opened almost directly into the firing-line.

5. After Père Teilhard's death, and even before, some readers were taken aback by the feeling expressed in this passage. Those who fought in the war of 1914 can vouch for its authenticity. Here, as in other contexts but with more clarity of analysis, Père Teilhard is expressing an experience that is not peculiar to himself, even though he took it into his life with no common intensity and nobility.

6. One cannot but note the similarity with Péguy, of whose poetry Père Teilhard was an admirer:

> 'Happy are those who died in the great battles,
> Resting on the earth, their faces turned to God.'

7. This paragraph is an advance summary of some of the considerations Père Teilhard was later to apply to the problem of war and peace. Cf. 'La crise présente', *Etudes,* 10 October 1937; 'The moment of choice, a possible interpretation of war' (Christmas 1939) in *The Activation of Energy,* 1963, p. 11. Cf. 'Mastery of the World and the Kingdom of God' in *Writings in Time of War,* p. 77 (1967): 'Transcending existing frontiers, a start is

being made in forging new links that nothing will henceforth be able to break'. Cf. also letter of 20 January 1941: 'There will be no real peace, I am sure, until men share a common understanding, at least as a first approximation, on what we should expect and hope for from the world's future' (*Letters from a Traveller*, 1962, p. 278). For the expanded version see 'The Salvation of Mankind: thoughts on the Present Crisis', in *Science and Christ*, pp. 128–60.

8. This last paragraph was not printed in *Etudes*. It already looks forward to 'The Great Monad', which was written three months later. Cf. 'Hominization' (1923): 'But just as in the life of individuals there are certain hours of awakening from which, by a sudden transformation, we emerge as adults, so in the general development of human consciousness, there come centuries during which the drama of initiation into the world, and consequently the inner struggle, suddenly occur. We are living at such a moment.' (in *The Vision of the Past*, 1966, p. 75.)

THE GREAT MONAD

A Manuscript Found in a Trench

In January and February 1918 Père Teilhard was with his regiment in the chalk country of Champagne. The letters written to his cousin during this period have been lost, but the date of *The Great Monad* and the place in which he finished it are given on the title-page: Vertus, 15 January 1918. Vertus is the chief town of a district to the west of Châlons-sur-Marne. The date would appear to be wrong, for the notebook in which Père Teilhard jotted down his thoughts from day to day shows that he was still working on the essay in the early part of February. For 15 January we should therefore read 15 February.

A note in the margin of the title-page tells us that the essay was written 'to run on from the last paragraph (cut out in the printed version) of *Nostalgia for the Front*'. In style it is closer, however, to the *Three Stories in the style of Benson*; again, in Benson's *Lord of the World* he found something of what he himself attempted to describe in *The Great Monad*. Thus in a letter dated 12 September 1918, we read:

'I've come across some odd numbers of the *Revue Hebdomadaire*, containing the end of *The Lord of the World*. I was delighted by the exact way in which Benson describes pantheistic mysticism and the possible unification of the "Great Monad". At the same time I was very aware (though I had not noticed it in 1910) of all the difference in point of view that separates me from Benson.' *The Making of a Mind*, 1965, p. 236.

'The Great Monad' is one of the names Père Teilhard introduced before 'the Noosphere'. In between the two came 'the Anthroposphere'. In February 1920 he was to write, 'Who will be the Suess of the anthroposphere?' By its combination of formal beauty, symbolic force and depth of thought, this "serious fantasy"[1] seems undoubtedly, for all its brevity, to be Père Teilhard's literary masterpiece.

I have just seen the moon rise over the ridge of the neighbouring trenches. The slim, hesitant crescent of the last few twilights has gradually turned into a full, luminous disc. The moon, invisible a fortnight ago, detaches herself, unique and glorious, from the black earthen parapets; she seems to be gliding through the barbed wire.

On these same uplands, the scene of our conflicts, on these flats, hardly different from what they are now, there was a time when no man yet trod. There were only herds of ruminants to animate the solitude in which thought did not exist – in which nothing stable was taking shape.

And then one day, after the horses, the antelopes, the elephants – hunting the wild animals of the open country and hunted themselves by life, thinking beings appeared here, coming from somewhere in the East.

The instinct for discovery, the need for space, flight from the stronger – these drove them on, until their flood came up against the sea's flood. It was through these wandering hunters that Mankind was stretching the first threads of its network over the face of the Earth.[2]

... However far we can look back into the past, there has been no change in the story of our race. It is a story of successive waves which, starting from some undetermined centres, have spread their layers over the surface of the continents.

For a long time these layers never succeeded in joining up and covering the whole: they died out before they were able to enclose the Universe; or else their advanced elements remained isolated after a period of falling back, like pools of still water or solid individual blocks. Elsewhere, too, their streams came into conflict and boiled up in formidable eddies.

In spite of these vicissitudes, the flood continued to rise; and now it covers the Earth. There is nowhere today where men are not in contact with and exerting pressure on men. Like some molten alloy, the tumultuous human mass, still violently jolted and shaken by explosions, needs only to find the laws that govern its own internal equilibrium.

Mankind in armed conflict with itself is a Mankind in process of solidification.[3]

What is it that is rising up this evening from the dimly outlined trenches to my front? Is it the Moon, or is it rather the Earth, a unified Earth, a new Earth?

When the great war broke out which at one blow brought crashing down the whole structure of a decrepit civilization – the short-sighted or the ungenerous-minded, those with no faith in the World,[4] knew a bitter triumph. Like Pharisees, they jeered at the bankruptcy of Progress and the exposed vanity of all social betterment.

As though every greater order has not always emerged from the ruins of the lesser! . . . as if a new and fresh surface did not force its way up through the tattered fragments of the old crust!

The whole of History teaches us this lesson, that after every revolution and after every war Mankind has always emerged a little more self-cohesive, a little more unified, because the links that hold its organism together are more firmly locked together and hope of a common emancipation has become strengthened.

. . . After every crisis Mankind is more differentiated and at the same time more one whole.

What, then, can we expect from this crisis?

If we are not as yet witnessing today the last outburst of discord, then we shall be doing so tomorrow; for the last act in the drama is rapidly approaching. It will not be long before the human mass closes in upon itself and groups all its members in a definitively realized unity. Respect for one and the same law, one and the same orientation, one and the same spirit, are tending to overlay the permanent diversity of individuals and nations. Wait but a little longer, and we shall form but one solid block. The cement is *setting*.[5]

Already, in the silence of the night, I can hear through this world of tumult a confused rustling as of crystalline needles forming themselves into a pattern or of birds huddling closer together in their nest – a deep murmur of distress, of discomfort, of well-being, of triumph, rising up from the Unity which is reaching its fulfilment. My heart was trembling with an emotion that embraced everything in the world . . .

. . . when, over the torn and blackened earth, there rose the great Monad.

The elements that had at last been reunited were swarming together, were rejoicing, were triumphing in the bliss of having succeeded in flooding over the whole Earth . . .

For my own part, I was filled with fear and overcome by dizziness when I marked the narrow limits within which the radiant globe was enclosed, and suddenly became conscious of the incurable isolation in which the glory of Mankind is lost.

It is something so new for man to find himself absolutely alone, eternally alone, and no longer to have anything before him to which he can direct his steps.[6]

Hitherto men have always lived in the shadow of human realities greater than themselves. They worked in order to combine with one another and to expand – to occupy still more countries and, by their multiple alliances, to form a people greater than their own. For their triumphs, they had spectators to applaud or envy – to direct their steps, they had guides – to govern their conflicts, they had an external power and potential judges. They never turned their eyes *outside* their own society; above them they always saw the leafy dome of the human forest.

This evening, as I saw the single block into which we are all on the point of solidifying, for the first time I had the feeling of *emerging* from our race and of seeing it as a self-contained whole –

and I felt as though we were all linked together and floating into the void.

This solitude had nothing of that initial isolation, still thronged with hopes, experienced by a handful of men lost in desert country: such men would have before them an emptiness to conquer and fill ... What I felt was the weight of an ultimate and definitive isolation, the misery known to those who have searched all around their prison and found no way out.[7]

Man has man for a companion. Mankind is *alone*.

Only a little more, and society will no longer have to look to any influence external to itself for the regulation of its all-inclusive harmony – it will need no admirer to wonder at its progress ... It will then have to find the driving force behind its improvement and the right ordering of its equilibrium without moving outside itself. When the thinking Earth has completed its closing in upon itself, then only shall we know the true nature of a Monad![8] ... – This evening, in the agony of the bloody schism which at this moment is dividing the World *with no possible recourse (already!) to any arbiter* – in the light, too, of the pronouncements in which our leaders, for the first time and under the pressure of an irresistible necessity, are drawing up the plan for a *universal* civilization – this evening I saw *the frontiers* of Mankind – I became conscious of the blackness and emptiness around the Earth.

A perfect circle in the vast sky, the Moon was riding over the trenches ...

The moon herself feels the pull and the heat of the stars in whose company she moves. But what friendly thought will be able to find its way through space as far as us?

I thought then that as soon as men saw the great Monad, *their own work*, rising over the battlefield like a prize to be won, they would forthwith bow down before it, in the wonder and pride of their satisfied power. Man is already so proud when he can master the forces contained in his own wretched person ... What limits can there be to this gesture of independence when he has succeeded in concentrating in one sphere the power contained in the whole of his species!

Soon, however, I understood that the uneasiness which from the first had impregnated my vision of the great Monad – the agony of feeling myself *shut in* – would, drop by drop, filter into the heart of this sense of satisfaction and sufficiency.

The feeling of the limits of our domain will inexorably make its way into the consciousness of the most heedless of us – it will insensibly chill the soul of the most enthusiastic. All, in the end, will feel, and feel *as one*, what I am going through now.

It will be a critical moment when human beings wake up, no longer at this point or at that point but as one whole, to *collective* consciousness of their isolation under the wide heavens – when raising their eyes to embrace the complete configuration of their world, see that they are *encircled* ...

Tell me, O thinking World, gravitating in the spiritual void, laden with the soul of all peoples, what force keeps you con- solidated upon yourself? and what pull, checking your fall, acts as your guide?[9]

I imagine that when Mankind has understood *en bloc* that it is sealed in upon itself and that in all the world (if not in the heavens) there is only itself on which it can rely to save itself (experi- mentally, I need hardly say)[10] it will first feel a great thrill of charity vibrate in the fabric of its being. – There are times when, in a sudden flash, we see what treasures of goodness towards his fellow-man lie hidden in the heart of man. But these treasures are nearly always locked up, so that what we know of society is hardly more than its conflicts and tyrannies: the men of today live as chance dictates, they do not seek one another out nor love one another ... If the pressure of an undeniable necessity could succeed in overcoming our mutual repulsions and in breaking the barrier of ice which isolates each one of us, who can judge what well-being and what tenderness would not emerge from the harmony of such vast numbers? – When men feel that they are really alone in the world, then (unless they tear one another to pieces) they will begin to love one another.[11]

Moreover, I like to think, instead of withdrawing into despairing inactivity, they will see how fruitless and chaotic has been the work to which they have so far applied themselves. – Even in this century, men are still living as chance circumstances decide for them, with no aim but their daily bread or a quiet old age. You can count the few who fall under the spell of a task that far exceeds the dimensions of their individual lives . . . At this very moment we are being given a glimpse of what a *national effort* can mean. Even so, unless adult Mankind is to drift aimlessly and so perish, it is essential that it rise to the concept of a specifically and integrally *human effort*. After having for so long done no more than allow itself to live, Mankind will one day understand that the time has come to undertake its own development and to mark out its own road . . .[12]

As the specific consciousness of the Monad spread over the earth, so its disc seemed to me to concentrate and grow brighter, while its track was aimed more directly to the Zenith. The great Monad had undoubtedly found one single, collective, *human* goal for its existence – and, each in its own degree, all individual efforts were co-operating in this supreme vital task . . .

The ancients believed that the stars were alive, like great animals or spirits. I can see what truth there was in their misconception. It may well be that the stars are scattered in space, with no possibility of inter-communication, in order that each one may carry a special soul, the soul of the peoples that multiply on its surface – the common soul of all those whose cosmic isolation concentrates into love and effort, until a mysterious organism is born of their coalescence.[13]

When the final spasms that are racking civilization today have come to appear as strange and distant to our descendants as the invasion of this corner of France by the first nomads appears to us, then, O Moon, you will rise over a Mankind concentrated on its ideal of progress, as this evening you are rising over the smoke-wreathed trenches – the same Moon, rising over our great-great- . . . grandchildren. And your melancholy smile will fall on the living, those who have completed their daily task and are wrapped in sleep, and those, too, who are keeping the night watches.[14]

Pale Moon, icy Moon, will those men – full of vigour on an ageing Earth – who look up to you in those days, will they understand the ultimate meaning of your silent face?

The ascetic keeps before his eyes the grim image of a whitened skull.

And of what does your wan countenance remind us, you burnt-out star, held up as a sign to all the ages, if not that Mankind grows, lashed to a corpse? . . .[15]

'Work' is what you seem to be saying to us, 'work with all your might, to make your dwelling-place fit to be lived in and lovely, rouse yourselves in a passion to disclose its secrets and to create beauty . . . What awaits you, in your turn – you and your works – is the rigidity of my stark crust.'

Is it a challenge to us, O Moon, that you hold in your death, is it the implacable mirror in which our future is to be read – or is it, rather, the last lesson that you have to teach us?

If that be a challenge, if you died because you failed, so be it! We shall fight for what your will lacked the intensity to win. We, in our turn, shall try to force the barriers of our isolation.

The World, maybe, is easier to mould than we think: upon its determinism, its limits, we shall bring to bear the convergent ardour of our action and our thought in an attempt to make it more pliable and expansible . . .

Perhaps, in spite of its impressive bulk, this Colossus has feet of clay? ... We are going to batter at its foundations like a ram, with the whole combined force of our shoulders. Suppose we could overturn it and make our way out through its shattered fragments?

Perhaps, at least, the ocean of space which imprisons us can be crossed by our thought or even by something in our life? ... Shall we launch a ship upon those waters and let the Earth founder behind us?

– But no: it is madness to hope to come out alive from the doomed enclosure that holds us – madness to hope to try to communicate to the whole Universe the life of the great Monad! ... What Titan could prevent Matter from continuing inexorably to fold back upon itself and so lock itself around us?

The day will come when Earth, too, bleached to a uniform whiteness, like a great fossil, will be a mere gravitational cipher; there will be no more movement on its surface, and it will still hold all our bones.[16]

What is descending upon us, therefore, from the sky in the clearness of the nights, is not a challenge to an insensate duel ... It is a supreme warning.

Down here, flesh – elaborated by spirit in order to act and develop itself – inevitably becomes, sooner or later, a prison in which the soul suffocates; and in consequence there is only one way into the greater life open to natural organisms, whether they belong to the individual or to Mankind – and that way is Death.[17]

Incessantly, like a trembling haze that vanishes, a little spirit is released from the Earth and evaporates around it: the soul of those who have passed away. By that same road must depart the fully formed and matured Spirit of the great Monad.

Every star (if it be true that they all live, every one in its own turn) will know its own individual death: in cold or conflagration, in intestine struggles or in slumbering happiness.

The only true death, good death, is a paroxysm of life: it is obtained by a desperate effort on the part of the living to be more pure, more stripped of everything,[18] more tense in their determination to escape from the zone in which they are confined.

Happy the World that is to end in ecstasy! . . .[19]

My vision, then, was incomplete.

Even when we contain within one single form the totality of our race, it is mistakenly that we see a true monad rise up before us. What we see is only the impermanent whirlpools produced by two streams that run separately.

While the remains of life gradually revert to a single mass, the final receptacle of all inert matter (later to disappear, perhaps in some extreme pulverization), Spirit emerges from every cosmic unit, and is drawn towards the pole proper to soul. – There we have the history of the World.[20]

One by one – each bearing the special colour, the particular properties, the individual vision of the World in which they have flourished – distinct groups of living beings join the Centre in which, we can be sure, the spiritual nectar extracted from the countless bodies scattered throughout the firmament, is combined into one single Thing.

Thus our isolation is only partial in its relation to the terrestrial organism which is for a time our common matrix . . . One and the same influence animates and holds together everything that thinks . . . One single circle embraces all spirit, and *imprisons nothing* . . .

We can hardly perceive this higher and uncircumscribed unity of the Universe . . . the most we can say is that at certain times a wind greater than we, coming we know not whence, passes through our soul . . . But we may well wonder what understanding of our personal life, or even of the life of one of our cells, could be attained by infinitesimal beings presumed to exist, and distributed among the molecules of our body . . .

O wonder-laden Centre! O immense sphere! O God![21]

*

On that war-time evening, everything was enveloped for me in
the plenitude of the great Monad – in the light of the moon.

Vertus, 15 January 1918

1. The author had added a sub-title, 'A serious fantasy . . . in the moonlight', but he
crossed this out and substituted another (A ms. found in a trench). The manuscript shows
many erasures and the writing is less firm than in others, so that this would appear to be
a first rough draft.

2. These first migrations of man are described in Henri Breuil's *Les Primitifs actuels et
préhistoriques*, Congrès de l'Association pour l'avancement des sciences, 1928. We know
that well before the war Père Teilhard had been closely associated with Breuil, who was
attached to the Institute of Palaeontology, while Père Teilhard himself was working in the
palaeontological laboratory of the Museum. Cf. Claude Cuénot, *Pierre Teilhard de Chardin*
(1958) p. 34–5; Edouard Le Roy, *Les Origines humaines et l'évolution de l'intelligence*(1928)
ch. 12 (pp. 234–54).

3. Here we already meet an idea which was to be expressed more clearly in Père
Teilhard's later work, notably in 'A great event foreshadowed, the Planetization of
Mankind' (25 December 1945), in *The Future of Man* (1964) p. 127, Fontana edition p. 132.

'During these six years, despite the unleashing of so much hatred, the human block has
not disintegrated. On the contrary, in its most rigid organic depths it has further increased
its vice-like grip upon us all. First 1914–18, then 1939–45 – two successive turns of the
screw. Every new war, embarked upon by the nations for the purpose of detaching themselves from one another, merely results in their being bound and entangled in a more
inextricable knot. The more we seek to thrust each other away, the more do we inter-
penetrate.'

4. This 'faith in the World' lay behind his later apologia, 'How I believe' (1934). Here
we find him asserting and vindicating it before developing the concept more fully.

5. In 'The Heart of Matter' (1950), p. 31 above, we read: 'This gift or faculty of
perceiving, without actually *seeing*, the reality and organicity of collective magnitudes is
still comparatively rare: but I have no doubt at all . . . that it was the experience of the
War that brought me this awareness and developed it in me as sixth sense'. To this he
adds a note: 'This awakening is unmistakably apparent in a rather over-free fantasy,
entitled 'The Great Monad', which was written in the trenches, about 1917: the full
moon emerging over the barbed wire – symbol and image of the thinking Earth – and
more clearly still in the last paragraph (omitted by the editors) of 'Nostalgia for the Front'.
See also 'Cosmic Life' (*Writings in Time of War*, p. 15), 'A summons, rising from some
hidden depth within ourselves, that calls on us to broaden our self-regard, and realize that
in virtue of our immortal souls, we are the *countless centres of one and the same sphere*'.

6. Teilhard was never to abandon this concept. On 12 October 1926 we find him
writing from Tientsin to the Abbé Gaudefroy, and confiding to him his dream of writing
'a sort of *Book of the Earth*' in which he hoped to describe 'the confidence, the ambitions,
the sense of plenitude, and also the disappointments, anxieties, the sort of dizziness of the
man who becomes conscious of the destinies and concerns of the entire Earth (entire
Mankind). I would not try in this essay to fall into line with any of the accepted trends, but
simply to express my own feeling and communicate my faith in man's work and man's

unity – my anger at the hard and fast divisions, both vertical and horizontal, that still compartmentalize spiritual fragments whose final end must be unity – our chagrin when we see ourselves imprisoned on a globe whose limited importance is being exhausted – our agony in finding ourselves all alone, the whole mass of us, in the middle of stellar space'.

7. *Issue*: This and similar words were much favoured by Teilhard. 'Creative Union' in *Writings in Time of War*, p. 173. 'The atomism of Spirit' (1941) in *Activation of Energy* (1970), p. 46: 'the way out opened for consciousness in the heart of things'. To the Abbé Gaudefroy, 16 June 1929: '. . . There is no possible way out for the Noosphere apart from the Christian axis'. 'The Christic' (above p. 92) (1955), 'we can . . . distinguish above us the positive gleam of a way out'. 'The end of the species' (1952) in *The Future of Man*, p. 303, 'an *outlet* appears at the peak of Time'. 'Reflections on the compression of mankind' (1953) in *Activation of Energy*, as above, p. 342. In that last essay and in 'The death-barrier and co-reflection' (1955) in the same volume, we have an analysis of the 'suffocating' world and the world 'closing in on itself' (pp. 341-6, 397-406). Cf. 'The human rebound of evolution' (1947) in *The Future of Man* (as above) p. 210, etc. Letter of 1 January 1917, in *The Making of a Mind* (1954, as above), 'The former cosmic framework no longer suffices to contain (to satisfy) the new activities born with the human soul', p. 160. 'The Singularities of the human species', Introduction (1954), in *The Appearance of Man*, pp. 208-9.

8. The sentence 'When the thinking Earth . . . Monad!' is written here in the MS., enclosed in brackets and marked for insertion above.

9. Père Teilhard still keeps up the deliberate but silent assumption that God is absent from this human universe, from the Great Monad. Here the apologist gives a hint of the plan he will realize in his concluding pages.

10. The bracketed words have been added in the margin.

11. Cf. Dostoyevsky, *The Raw Youth*: Versilov is telling his son Dolgoruky how men have driven out God. They have suddenly realized, he goes on to say, that they are now completely alone, utterly abandoned, like orphans. So, what can they do? And Versilov, as he muses, thinks to himself that, if men understood this, they would quickly find some object of love in order to allay the deep pain of grief in their hearts. Every man would tremble for every other man's life and happiness. As they met they would look at one another searchingly and with great understanding, and their eyes would be filled with love and sorrow. That, however, was a mere dream.
– Or Péguy, *Le Porche du mystère de la deuxième vertu*, *The Porch of the mystery of the second virtue*, (Pléiade edition, p. 127): *Ces pauvres enfants sont si malheureux qu'à moins d'avoir un coeur de pierre*
Comment n'auraient-ils pas charité de leurs frères,
Comment n'auraient-ils pas charité les uns des autres.
So hapless these poor children, that unless their hearts were of stone
How could they not know charity for their brothers,
How could they not know charity for one another.

12. This idea was to be, worked out more fully in the title-essay of *Human Energy*, part IV, 'The conscious organization of human energy', pp. 125-37 (1969).
Forty years later, we began (take, for example, the geophysical year of 1965-6) to fulfil to some degree the prophecy contained in 'The Great Monad'.

13. The word 'coalescence' recurs later (1950), in almost the same sense: 'How may we conceive and hope that human unanimity will be realized on Earth?' in *The Future of Man*, (1964), p. 284: 'An enforced coalescence of all Thought in the sum total of itself'. But the 1950 essay distinguishes between 'an enforced unification, by force or compression' and a 'free unification, through attraction', and it is in connection with the former that Teilhard uses the word 'coalescence'. Here, on the other hand, his point of view is somewhat

different and both forms of unification are included.

14. At this point the symbolism changes. The Moon is no longer the symbol of the Great Monad, of unified Mankind rising up in a gigantic common effort: it becomes the symbol of cosmic death.

15. Cf. M. Barthélemy-Madaule, *Bergson et Teilhard de Chardin*, p. 88: 'It is a sort of solemn dirge that Teilhard hears on the field of death lit by the dim light of the small hours'. Earth, which bears Mankind, will suffer the same fate as the Moon to which she is bound.

16. Cf. 'The end of the species' (1952): 'We shall gain nothing by shutting our eyes to this shadow of collective death that has appeared on our horizon. On the contrary, we must open them wider'. (*The Future of Man*, 1964 (as before), p. 300, Fontana edition p. 314.) 'Is not Man even now in process of developing astronautical means which will enable him to go elsewhere and continue his destiny in some other corner of the firmament? That is what they say, and for all I know there may be people for whom this sort of reasoning does really dispel the clouds that veil the future. I can only say that for my part I find such consolation intolerable, etc.' (pp. 300-1, Fontana edition p. 315). Cf. Péguy, *Zangwill*: 'Mankind will leave behind the first dirigibles just as it left behind the first locomotives. We shall be able to circle the earth in a mere flash. But it will always be only the temporal earth.'

17. Cf. letter of 13 November 1916 in *The Making of a Mind* (as before), pp. 144-6. 'Mass on the World' in *Hymn of the Universe* (1965) and above p. 119. *Le Milieu Divin*, pp. 68-70.

18. We should possibly read the MS. as 'plus uns' (more one) rather than 'plus nus' (more stripped).

19. Cf. 'The atomism of spirit', in *Activation of Energy* (1970), p. 46: 'Escape in depth (through the centre) or, which comes to the same thing, ecstasis.' 'Life and the Planets' (1945) in *The Future of Man*, 1964, pp. 122-3, Fontana, pp. 126-8: 'We cannot resolve this contradiction, between the congenital mortality of the planets and the demand for irreversibility developed by planetized life on their surface, by covering it up or deferring it: we have finally to banish the spectre of Death from our horizon . . .' Let us now suppose that, from Omega Point "there constantly emanate radiations hitherto only perceptible to those persons whom we call 'mystics'!" Let us further imagine that, as the sensibility or response to mysticism of the human race increases with planetization, the awareness of Omega becomes so widespread as to warm the earth psychically, while physically it is growing old. Is it not conceivable that Mankind, at the end of its totalization, its folding-in upon itself, may reach a critical level of maturity where, leaving Earth and stars to lapse slowly back into the dwindling mass of primordial energy, it will detach itself from this planet and join the one true, irreversible essence of things, the Omega point? A phenomenon perhaps outwardly akin to death: but in reality a simple metamorphosis and arrival at the supreme synthesis. An escape from the planet, not in space or outwardly, but spiritually and inwardly, such as the hypercentration of cosmic matter upon itself allows.'

20. Cf. letter of 6 January 1917, 'Everything we give out from ourselves except to another soul is no more than dregs. In a way, the whole tangible universe itself is a vast residue, a skeleton of countless lives that have germinated in it and left it, leaving behind them only a trifling, infinitesimal, part of their riches. True progress never makes itself felt, is never realized, in any of the material creations we try to substitute for ourselves in the hope that they will survive our life on earth: it is in souls that the advance is made, the real sparks in which the inner fires of the world are concentrated and embodied, and it disappears with them', in *The Making of a Mind* (1965), p. 163. Wedding address (1928), 'For Odette and for Jean,' see above, p. 138. 'Far from being impermanent and accidental,

it is souls, and alliances of souls, it is the energies of souls, that alone progress, infallibly and it is they alone that will endure'.

21. Cf. letter of 29 September 1918: 'Isn't the particular attraction of his (Christ's) being, precisely the uniting in him – if I may put it so – of the centre and the sphere' (*The Making of a Mind*, p. 241).

This is the classical teaching, already to be found in St Gregory the Great, *Moralia in Job* I.2. c.12, n.20: 'He remains within all things, outside all things, above all things, below all things ... Encompassing without, penetrating within ... penetrating by encompassing, encompassing by penetrating'.

'It is precisely *because* he is at once so deep and yet so akin to an extensionless point that God is infinitely near, and dispersed everywhere. It is *precisely because* he is the centre that he fills the whole sphere. The omnipresence of the divine is simply the effect of its extreme spirituality and is the exact contrary of the fallacious ubiquity which matter seems to derive from its extreme dissociation and dispersal. In the light of this discovery, we may resume our march through the inexhaustible wonders which the divine *milieu* has in store for us.' (*Le Milieu Divin*, pp. 101–2.)

Cf. note to 'Le Christ dans la matière' in *Ecrits du Temps de la Guerre*, Oeuvres XII p. 126: 'On more than one occasion Père Teilhard stated that God is simultaneously the Centre (the Heart) and the Sphere. Thus, in 'The Great Monad', above, p. 191, 'O wonder-laden Centre! O immense Sphere! O God!' And again, in 'Cosmic Life' *Writings in Time of War*, p. 70, 'Jesus, the Centre to which all things are moving'. His language is akin to that of de Bérulle in his *Discours de l'état et des grandeurs de Jésus* (5th edn., 1639, pp. 152–3) and his *Vie de Jésus*, discours 1, no. 21 (3rd edn., 1630, p. 29).

MY UNIVERSE

This is a key-text for an understanding of Père Teilhard's fundamental attitude and of the degree of importance he attaches to the various concepts he develops in his writings. Moreover, it is exceptionally clear.

We have two autograph manuscripts, showing only comparatively slight differences. Anyone familiar with the author's methods who compares the two carefully, will have no doubt but that one is a first draft and the other the revised version (cf. *The Making of a Mind*, p. 240). The draft was sent to his cousin Marguerite Teillard; the revised version was evidently intended for one of those who, in the author's words, 'have the right to guide me'.

We must wait for a critical edition to give us the variant readings and for stylistic experts to examine their nature. It is the revised version, we need hardly add, that is printed here.

The bewilderment, accompanied by a certain disquiet, experienced by my best friends when reading my most recent essays (*Cosmic Life, The Struggle against the Multitude*) has impressed on me the necessity of providing some clarifications of my ideas.

In order, therefore, to be more certain in my own mind of what precisely I am putting forward, and to simplify the task of criticism and correction that falls on those who have the right to guide me, I have tried to define the basic essential characteristics of my 'vision of the World', and to allow them to emerge from the philosophical idiom in which, for lack of any better, and provisionally, I have expressed them.

What follows is the result of this process of refinement and discrimination.

I shall begin by describing the *fundamental tendency*, the natural cast, of my mind, which cannot, in practice, be changed.

Then I shall describe how these innate dispositions gradually changed, for me, into a *particular way of seeing everything*, whether earthly or divine.

Finally, I shall show how, in its turn, this vision or experience (belonging, more properly, to the mystical order) came to be contained as a secondary development in a certain ascesis (= *ascesis* 'of total effort') and a certain philosophy (= 'philosophy of Union').

Thus the complexity of my internal attitude will be seen to proceed in successive steps – less and less vital for me, but at the same time easier to contest and correct.

May Our Lord Jesus Christ enlighten, for their own sake and for mine, those who read this brief apologia!

I. INNATE TENDENCIES

However far back I go into my memories (even before the age of ten) I can distinguish in myself the presence of a strictly dominating passion: the passion for the Absolute.

At that age, of course, I did not so describe the urgent concern I felt; but today I can put a name to it without any possible hesitation.

Ever since my childhood, the need to lay hold of 'some Absolute' in everything was the axis of my inner life. I can remember very vividly that, for all my youthful pleasures, I was happy only *in terms of* a fundamental delight; and that consisted generally in the possession, or the thought of, some more precious, rarer, more consistent, more immutable object. At one time it would be a piece of metal; at another, I would take a leap to the other extreme and find satisfaction in the thought of God-the-Spirit (the Flesh of Our Lord seemed to me at that time to be something too fragile and too corruptible).

This may well seem an odd preoccupation. I can only repeat that it was a fact, and a *permanent* fact. I was never to be free from the irresistible (and at the same time vitalizing and soothing) need to find *unending* rest in Some Thing that was tangible and *definitive*; and I sought everywhere for this blissful object.

The story of my inner life is the story of this search, directed upon continually more universal and more perfect realities. Fundamentally, my underlying innate tendency (the *'nisus'* or 'thrust' of my soul) has remained absolutely inflexible, ever since I have been aware of my own self.

It would serve no purpose here to give a detailed review of the various altars that I have successively raised to God in my heart. I shall only say that as I found every *individual* form of existence to be unstable and subject to decay, I extended the range of my search: to elementary Matter, to the currents of physical energy, to the totality of the Universe – always, I must confess, with an instinctive predilection for matter (regarded as more absolute than the rest) that I corrected [in myself] only much later. (Cf. 'Creative Union, True Matter' in *Writings in Time of War*, p. 166, 1968, and below pp. 205–6.)

Since my childhood, and in later days ever more fully and with a greater sense of conviction, I have always loved and sought to read the face of Nature; but, even so, I can say that my approach has not been that of the 'scientist' but that of the 'votary'. It seems to me that every effort I have made, even when directed to a purely natural object, has always been a religious effort: substantially, it has been one single effort. At all times, and in all I have done, I am conscious that my aim has been to attain the Absolute. I would never, I believe, have had the courage to busy myself for the sake of any other end.

Science (which means all forms of human activity) and Religion have always been for me one and the same thing; both have been, so far as I have been concerned, the pursuit of one and the same Object.

II. REVELATION OF THE UNIVERSE (COSMOS)

Under the constant pressure of my mind, which endeavoured to extract from Things a soul made up of consistence and the Absolute, the Universe was ultimately revealed to me as a Reality with an extraordinarily insistent claim for recognition.

As I write now, I can see, in what has become my most habitual outlook on the world, in my normal day-to-day life:

1. First, the Universe as a certain *eminently great* and precious Entity. I am habitually conscious (in some way) of its Totality, of its 'Becoming', of the countless potentialities (*virtutes et potentiae*) it contains. And in the presence of this majesty, I must confess that many restless human activities seem to me singularly unworthy of notice.

2. Secondly, I see the Universe as *supremely inclusive* and dominant. I feel that I am involved in it, locked into it, contained within it. I feel that I cannot take full possession of my own self except by extending my self into a certain perfection which runs through all things – so that my own fulfilment must be in, and with, the universality of Creation.

3. This means that I believe I can distinguish in the Universe a *profound*, essential *Unity*, a unity burdened with imperfections, a unity still sadly 'pulverulent', but a real unity within which every 'chosen' substance gains increasing solidity.

Thus a first, inextinguishable Core of fire is radiant within me, and in this all my activity finds warmth: the vast, intimate, single World. In its heat *the passion for the universal Real* is kept alive deep down in my being. – *Human action* seems to me to be completely satisfying and conscious only when it is carried through in union with the fulfilment of all cosmic perfection.

This disposition of mine is the result of an innate tendency. I should have to make a positive (and perhaps impossible) effort to resist it.

III. CONJUNCTION OF THE UNIVERSE AND GOD

God Our Lord, the revealed End of the Universe, is the second Core of my soul.

The whole problem of my interior life – and all, too, that gives it value and delight – has consisted, and still consists, in knitting together in myself the influences that radiate from each of the two Centres (God and the World) – or, to put it more exactly, in making them coincide.

I shall describe later at what particular, explicit, solution to the problem I came to rest, after more than twenty years of feeling my way and experimenting within myself. – What I wish to draw the attention of my guides to above all is that, before seriously reflected considerations came into play, the reconciliation and fusion of the two fundamental loves (love of God and love of the World) was realized in me, intellectually and affectively, by itself alone, *vitally*.

Without any effort, through a sort of natural expansion of creation, I came to see God as an extension of the attributes (magnitude, intimacy, unity) in the Universe which had made so vivid an appeal to me. In some way he was revealed to me through those attributes (shining through them, reaching me through them – impregnated with them, if I may so express what I mean), fulfilling them, going beyond them, and yet *not destroying them*.

Through dilation of the World's charms – and also, I may add, through the need to find an absolute principle for the World's successful issue and for its unity (*a remedy for its contingence*) – knowledge and love of the Universe developed *spontaneously* for me (with great clarity, but in a way that is difficult to express) into knowledge and love of God.

Today I can, I believe, see and feel how the two Centres of all human love insist on their need for one another and complete one another in an astonishing way: God using the World so that he may be attained by us and himself attain us (that is to say, receiving from the World, in relation to us, a sort of *esse tangibile*); and the World, in turn, relying on God in order to overcome its contingence and plurality (that is to say, receiving from God, by participation, a sort of *esse absolutum* – the consecration of its reality).

What is Our Lord Jesus Christ if not this synthesis of the created Universe and its Creator?

This fundamental experience, the support of my whole religious life, can be formulated in the following *wish*, in which is expressed the most general necessary condition of my personal sense of balance and of my interior joy:

'To be able to admit a certain co-extension of Christ and the Universe, such that:

1. Christ may succeed to the magnitude and all-enveloping power of the Universe.

2. Meritorious action can be effected with the consciousness of acting in union with the whole Universe.'

In all my ideas, this is the only point to which I really cling. And it is this above all that I wish to have either approved or corrected.

In understanding the value I attach to the orthodoxy of the thesis I have just put forward, it should be noted that it is not merely the expression of the psychological need I feel of preserving my love of the Universe (in some way the initial *substance* of my love of God). It is an even more categorical statement of my faith in the Plenitude of Christ.

My irresistible tendency is to *universalize what I love, because otherwise I cannot love it*.

Now, a Christ who extended to only a part of the Universe, a Christ who did not in some way assume the World in himself, would seem to me a Christ smaller than the Real . . . The God of our Faith would appear to me less grand, less dominant, than the Universe of our experience!

How, then, could I love him more than all things, more than the World?

On the other hand, I have no words to express the ever fresh treasures of strength, of light, and of peace that are constantly made available to me by the fundamental vision *of Christ in all things.*

In very truth, *venerunt mihi omnia bona cum illa.*

IV. POSSIBLE NATURE OF THE CO-EXISTENCE OF CHRIST AND THE UNIVERSE

In order to follow the logic of my nature, in order to be true to my own self (and that means, I hope, true to my vocation) I have had to try to become perfectly clear in my own mind about what this universal Presence of Christ consists in: the Presence that I felt and loved above all things.

This was a task that I could not shirk.

At the same time it plays only a secondary part in my 'teaching', a somewhat artificial part, and one much more disputable than the innate state of mind that it seeks to legitimize and interpret.

Let me describe how I picture to myself, for the moment, the relationship between Christ and the Universe.

In a general way I think that the co-extension of Christ and the World must be understood primarily in the sense of a physical, organic, influence exerted by Christ on the essential movement (or the sum total of the essential movements) that causes the Universe to grow (= *creative or transforming action*).

That being so, let us, to simplify matters, say that: $o =$ the natural term (x) of human (and cosmic) advances; and $\omega =$ the supernatural term (plenitude of Christ) of the Kingdom of God.[1]

I conceive three principal relations between o and ω:

1. Either o and ω are two disparate (independent) terms developing on two different planes within the same created activity

(for example, ω is the product of human actions regarded as moral and 'effected for God'; and o is the fruit, with no value for the supernatural world, of those same actions in so far as they achieve their end in this world of time).

2. Or o and ω *are two antagonistic terms*, each tending to eliminate the other, so that every point at which created activity comes in is a place where there is a choice between, and a separation between, o and ω ($=$ the doctrine of renunciation, pure and simple).

3. Or, finally, o and ω *are two hierarchically ordered terms*, ω being a magnification of o, which it has taken to itself and sublimated, 'along its initial axis'. (For example, we can conceive how natural human effort and grace work together, *each for an essential part*, in the development of Spirit: Spirit *continues to produce itself in its natural substance* at the same time as God elevates it to the supernatural order. In such conditions, the World is not merely an exercise-ground: it is *a work* to be carried through.)

The first of these hypotheses seems to me to be dualist and spurious, neither one thing nor the other. (I have criticized it at length in *Cosmic Life*.)

I find the second theoretically attractive; but in practice it seems to me inhuman and impossible to reconcile:

1. either with the practice of the Church, which has always openly encouraged human work and given it her blessing;

2. or with the most elementary religious psychology, which discloses a strict connection between the natural expansion of human faculties and their capacity for love of God. The Universe stimulates the 'zest for being', and provides the nourishment which are transformed into love of God. To my mind, at least, this process is extremely clear: Heaven cannot dispense with Earth.

Until further orders, therefore, I hold to the third solution, which has the advantage of being directly suited to my double instinctive need:

1. to feel God underlying all natural energy, and

2. to find a universal, absolute, value in all human action (*non solum quoad operationem, sed etiam quoad opus*).

In a real and literal sense we may say, if we accept the hypothesis of Christ's adopting and supernaturalizing of the natural evolution of the World, *quidquid patimur, Christus agit* and *quidquid agimus, Christus agitur* – whatever is done to us, it is Christ who does it, and, whatever we do, it is to Christ we do it.

This way of looking at human activity and passivity as integrally sanctified and divinized has become so familiar to me that it is no effort to me to live with it. I find in it an ease and breadth of movement, a clarity of judgement and decision, which make me earnestly wish that many others besides myself should understand and adopt the same position.

It is most important to note that this concept of the World's *conjoined ends* (natural and supernatural) has nothing in common with a theory of hedonism or 'hold fast to all you have'.

Its aim is, no doubt, to channel towards God, to harness for Heaven, *the whole* of the World's drive towards the Beautiful and the Good. But it maintains (as does every theory of true transformation):

1. that natural progress, as well as supernatural, underlies individual work and renunciation.

2. that natural development is subordinated to the kingdom of God.

3. that the centre of gravity of human effort gradually shifts towards the concerns of heaven as certain fields of lower activity are left behind or exhausted (it is thus that virginity tends to replace the marital state).

V. THE PHILOSOPHY OF UNION

Having admitted that Christ coincides with the Universe, by virtue of being the *universal Centre* common to cosmic progress and gratuitous sanctification, we have now to discover whether we can go further in our elaboration of his divine co-extension with the World: in other words, we must form an idea of *the law of the transformation* of all things *in Ipso* and *per Ipsum.*

Such a formulation has seemed possible to me.

I have thought (cf. 'Creative Union') that the entire development of the supernaturalized World, seen through man's experience, might well assume the form of a vast movement of unification, converging towards Christ.

I have tried, accordingly, to show that the successive advances of created being, from its first appearance out of Non-being until the formation of rational soul, until the incorporation of the elect in the mystical Body of Our Lord, are *connected with* (if not due to) the progressive reduction of an initial plurality. On this hypothesis, the differentiation of beings (which is the immediate term of their individual perfection) is no more than the preliminary to an ever closer and more spiritual union of the elements of the Universe. The *unique attraction* of Christ animates this great effort towards self-concentration made by created Spirit.

The *advantages* of this theory (of creative Union) are as follows:

1. Firstly, *philosophically:*

a. it satisfies simultaneously the *monist* and *pluralist* tendencies which clash so distressingly, I believe, in every mind that is impressed by the REAL need to reach some small understanding of the World (*the unity* of the World is brought about by our fidelity in *individualizing ourselves*);

b. it also reconciles the postulates of *materialism* and (using the word in the wide sense) *spiritualism*. Although matter is not volatilized (a temptingly easy solution, but one contrary to dogma), it is dethroned by Spirit, to which, nevertheless, it serves as a support. The whole coherence and ontological value of the

Universe depend, in fact, upon Spirit, which alone locks together in itself, and interlocks, the elements that constitute the World . . . This perception of the soul's annexation of the attributes that most attracted me in Matter, has been, I believe, one of the last great advances in my thought.

2. Secondly, *mystically*: creative Union satisfies me (though I should rather say that 'I find satisfaction in it') because it reduces all the World's movement to a communion. *Communion* becomes the *unique and essential act* of the World; in other words, it takes on the qualities of universality and the absolute that I persist in trying to give to everything I love 'absolutely'. The fact is that the system of 'creative Union' was born in my mind from the need to *generalize*, and to *link indissolubly to the structure of the World*, what we know of the mystical Body and of union with Jesus.

For me, the *best philosophy* will always be that which allows me most fully *to feel Christ, necessarily*, and *everywhere*.

I can readily understand that the theory of creative Union calls for rectifications, if not in its central core (where it is close to Christ), at least *in its extension* to the initial creation and the formation of the soul.

Nevertheless, I must emphasize here:

In seeking to reduce everything to union, my aim has not been so much to find a metaphysical solution for the Universe as to discover an historical pattern, practically applied, in the developments of Creation.

Supposing it were proved that the creation and spiritualization of beings can in no way be reduced to the mechanism of a union:

It would even then be true that a progressive unification of things accompanies, and is the measure of, their entitative augmentations.

Union would still be the *apparent*, empirical, *law* that governs the perfection and sanctification of creatures.

That is all I ask.

VI. THE NECESSITY OF A SOLUTION

Whatever may be the corrections, more or less radical, that must be applied to the solution I have found for the 'problem of my life', one point will remain indisputable: and that is the concern to *unify my interior vision*, of which I am so vividly aware that many others must, I am sure, feel it as strongly as I do.

The supernaturalization of the World does more than provide theologians with abstract difficulties.

It introduces into the heart of practical life an appearance *of duality* which, to my mind, it is important to express in definitively precise terms, and to reduce, so far as possible, by a complete, systematic, solution.

1. The man who really wishes to live his Christianity immediately finds himself confronted by a most perplexing dualism in *effort*; how is he to reconcile renunciation of the World (necessary to life in Christ) with ardour for the Earth (indispensable to man's effort)?

2. And this dualism in action has its source in (or extends into) a much more serious *dualism of religious feeling*. The soul feels itself caught, in no metaphorical sense, *between two absolutes*: that of experience (the Universe) and that of Revelation (transcendent God).

Judging by my own case, I would say that the great temptation of this century (and of the present moment) is (and will increasingly be) that we find the World of nature, of life, and of mankind greater, closer, more mysterious, more alive, than the God of Scripture.

The tendency to pantheism is so universal and so persistent that there must be in it a soul (a naturally Christian soul) of truth which calls for 'baptism'.

I am convinced that the dogmas and practice of the Church have long provided us with all the elements required for this conquest.

For the glory of Our Lord and the triumph of his Truth, for

the peace of many men of good will, I therefore cry out with all my strength for the moment when the age-old rules of Christian ascesis and direction (still, maybe, too empirical) will be brought together into a more organic and more rational code.

And I wish too – with all the longing I have to love God – that the elements of truth, universally believed and professed by the Church, relating to the action and universal presence of God and of Christ – that these may at last be examined *as one whole*, and *with no dilution*.

Then, perhaps, we shall be astonished to see how many of those considerations that have appeared in my writings to be forced, hazardous, or extravagant, derive quite naturally (they or their equivalents) from the most authentic and most practical beliefs of our faith – *once we take the trouble to bring those beliefs together*, not simply into an idiom, but into a coherent *reality*.

NOTE

It is not difficult to see how the tendency whose predominance I favour in Christian practice and in the interpretation of dogma, is exposed to a double danger:

1. So to magnify the Universe as to eclipse or 'materialize' God.

2. Cause the natural resources and affective powers of life to be used even to the point where we are allowed to profit from them and enjoy them, *in a merely pagan spirit*.

Both these mistakes would be *exaggerations* such as every truth is liable to suffer from.

Their avoidance is a matter of Catholic good sense and of Christian prudence.

Ay (Marne), 14 April 1918

1. For this distinction and Père Teilhard's later elaboration of his theme, see the Note at the head of 'The Soul of the World' (in *Writings in Time of War*, p. 177). There it will be seen how o finally disappeared, absorbed by ω, in virtue of o's representing the end of the Universe's natural evolution.

NOTE ON THE PRESENTATION OF THE GOSPEL IN A NEW AGE

This piece was written in Strasbourg immediately after *Forma Christi*. When making a fair copy (and the manscript we have before us shows hardly any erasures) Père Teilhard dated it the feast of the Epiphany. In fact, it would appear that it was some days later that the essay was completed, for we find him writing to Marguerite Teillard-Chambon on 8 January:

'I've let myself get a bit behind-hand with you because of drawing up my little "manifesto", which I've almost finished today. Here and there, I've used rather forceful language, but I believe I've never said more than I sincerely believe, nor written without an over-riding love for the Church that alone can assure us the joy of possessing Our Lord. What I have primarily tried to do, is to make myself understood by friends: and so I've sought above all to be straightforward and clear.'

He then mentions his intention of sending what he has written to Père Léonce de Grandmaison, but not, on this occasion, with a view to publication in *Etudes* or *Recherches de science religieuse*: 'I trust him to guide me, to suggest practical methods (if occasion arises) and also at the right time to influence my superiors' decisions. Don't forget to pray a little for me, will you?'.

Again, on 11 January, he writes:

'About my *Note sur l'Apostolat*, I sent it yesterday to Père de Grandmaison with a very frank letter . . . I felt it was better to speak frankly in an explanation that amounts, in fact, to a disclosure of conscience. Before sending it to anyone else, I'll wait to see what Père Léonce thinks about it.' (*The Making of a Mind*, pp. 273–5.)

What we have, then, is a confidential document. In content, it is of more or less the same nature as 'Mastery of the World'. Throughout all Père Teilhard's life, he was to persevere in returning to the same theme, without substantial modifications, in particular in his answer to the questionnaire on modern unbelief sent out by *La Vie Intellectuelle* (1933), in his 'Reflections on the conversion of the World' (1936), 'The Awaited Word' (1941), and 'The Heart of the Problem' (1949). It was only that the 'faith in the world' he hoped to see more heartily welcomed by those who have authority in the Church was to assume for him, ever more distinctly, the form of a 'propulsive' faith, driving 'towards the Ahead'. See also 'Faith in Man' (January 1947), in *The Future of Man*, p. 185; address to the international congress of the Society of Jesus, Versailles (August 1947) in *Science and Christ*, p. 199.*

* The text published here follows Père Teilhard's manuscript, as do all the others. That printed earlier in the *Cahiers Pierre Teilhard de Chardin*, no. 4 (1963) reproduces a typed version authenticated by Père Teilhard's signature; it is, however, considerably shorter and contains slight but numerous variations. In two or three instances these would appear to be explained by the author's wish to express himself more exactly (for example, 'the adherence of unbelievers to the faith' – *l'adhésion des incrédules à la foi* – for 'the fideist adherence of unbelievers' – *l'adhésion fidéiste des incrédules*). At other times, by the wish for greater simplicity (e.g. 'in the Church' for 'in Israel'); and at other times, again, by inadvertence or misreadings.

The great converters, or perverters, of men have always been those in whom the soul of their age burnt the most intensely.

INTRODUCTORY NOTE

Effectively to influence a vital current, whatever it may be, a man must himself belong to that current. It is only a craftsman who can be understood by craftsmen. Only a geologist or a soldier can speak to geologists or soldiers. Only a Man can make himself heard by Men.

We have in our day, as I shall show, a *natural* religious movement of great force.

We Christians, we priests, do we realize that if we are to influence it and supernaturalize it (and that is what is really meant by the conversion of the world) it is essential that we share – *non verbo tantum, sed re* – in its drive, in its anxieties and its hopes?

So long as we appear to wish to impose on the men of today

a ready-made Divinity from outside, then, surrounded by the multitude though we may be, we shall inevitably be preaching in the desert.

There is only one way of enthroning God as sovereign over the men of our time: and that is to embrace the ideal they reach out to; it is *to seek, with them,* the God whom we already possess but who is as yet *amongst us* as though he were a stranger to us.

Who is the God whom our contemporaries seek, and how can we succeed in *finding him, with them,* in Jesus?

It is of this I wish to write, *for this is something I have felt.*[1]

I. THE MODERN IDEAL OF THE DIVINE

The deep-rooted religious movement of our age seems to me to be characterized by the appearance (in the consciousness of man) of *the Universe* – seen as a *natural* Whole, *more noble* than Man – and *therefore equivalent,* for Man, *to a God* (finite or infinite).

The features of this God are still indistinct. It is not so much his brilliance we see as that of the aureole that surrounds him, in that quarter where lie Life, Truth, and Spirit. – But his radiance is beyond all doubt.

A more exact view of things – replacing a certain illusion (geo-, anthropo-, europeo-centric)[2] – is showing us today our own being lost in such a reservoir of energies and mysteries, our own individuality subject to so many ties and extensions of itself, our civilization surrounded by so many other cycles of thought, that the feeling of the crushing dominance of the World over us as persons is being impressed upon everyone who shares in the vision of his own time.

Today, thanks to advances in our methods of observation and the development of our thinking, the Reality which the so-called pantheist[3] mystics have always felt rising up in the heaven of souls, is beginning to win recognition even in the mass of mankind.

Next, although modern Man cannot yet give an exact name

to the great Being who is being embodied *for him* and *through him* in the World, he already knows that he will never worship a divinity unless it possesses *certain attributes* by which he will be able to recognize it.

The God for whom our century is waiting must be:

1. as *vast* and mysterious as the Cosmos.
2. as *immediate* and all-embracing as Life.
3. as *linked* (in some way) *to our effort* as Mankind.

A God who made the World less mysterious, or smaller, or less important to us, than our heart and reason show it to be, that God, – less beautiful than the God we await – will never more be He to whom the Earth kneels.

Of this we must be quite clear: the *Christian Ideal* (as normally expressed) has ceased to be what we still complacently flatter ourselves that it is, the common Ideal of Mankind.

More and more men, if they wish to be sincere, will have to admit to the man in the pulpit that Christianity seems to them to be inevitably *inhuman* and *inferior*, both in its promises of individual happiness[4] and in its precepts of renunciation. 'Your Gospel', they are already saying, 'leads to the formation of souls that *have an interest in* their own selfish advantages – *with no interest* in the common task; and so it has *no interest* for us. Our concept is better than that: and therefore there is more truth in ours.'

The precedence assumed, in modern consciousness, by the Whole over the individual is rapidly tending to produce a new *moral Ideal*, in which justice ranks higher than charity, work than detachment, whole-hearted effort to develop than mortification.

'Christian' and 'Human' are tending no longer to coincide. In that lies the great Schism that threatens the Church.

Let no one declare that this schism is imaginary – or at all events that the blame lies entirely with those who are going their own way.

Life, as a whole, makes no mistakes. And where is Life to be found today? Can we really say that it is to be found with us?

What books are bought by the thousand, if not those which outline the religion of a God who is close to us, is progressive, is universal – the religion expounded by such sincere and ardent thinkers as William James, Schuré, Maeterlinck, Bergson, Wells, and so many others?[5]

What voice is listened to in Rome (and in vain do we smile at it from our Olympus) if not the voice that says: 'I feel that the time has come when men must forget their local attachments and unite in a single great enterprise that will unite all free men for ever, so to become a single body of free minds'? (President Wilson, 2 January 1919.)[6]

And what, above all, is the summons of the spirit within us?

For my part, I assert before God, in the hope that my testimony may enlighten some of my brothers who have confidence in my zeal for perfection but who do not perhaps 'experience' the soul of their time to the same degree as I do:

'Since, as a result of certain experiences (dating back to my childhood, and analysed over many long years), I have succeeded in "integrating" with my Faith, in (as I shall explain) introducing into it, this passion for the Universe which today animates "natural" Mankind – since that time, I have the feeling of having entered a new World. Compared with the satisfactions and the desires I now experience, my former religious life seems to me mere childishness.'

The truth is that when, after having for some time shared the anxieties, the hopes and the activity that give life to the peak of Mankind, we come back to certain of our own religious circles, we feel we must be dreaming, as we consider what efforts are *absorbed* there in the beatification of a servant of God, in ensuring the success of a particular devotion, in the subtle and impossible analysis of a mystery.

We are building our abode in the clouds, and we cannot see that Reality lies outside and is striding away from us.

*

And yet, if Reality is to reach its fulfilment it has need of us Christians. The God of the Bible is not different from the God of Nature.

What, then, does our generation need, for the pantheism of one part to be supernaturalized and the Faith of the other to be humanized? For the Schism that threatens us to be replaced by the Union that vitalizes?

What is needed is that, in the name of the purest essence of Revelation, we shall seek to forward, by prayer, by meditation, and by example, the conjunction of the two stars whose conflicting attractions disturb, it would seem, *the peace of men of good will.*

We must preach and practise what I shall call 'the Gospel of human Effort'.

II. THE GOSPEL OF HUMAN EFFORT

The special apostolate I urge – which aims at sanctifying not simply a nation or a social category, but *the very axis of man's drive towards Spirit* – includes two distinct phases: the first, and natural, phase providing an introduction to the Christian Faith; and the second, supernatural, phase showing (in the light of revelation) how far and in what direction earthly activity can be carried.[7]

1. In a first introductory phase, I believe that we must develop – in those who believe in Jesus Christ just as much as in unbelievers – a *fuller consciousness of the Universe* that encompasses us, and of our capacity to influence its development by our action.

This religious, mystical, passion smouldering in us, this passion for the natural Whole of which we form a part, must (to judge from my own case) be nourished and systematized: as much to vitalize the religion of the faithful believers as to pave the way for the faith-adherence of unbelievers.

We may conceive a special 'training' for those who are *absorbed* by the narrow view of *the individual*; this would aim at arousing in them the feeling (fundamental, to my mind, and adding such breadth!) of supra-personal Realities.

As for the others, those who already possess the dominating intuition of the Universal, I am convinced that we cannot do more useful work for the Kingdom of God than by encouraging and confirming them in their vision.

Going beyond the limited and precarious associations effected among nations – the alliances, the large economic or scientific unions – I believe that it is the part of the Christian (*'christianorum est . . .'*) to raise men to the idea of *some human Effort*, unique and specific, which would bring together all activities: no longer merely in the defensive (as we saw at times during the war) but in the positive pursuit of a supreme Ideal – an Ideal that cannot fail to reach exact definition through our patient and convergent efforts towards a larger measure of Truth, of Beauty and of Justice.

To present to men the brilliance (which fits in with what they have today a presentiment of), and *to share with them* the hope, of some crowning glory for the Universe – and, in order to do this, to neglect nothing when it is a question of associating them in the unity of one single terrestrial faith: such, to my mind, should be the human, preparatory, form of our zeal and our preaching.

And, working in this field, we Christians would be fully associated with the most noble and most vital section of our contemporaries, whatever their religious convictions.

2. Revelation can then be introduced[8] into a Mankind that has thus been sensitized and unified by the religious expectation of some *soul of the World*.

The strictly Christian, 'esoteric' phase of the Evangelization 'of human Effort' would consist (as I see it) in presenting Jesus Christ to men as the very Term, already vaguely apprehended by them, of universal development: men being able (by virtue of the supernaturalization of the World) to reach consummation only in his Unity; and he needing, in order to attain his plenitude, to drive his roots into the totality of each one of them.

Surely it is the very core of the teachings of St John and St Paul that *'every creature, in the whole of its self, acquires its full development, its full determination, its full personality, only In Christo Jesu*'?

'Everything in the Cosmos is for Spirit'; that, in natural terms, is the verse,

'Everything, in Spirit, is for Christ': and that, in supernatural terms, is the verse of the Gospel that our modern World needs.

In this revelation, it is clear, lies the supreme consecration of human Effort. – It is not only that by a 'good' intention Man can invest all he does with a certain merit: the substance of his handiwork (*even the natural substance*) – that is to say each new step in vital fulfilment that he makes good, for himself or for the Species – appears to be such that it can be integrated in an absolute Term to the World: Jesus Christ, the individual head, and 'universal Form' of the Elect.[9]

There is, in truth, a secret message, explanatory of the whole of Creation, which, by allowing us to feel God in everything we do and in everything that is done to us (God creating in all things and being born in all things) can bring true happiness to our generation . . . That man hears the message by whom the Universe is seen to be the universal Species in which – by infinitely diverse but real ways – Christ is incarnate: incarnate through the combined action of determinant and liberating factors, and of grace.

And that secret message is: *Hoc est Corpus meum.*[10]

The universal 'consecration', the universal communion, that is to say the possible convergence of all created efforts (*opus* and *operatio*) upon God, and their adoption into the final Reality of Christ – that is what we have to show to the Men of our day if we wish them to make their way to God, and to do so *ex toto corde suo.*

It is, in fact, from this point of view *alone* that Christ is seen *in the extension* of the human Ideal – and the God of the Christians emerges as identical with the deity of whom the Earth dreams: as great, as immediate, as concerned in our progress, as the Universe.

It is not enough that we demonstrate the theoretic possibility of the coincidence of the two Ideals, the natural and the revealed, (the one extending beyond the other, but running along the same axis). The decisive argument that will convince the World of the reality of our God will be the demonstration of the *conjunction of the two attractions*, the heavenly and the earthly, *realized* in a life that is *fully human because fully Christian*.

After we have meditated in our own minds, and preached to those we move among, the Gospel of human Effort, we shall have to *practise* it; and that means that our own behaviour must provide an example of what can be effected in man by his passion for the World when it has been transformed by the love of Jesus Christ.

1. In the first place I believe that a Christian has a sacred, priestly vocation, essential to the Church, to *associate himself* – in his passion for Christ and in order to fulfil Christ – with the *Artificers of the Earth*.

We have had many examples of men who have devoted themselves to study *within* Religion, *in order to* exalt or defend Religion. But when shall we find priests and religious who will leave behind this externalism and will seek and study *through* religion, *religiously*; by that I mean with the distinct and professed consciousness that the least of their achievements in the natural field provides nourishment for souls and thereby serves, in a word, to bring about the growth of the Body of Christ?

I pray that the number of those will soon be legion, who understand that a priest, *as priest*, can devote himself to Science or Sociology – and that his real work lies there just as much at least as in concentrating on funeral services.

How sad it is and how disastrous that we have allowed the Ministers of life to become for the vast majority almost exclusively 'the people who bury you'.[11]

2. In the specific domain of religious truths, we shall have to remain faithful to the belief in the sanctity of human Effort, which we will have proved by our concern to be the first to arouse the Earth, *in the name of our Christianity*.

217

We have been taught habitually to regard Revelation as a splendour that sheds a clear light on the whole structure of the World. If we are not to win no more than a smile from the Gentiles, and above all if we are not to discourage them from joining us as being over-ingenuous or too ready to under-estimate the Universe, we must with all urgency restore to their just proportions the gifts God has given us in Scripture. The divine Truth is still not a Sun for us; it is no more than a small star shining in the depth of night.

We have learnt from Jesus Christ and the prophets in what direction and towards what term the centre (the kernel) of our petty being is moving. Of the extensions into which the World and our own person develop, of the historical phases and physical conditions of our return to God, *we know* practically *nothing at all.* We are moving through *darkness* towards a luminous point; and if we do not defend our vision with real determination, if at every moment we do not recapture it, *the very sight of the star will escape us.*[12]

There you have the beauty of real fact.

The man who wishes to hold on to his vision must fight unremittingly for light. The Christian, too, is subject to that noble and austere law which links together mind and Truth.

That is why a Church that did not continually (impossible though such a concept is) look for her God *as though* she might lose him (I was on the point of saying 'as though she did not already possess him') would be a dead Church, melting into nothingness in the ocean of human Thought.

Could we but say such things to men, a little more clearly – could they but feel that we know as intimately as they do the anguish and the richness of doubt – would they hate us so bitterly as tyrants over their minds and strangers to their souls?

One conclusion emerges unmistakably, I believe, from what I have said above: that at this moment the great task that Theology must undertake is precisely to ensure that the star of Bethlehem is not eclipsed by the new star (the World) rising over Mankind. – In all branches of sacred Science the time has come to examine, through study and prayer, *the area in which God and the Cosmos come together*.

a. In *dogmatics*, our teachers, after having for so long analysed divine relationships '*ad intra*', must at last *sympathetically* embark on the study of the *relationships ad extra* that subordinate the Universe to God. Modern thought demands this imperatively: and the persistence of heresies, all thrusting in this direction, is the sign of a deep-seated human anxiety that looks for satisfaction.

While pagan mythologies are shot through with vague but illuminating suggestions of the involution of souls, of divine incarnations, of the association of Evil and Being, it is astonishing, as we look around us, to note how artificial, and almost infantile, is the normal Christian way of presenting the origins and vicissitudes of the World.

In making God personal and free, Non-being absolute, the Creation gratuitous, and the Fall accidental, are we not in danger of making the Universe *intolerable* and the value of souls (on which we lay so much emphasis!) inexplicable?

Is it really true that there is nothing to be found in Scripture that could give us a more elevated picture of the events that sweep us along with them and of the real values contained in our own selves – a picture with more meaning and more in harmony than of old with the grand idea we are building up of the Universe?[13]

There was some good, maybe, in Gnosis.

b. In *morals*, I take it that the time has come when (without even in the least degree rationalizing the Christian virtues) we must nevertheless examine in what ways they harmonize with the experiential orientations of human progress: what, for example, is the 'physical' function of Charity in the formation of the Body of Christ, or what is the role of chastity in the spiritualization of the soul?

Love (ἔρως—eros) underlies so many things that matter to

Man, his salvation or his loss; it is the very stuff, maybe, of all our important desires. Is it not incredible that after so many centuries of frowning on it and curbing it not one of our writers has continued Plato's work and considered whence that passion comes and whither it leads, what it contains of evil or impermanence, and, on the other hand, what element in its power should be carefully nursed so that it may be transformed into love of God![14]

From another angle, the ever vaster organizations that are being formed (or disclosed) in the World are tending to produce a new category of duties; and room must be made for these alongside the old commandments. Morality has hitherto been individualistic (the relations of individuals to individuals). In future more explicit emphasis will have to be laid on Man's obligations to collective bodies and even to the Universe: on political duties, social duties, international duties – on (if I may be allowed the expression) cosmic duties, first among which stands the Law of Work and Research.

In the sphere of responsibilities, a new horizon is opening up for our contemporaries, and into this Christianity must, as a matter of absolute necessity, extend the radiance of its light: otherwise it will have *to pay the price* of lagging behind in its teaching and of *allowing man's conscience to shape itself with no reference to our faith.*

c. Finally, *in ascetics*: we can see that if many in Israel are to enjoy peace and be free to expand, we must find a truly comprehensive formulation of *Christian renunciation*; without in any way minimizing the doctrine of the Cross, this must nevertheless integrate in Christian effort all the dynamic contained in the lofty enthusiasms of the human race.

In their preoccupation with speculative arguments, theologians forget this: that to reconcile, with practical effectiveness, natural and supernatural in a single harmonious orientation of human activity is a problem a thousand times more acute than all the difficulties we may accumulate about the essential nature of Grace.

If we are to solve that problem we must show that Renunciation is far from robbing nature of its richness, nor does it make the Christian despise the Universe: it *proceeds* essentially from *human Effort*, – true Chastity and true Contemplation being the magnified forms, extended in their innate directions, of human activity and love.

The Christian choice, therefore, should be presented as one not, in fact, between Heaven and Earth, but between two efforts to fulfil the Universe *intra* or *extra Christum*.

The results of such a demonstration would be immense.

Quite apart from the dissipation of obstinate prejudices in hostile hearts, there would be what nobody, I believe, now realizes: the solace brought to many righteous souls, and the new impulse towards Jesus Christ they would feel if it was taught unambiguously that Our Lord can really be sought and attained by all man's vital forces – sought and attained '*like a World*', taking shape from a starting point in our World.[15]

I am convinced that every doctrinal progress that, on any point at all, will thus contribute to *harmonizing* the image and the love of the God of our Faith with the natural aspirations and beliefs now rooted in the heart of man – that every such progress means one more harvest of souls for the kingdom of God.

To *extend* the kingdom of God to new peoples is well enough. But it is still better, and more direct, to *make it penetrate* into the deep-rooted 'nisus' or 'thrust' in which Mankind's desires are today combining. If we could succeed in planting love of Jesus Christ at that exact point, we would be amazed at seeing the torrent of peoples who would spontaneously take the road back to Jerusalem.

The World can be converted and saved *only by the supernatural*, but it must be by a supernatural *harmonized* with the *natural* religious tendency proper to each century.[16]

There is a chapter in the *Spiritual Exercises* of St Ignatius entitled *ad sentiendum cum Matre Ecclesia*'. – Let us remember that, to be a true Mother, the Church, in turn, must be able '*sentire cum homini-bus*'.

For the past century (and more recently, during the war) there have been many points on which there has been a failure on our part to understand the anxieties and desires of the Earth: by not sharing in the great instinctive currents that control the direction of natural Life, we have found ourselves obliged to fall back on the anaemic counsels of 'human prudence'.

Because I am conscious of experiencing with great intensity the aspirations (as others experience the frequent sense of compassion) that dwell in the soul of my time, I regard it as a duty to bear this witness to my brothers in the apostolate (the fruit of a personal, prolonged, and unmistakable experience):

'The only Gospel that can draw our society towards Jesus Christ (and the only Gospel, in fact, whose influence I can feel) is that which will show God at the term of a *greater* Universe, one in which there will be *more* for Man *to work upon*.

'If we, who are Apostles, wish to reach the mind and heart of Mankind for the sake of Jesus Christ, then we – seekers, ourselves, for the Truth, – must bring *to those who are seeking*, the news *of a greater work to be accomplished* that calls for *the whole entire body* of their effort.'

Strasbourg, Epiphany 1919

1. With this we may compare a sentence, for example, from the beginning of 'How I Believe' (1934), in *Christianity anh Evolution*, p. 97: 'On an individual scale, may we not see in this the particular solution, at least in outline, of the great spiritual problem which the vanguard of mankind, as it advances, is now coming up against?' Or again, the following from 'The Christic' (1955), above, p. 82: What follows 'constitutes the evidence brought to bear, with complete objectivity, upon a particular interior event, upon a particular personal experience, in which I cannot but distinguish the track followed by a general drift of the Human as it folds in upon itself.'

2. At this date Père Teilhard had left Europe only to go to Egypt; but he was already universalizing his view of facts and problems.

3. This same suspicion of pantheism was attached to Père Teilhard, whose language is often very close to that of Christian mystics.

4. Wells, in *God the Invisible King*, expresses no desire for personal immortality. The same admission could be found in Maeterlinck, William James, and many other writers.* It is open to argument. What matters is that the assertion put forward by these writers (who are seekers) should be sincere and that it should stimulate a far-reaching echo in their circle.

This example shows to what an extent some of our *'proofs of Christianity'* are being transformed. (Note by Père Teilhard.)

* That is why Père Teilhard was constantly to insist on collective, universal, death, as he had already done at that date in 'The Great Monad'.

5. These, again, are writers whom Père Teilhard had read attentively. He speaks at length of Schuré in his letter of 13 December 1918 (*The Making of a Mind*, pp. 267–8) and of Wells in letters of 1, 5, 11 and 14 January 1919 (*ibid.* pp. 270–1, 273, 276, 277). A number of passages in his essays, without saying so in so many words, outline their refutation.

6. Even in Bolshevist extremes we can detect this modern concern to approach all problems *sub ratione Universi*! (Note by Père Teilhard.)

7. Through all the successive variations in his point of view, Père Teilhard was always to retain in his apologetic work this distinction between the two parts. Here we may note the metaphor of the 'axis' which was to recur frequently in his last years.

8. A deliberately vague expression, used with an eye to a possible Christian revelation. A year before, he had written 'The Soul of the World' and placed as an epigraph: '*Et vocabitur nomen ejus Emmanuel*', but he appeared still to distinguish between this 'Soul' and 'Emmanuel': '. . . the soul of the world and Christ are not in opposition: they carry their being further in the identity of one and the same Reality'. When writing the essay printed here, his point of view is less theoretical, but he seems to be more fully aware that there is no initial unification of the world apart from Christ. Cf. Introduction to 'The Soul of the World' in *Writings in Time of War*.

9. The supernatural subsists by transforming (re-creating or ultra-creating, *ultra creando*) a vital sap which has to be constantly supplied to it by the natural effort of life. (Note by Père Teilhard.)

10. This passage is, in a way, an advance summary of the whole of *Le Milieu Divin* (intention and work; activity and passivity; growth of Christ and consecration of the world becoming for the believer the divine milieu). He has not yet, however, achieved a proper balance in his expression.

11. In the exaggerated language and the rather far-fetched contrasts we see that Père Teilhard is anxious to impress his view on the minds of the responsible authorities to whom this memorandum is addressed.

12. Cf. Psalm 118. 105: *Lucerna pedibus meis et lumen semitis meis*, a lamp to my feet and a light to my paths.

13. Here we have a summary of the metaphysical programme Père Teilhard was to put forward in 'My Universe' (1924) and return to in 'My Fundamental Vision' (1948), without ever developing it fully.

14. We meet the same problem in 'The Eternal Feminine', and it recurs more than once later: 'The Spirit of the Earth' (1931) in *Human Energy*, pp. 29–47; 'Sketch of a personalistic Universe' (1936), *ibid.* pp. 48–92; 'The Phenomenon of Spirituality', *ibid.* 93–112; 'Human Energy' (1937) *ibid.* pp. 113–62; 'The Atomism of Spirit' (1941) in *The Activation of Energy*, pp. 51–3. We should note the word 'transformed', which establishes an equivalence between transformation and supernaturalization (cf. Père Teilhard's note 9, above).

15. We find the same later in his correspondence with Blondel, 12 December 1919, where he says that he agrees with Blondel in thinking that 'Christ must be loved as a World, or rather as the World, that is to say as the physical centre of ultimate deter-

mination and of true consistence imposed on everything in Creation that is to survive.' (*Archives de Philosophie*, 1961, p. 135; vol. 24.)

16. We may say that the complete cycle of interior (and apostolic) life for the Christian comprises three phases:

1. *Participation* in the hopes and troubles of his time (that is to say 'incarnating himself in them').

2. *Integration* of this human force into supernatural life in such a way as to develop a single effort towards the spiritualization of being.

3. *Sublimation* of human effort by causing it to attain (through an extension of itself) the higher forms of activity,* which are purity, contemplation, death *in God*.† (Note by Père Teilhard.)

* That which seems the less active is, to the eyes of faith, the 'higher form of activity'.

† In this 'Note on the presentation of the Gospel' Père Teilhard, contrary to his normal practice, has enlarged on only one aspect of things, because he is addressing Churchmen who have no need, he thought, to be reminded of the second aspect.

THE NAMES OF MATTER

To Marguerite Teillard-Chambon, from Paris, 20 April 1919: 'For some mornings now I've been writing *The Names of Matter*. I expect I'll finish it tomorrow. It makes quite a readable little essay, and could serve as an introduction to *The Spiritual Power of Matter*.' (*The Making of a Mind*, p. 294.)

It will be noted that all Père Teilhard means to do in this essay is 'introduce some sort of possible order' into the various ways in which matter is understood, or the various sorts of matter, and to show how we may 'picture' their relationships.

Nothing is at the same time closer to us and further away from us than Matter. We can touch it, we believe; we might say that it even penetrates into our minds; at every moment, as we shall see, it is in some way being born in our minds. And then, when we try to take hold of it, to rationalize it, to understand it, it evades us; it retreats indefinitely into the background (as God withdraws ahead) as we analyse and grasp it, putting an ever greater distance between itself and our intellectual constructions and our sense of fellowship.

And the reason is that while Matter is welded into our being, it lies at the same time at the opposite pole from our soul.

While we cannot distinguish, as we look ahead, where our road is leading us, we can see, as we look down, the abyss from which we are emerging. All around our spirit, Matter is the deep from which our substance emerges. When we examine it, and think that it is so close as to be touching us, we find in fact that our eyes are travelling over and seeing as one blur an immensely thick layer of existence: they are lost in the infinite that lies behind us.

So distant and so complex, for all its appearance of unity and intimate closeness, Matter cannot but puzzle and disturb us. This it has always done. Our empirical knowledge of it and our instinct (since we cannot understand it) causes us alternately to exalt and vilify it. We say that it is eternal, or at least indestructible – stable, unifying, powerful, overflowing with life – but then we add that it is evil also, maleficent, distressful, mechanical, dead, subject to decay . . .

What I wish to do here is to introduce some sort of possible order into the various contradictory names that have been given to Matter over the centuries. And to this end I shall use (as a 'key' to classification) the point of view of 'creative Union'.

This, I may remind you, consists in admitting that in our Universe every further degree of being (that is to say of spirituality) coincides with a further degree in the unification of an initial and extremely dispersed Multiple, which is the lowest aspect of the World, the form in which it comes closest to Non-being. '*Plus esse est plus, a pluribus, uniri.*' (More being is the uniting of more from more.) '*Deus creat uniendo*' (God creates by uniting). According to this hypothesis, each *more* spiritual monad is formed by the organization of a pleiad of *less* spiritual monads, following a completely new principle of union. This *forma uniens*, unitive form, which is distinct from the pleiad it spiritualizes (= which it is its essence to spiritualize) can itself be diffuse: and then, when the structure it has made to cohere disintegrates, it also disappears – or (as in the case of Man) it may be perfectly centred (owing to the very complexity of the body it animates), in which case, after appearing in the operation of an act of union, it can survive the dissociation of the elements which it brought together. – It can subsist 'unanchored', even without uniting anything *actu* (actually) – it is immortal.

If we accept this view, and position ourselves in a phase of the Universe (our own phase here and now) in which the Multiple is in process of reduction or convergence (= an *in*volutive, as opposed to an evolutive phase) we may picture to ourselves as follows the various circles of Matter that are formed, acquire complexity, and disintegrate.

I. (FORMAL MATTER)

In a being (in a monad) Matter is fundamentally *that which makes* the monad *capable of being united to other beings*, in such a way as to form with them a new and *more simple Whole*. It is not Matter that unites (Spirit alone can do that); but it *serves as a hand-hold* for union. It is Matter, in other words, that makes the being (the Monad) into *Element:* into something, that is, which has to accept unification in order to be spiritualized. Understood in this sense, Matter (*Materia formaliter sumpta, s. Materialitas*, Matter taken formally, that is, Materiality) is a positive entitative principle. Defined as *that which can be united*, it is neither negative, nor evil (as the *dis-united*,[1] for example, would be) and so far from disappearing in Spirit, it is in Spirit that it is consummated.

II. (CONCRETE MATTER)

When we speak of the *pure unitable* we are, it is clear, introducing a co-principle (or, again, a modality) of existence. We are not speaking of anything that can subsist in isolation '*a parte rei*', apart from the thing, (any more than can the prime Matter of the Schools or the Thomist *essentia*). '*Materia formalis*' does not exist outside some principle of union; but it imposes on the beings it affects a certain way of coming into existence, a certain common original type. – Since the most material being is the being closest to the 'pure unitable', *concrete Matter* will appear in the form of the *supremely dispersed*. The initial state of the Cosmos is therefore, by virtue of its materiality, that of an immense multiple, of an extreme diffusion and distension. Or, to speak more accurately, concrete Matter has no *precise* beginning: it emerges from an abyss of increasing dissociation; in some way it condenses, starting from an external, shadowy sphere of infinite plurality, whose limitless and formless immensity represents the lower pole of being. So soon as we can recognize some consistence in it, we find that it is formed from an aggregate of monads, each of which has already been subject to, and bears within itself, an indefinite sum of unions.

III. (UNIVERSAL MATTER)

Vast and fugitive though the lower circles of *nascent Matter* may be, they delimit and 'inform' *some Thing*. So soon as our Universe acquires a recognizable contour, it is no longer (and has not been for a long time) a pure aggregate of dissociated elements. The interaction of its parts and its global consistence would be inconceivable unless some sort of great, inchoate,[2] vague Soul (a sort of *Forma cosmica*) made certain for the Pleiad (taken as a whole) the unity of *a* sphere, *a* current, *a* rudimentary Whole. The totality of the elements contained in this primordial envelope represents the *single, Universal, Matter*, that is to say the sum of the elements destined to enter into all the later unifications of being (inside the World under consideration).

IV. (TOTAL MATTER)

Within this 'first membrane' of the Universe, which is the most universal *Forma cosmica*, an infinite number of collective movements begin to assert themselves; they mark off (segment) the Multiple into so many currents (anastomosed or interlocked) along which the mass of primitive monads is drawn, following a variety of routes, towards the Centre of all unions.

The result of this is that at every moment each element of the World, taken in the *totality* of its being, is formed not only by what it is within itself, but also by what it serves to integrate above itself, within universal Matter. If we are fully to define the nature of each element of the Cosmos, we have to consider, besides the monad (which it constitutes), the pleiad or the pleiads (in process of union) of which it is a participating member. The richness of a creature depends both on the perfection of its form (the principle of union) *and* on the value of the collective (or cosmic) forms that use that creature (*temporarily or for ever*) to build up the higher degrees of union (= spiritualization) in the Universe.

We can understand, then, what an immense difference there is between even the humblest Matter, considered *in Mundo* (I was on the point of saying *in vivo*) and the Matter which we agree to call *physico-chemical*. *Physico-chemical matter* is an abstraction (in the strictest sense of the word) obtained by isolating the cosmic elements from everything that is a higher unification at a certain level.[3] As such, it does not exist in the Reality of Things. The most chemically pure nitrogen, taken in its totality, (that is to say with all its *real* extensions) includes essentially, besides the properties listed by the scientist, all the finalities (completely physical) in which it is involved *hic et nunc* by virtue of the general movements of the Cosmos and of Life. These immense convergences are necessarily impatient of analysis (since they are the framework of a higher organization). But they constitute, in part, the richness of concrete Matter. And it is the operation of those convergences, for example, (and not the value of the so-called physico-chemical properties of bodies) which will one day, perhaps, allow the synthesis of Life to be realized. – The elements of the World, taken together with the sum of their linkages as they converge on Spirit: that is what we might call *total Matter*.

V. (RELATIVE MATTER)

In relation to any monads that have reached a certain degree of internal concentration, the Universe is necessarily divided into two zones: the zone above, in spiritualizing union (= the desired but invisible zone) and the zone below, in the extreme of diffusion or relative plurality. The higher, simpler and freer zone is the domain of Spirit (relative). The lower, more obscure, more bound by necessity, represents Matter (relative).[4] To the animal, for example, the vegetal is relatively material, and Man (who, moreover, is unknowable because rational) is relatively spiritual.

For every being, the Matter that concerns it (the Matter it can feel and know by touch, and from which when the time comes it will have to suffer) is primarily, of course, that Thing, less unified than the being itself, which surrounds and dominates it. It is that above all that we have in mind when we speak of Matter. It is to that we address our praises or curses. Let us, then, examine it in the case that means most to us – the only one, moreover, of which we can speak – that of the human Monad.

In *our* Matter we must, I believe, distinguish three parts, that is, three different *Matters*, which I shall call Matter A, B and C.

A. LIVING MATTER. – *Matter A (or living Matter)* comprises the still *unifiable* (spiritualizable), but *not* as yet *unified*, portion of the Universe.

The principal part of this Matter A is formed of human souls themselves, taken collectively. However complete and autonomous a spiritual soul may be, it cannot exist in the World in isolation, and is not made ever to subsist separately. In reality our souls represent the elements, the atoms, of a further structure, still higher in spirituality than themselves. While this multitude of souls is waiting for higher unification under one and the same Spirit, it suffers all the ills of every incompletely organized plurality: it forms *a Matter*. The human mass, as a whole, still obeys the same laws of large numbers which allows Science to treat gaseous masses or any other particular grouping as a mechanical Thing. To a sufficiently distant observer the sum total of our free choices would appear overlaid by determinisms. And we ourselves, sunk in this Matter-of-Spirit, are painfully conscious of all the cruel discords and insoluble mutual externalities that subsist in it. Even in the intimate depths of our soul, the vanquished multitude we shelter under our completely new unity, is still distressingly at work. Who has not felt the rending of a nature in which contrary tendencies are developing simultaneously, tearing the Spirit apart by their hostile growth? – All this is fruitful pain, a suffering that comes with aggregation, an evil that comes with growth, within the being. *Omnis creatura ingemiscit et parturit:* every creature groaneth and travaileth.

Outside *the group of our souls, living Matter* still contains the countless *Elements of spiritualization* scattered and diffused throughout the Universe: energies for bodies, stimulants for soul, shades of beauty, sparks of truth. Through the World, God envelops us, penetrates us, and creates us. Like a little child still clinging to its mother's breast, our spirit sends down all sorts of tendrils and roots into *Materia matrix.* It needs that material mother in order to live; and the grand role of the soul is to extract – to the last drop, were that possible – the *spiritual power*[5] generously stored in the lower circles of the Universe. It is the vocation, and the supreme joy, of every Man (even as he builds up his soul) to add to this spiritual Reserve a truth, an impulse that works for good, a new Element of whatever nature, from which generations to come will draw nourishment until the end of time.

In virtue of its nature, *living Matter* is fated to suffer reduction, to lose its Materiality.[6] But as it advances towards the higher zones of Spirit, it leaves behind, like a long furrow, Matter B and Matter C.

B. INVERSE, OR DEAD, MATTER. – Matter B is *dead Matter* or *inverse Matter,* resulting from the disintegration (whether culpable or not, but always painful) of *living Matter.*

Because the 'life' of inanimate Matter is much longer than our own, it seems to us to be immortal. In reality it finally vanishes, like everything else, in so far as it does not succeed in entering into a principle of spiritual union. Everything in the Universe that is not assimilated by a rational soul is, it would certainly appear, doomed to destruction – and sooner or later it will re-descend the steps of union and vanish in pure Plurality. At all times there is a secondary current of descending being, within mounting being, in the Universe.

This dispersal threatens and attacks us most noticeably in our bodies – that is only too clear. But we should note that there is for Man (and even for the Angels!) a real dissociation and material-ization of spirit. – Vice (the flesh) cannot succeed in breaking up the spirituality (consummate and indestructible) of our soul, but it certainly introduces into it a principle of corruption and internal disintegration,[7] which destroys in it the seed of the unifications still to come and abandons it to the deathless canker of a decom-position that can never kill. – More subtly and more grievously, pride, which leads souls astray into selfishness and turns them against every principle of further unification, effects an identical materialization in us. Directly, by halting the convergent move-ment of the monads, (and so increasing the Plurality of the Universe) it endangers the future spiritualization of the World.[8] But secondarily, it condemns the soul, as the penalty of its false self-emancipation, to falling back, with the flesh, into the subsoil of being, exposed to the double torment of *external isolation* and *internal fissure*.

The sight of this evil and agonizing Plurality, abandoned by the World as so much waste material, readily explains the idea – so persistent among men – that the original multiplicity of the Cosmos is the trace of some pre-cosmic fall as a result of which a Spirit was 'fragmented'. On this hypothesis, the arduous *Evolution* in which we live is the expiatory phase that follows a culpable *involution*.

There is certainly a profound (and revealing?) analogy between these often extravagant beliefs and the dogma of original sin. The result of the latter, in any case, would appear to be that the loosening movement which continually brings about the birth of Matter B, is not a mere negative or relative phenomenon (as analysis of the concept of Materiality alone might suggest).

From the Christian point of view, the tendency to Pluralism, which asserts itself like a temptation in all our efforts towards unification, represents in fact a real *backsliding*, an evil *twist*, the *memory* of some earlier state (= *Fomes peccati:* the touchwood of sin). And this positive retrograde tendency is complicated by the equally positive part played by the Powers of Darkness.

Ex dogmate, evil Matter, which is initially an evil *direction* (the direction of disintegration) in Matter, seems finally to have been *embodied* in a group of *habitus* and fallen monads, which form a *real pole* of attraction to dissociation at the opposite extreme from God.

C. SECONDARY MATTER OR NEW MATTER. *Matter B,* we see, more or less represents in our human World, Manichaean Matter, the evil principle of the Universe. What I call Matter C corresponds, on the other hand, to the *Matter of the idealist philosophers* (or to that of the physicists[9]), that is, to the group of automatisms and determinisms in the World. This is *secondary or new Matter,* produced not by any fault or retrogression in being but by the progressive and normal operation of spiritual activity.

A first source of *Matter C* in us is the very functioning of our faculties, as *actively exercised faculties.* Every operation (as has long been noted) is mechanized at the same time as it is realized. Once deliberately made, the act clothes itself in a nascent habit. Perception has hardly become conscious before it shrouds itself in a familiarity that robs it of its freshness and makes it almost unfelt. Thus by a law specific to Life, *at the same time* as we are irresistibly driven (in order *to be able to continue to feel*) towards new forms of activity and perceptions,[10] – a new skin of determinism and unconsciousness is added, every time we act, to all the corporality we already bear within us. The two processes (spiritualization and materialization) are strictly tied together in our evolution, like the two sides of one and the same medal.

This first Materiality that our action 'secretes' *in itself* in the form of 'habits', simply by its own specific exercise, is joined by another (external to us, but no less rigid) which, on this occasion, is caused by the use of our freedom, by *our choice*.

At first, it is almost nothing – a decision we take. Its being is weak, inconsistent, completely enclosed in our heart – a wrinkle that a breath can disperse. Soon, the whole picture changes. As time passes and we turn away from the directions our choice has eliminated, as secondary choices are grafted on to our choice, and the lives that surround us become entangled in the ramifications of this axis, a very complicated structure of existence is built up – *a state is propagated* and *established* through the medium of these things that we are now powerless to suppress. Something is born by us, which holds firm without us, and is stronger than us. We have become the slaves of our freedom.

Interior *automatisms*, and exterior *situations*; we would do wrong to condemn unreservedly these two materialized forms of our spirit. They are the very conditions of Progress and of the organization of beings. They facilitate rapid action, and they ensure the stability of the gains made by the passing centuries. They provide enduring materials, and form an armature for the spiritual structure of the World. Without them nothing would be built in duration.

. . . And yet, in spite of the essential functions performed in our World by determinisms, we feel that they represent in us something that is precarious and transitory.

From the heart of *as yet un-spiritualized Matter* (Matter A), from the depths of Spirit *in process of continual materialization* (Matter B and C), human aspiration has always asked the same question: 'Who will deliver us from this body of death?'

VI. (LIBERATED MATTER)

According to which section of *relative Matter* concerns us, we obviously have to consider in very different ways the liberation that our soul longs for.

THE NAMES OF MATTER

Living Matter, we have seen, is essentially good, transformable and enduring. All that offends us in it (that is, the determinisms, the discords, the conflicts) is solely due to the insufficiently organized, or centred, state of the Elements of which it is made up. This inchoateness, this imperfectness, will disappear as the residue of pluralism which distresses us is harmonized and integrated under a higher unitive Principle. In order to spiritualize ourselves (here below or elsewhere) in that quarter, we have only to make the elements of our being and of the Universe converge faithfully, in us and around us, on God.

Inverse Matter, on the other hand, is committed to a very different lot. Its useless part, which cannot be assimilated by Spirit, returns to Plurality, to Non-being. As for its immortal part, the part to which guilt can be attached, it is true that all our efforts must tend to bring back towards the divine Pole its disjointed and divergent laminations; it is true, again, that the power to 'be converted' is generously granted to it by a Saviour-God – but we cannot hope *ex revelatione* that the *whole* of its mass will finally succumb to the attraction of Spirit. The movement that attaches the Universe to Christ is in reality a segregation. A portion of evil Matter, permanently cast out, will form the irreducible spoilage left by the universal operation of salvation. There remains a *Massa damnata*, in itself *not capable of liberation* – which will nevertheless one day *free* the Universe from its weight, when, like so much jettisoned ballast, it sinks to the lower pole of existence. Here we meet a formidable mystery.[11]

There remains *secondary Matter*. Relieved, by hypothesis, from parasitic determinisms (conflicts, blind collective movements and so on) which the spiritualization of living Matter will melt away, it represents essentially the *organic interconnections and determinations* contained, *vi originis suae* – in virtue of its origin – by spiritualized being. What freedom may we expect for this secondary Matter? An arbitrary revivification of its network would mean return to the amorphous or incoherent multiple. We may, however, conceive a state in which what is now blind and rigid slavery in us, would become supple, mobile and conscious equilibrium. *Logically*, this re-animation of *hardened* (materialized) Matter does not seem impossible. *In fact*, because of the intimate connection between our bodies and the vast portion of the Cosmos (Matter B) – which by nature or culpably is incapable of rising as far as Spirit – our release from determinisms would seem to be impossible to realize in this world. To win freedom, Man must die, which means that he must in the first place be cut off from all that is not destined to survive with him. In order to attain the higher circles of existence he must dissolve the mixed organism (made up of interlocking mortal and immortal) that earthly life has woven around him. *Matter C* is the essential constituent of the perishable portion of our selves (the chrysalis), the portion of which we cannot rid ourselves except by allowing it to drop away. At the same time, and strangely, when Matter C is born in our spirit we find that it has driven its roots so deep that we cannot detach it completely. Even in our 'separated' souls it will subsist by virtue of something in it which has the power to resuscitate it.

VII. (RESUSCITATED MATTER)

The fact is that something that is *material* must reappear in order to share in the final life of Spirit. Christian hope and Christian faith both look to this. In what, then, may we say that *resuscitated Matter* consists?

It cannot be, it would seem, the re-created sum total of the material monads that throughout our life will have served as the support of our soul. In the first place it is not clear what purpose would be served, in glorified existence, by this lower multiple whose power to enrich will have been exhausted in the course of the Universe's terrestrial phase. Secondly, why should we conceive a reconstitution in our substance of certain physico-chemical centres,[12] rather than a reconstitution either of all sorts of micro-organisms whose association has been needed for our life to be complete, or even of every living monad which has formed part of the same Cosmos as we ourselves?

Moreover, it would be too unorthodox to conceive resuscitated Mankind as formed solely by the association, in a spiritual body, of glorified souls. Something formerly and specifically fleshly must be re-born in us . . .

– If we are to form some sort of picture of the great and welcome transformation that is to restore our body, we have to go back to what we opened by saying about *formal Matter*, and consider what that has become in the course of time under the influence of creative action.

Matter, we said, is essentially what gives a being the *character of Element*. It is this that makes the being *unitable* (to other beings, in the perfection of a Whole).

Let us consider human souls, deprived of their bodies. In their nature they include the essential need (*Materialitas remota*) to fulfil themselves under the Unity of a common beatifying Principle. Morever, this need to be united is not without definition or form: *born* in the process of animating some Matter that has been worked upon for a long time, itself an element of an immense Universe, every soul possesses *in its spiritual unity* an individual *structure* of *extreme complexity, the mark that betrays the unions* of which it is the sum, and the *expression* of the *only form of contact* that can 'wed' it. Separated souls need to be united. They are constructed to do so in a very special way in which *their history* is completely reflected. But, so long as their links with Matter are broken, it is impossible for them to join together: *they are not* (immediately) *unitable*.

Suppose now that God, in realizing their need to unite, *according to the fabric proper to each one of them*, reconstitutes in one and the same Cosmos this dust-cloud of floating monads. When they have coalesced, they will be able to know the joy of having truly re-found *a* body and *a* World. Having so coalesced according to the very law of their earthly origin and existence, they will in real fact have regained *their* body and *their* Universe.

Without the determinisms, or the geometric rigidity, or the impenetrability which are the secondary and transient attributes of unorganized Plurality: but within all the real power to give completion, to inter-communicate, to know the immortality that is contained in Number – with no trace of useless multiplicity, but bearing in its simplicity the mark of all the multiple of all times (as an extension, that is, of *Universal Matter*) – in those conditions and on that day, the Flesh will be truly *risen* again.

Matter will have entered its last phase, and will have but one Name.

Paris, Easter 1919

1. Cf., however, paragraph 5 below (= p. 229). (Note by Père Teilhard.)

2. Cf. the note at the head of 'The Soul of the World' in *Writings in Time of War*, pp. 177–8.

3. This level is determined by the presence in the multiple of a sufficient proportion of determinism, which is due either to a statistical effect of 'large numbers' or to automatism appearing in the monads in a secondary mode. (Cf. above.) (Note by Père Teilhard.)

4. This relative materiality of a part of the Universe in relation to ourselves can perfectly well be *temporary* or *apparent*. Temporary, because what is at the moment more material than we are is perhaps on the road to a unification higher than our own (such is the case of the *collection* of elect souls in relation to an isolated soul). Apparent, because nothing can prove that any particular aspect of the Multiple around us is not the *under-side* of certain organic unities, more advanced than we, whose *point of convergence* and *specific life* are hidden from us. – What knowledge of my human life could be possessed by a being assumed to be small enough to live in a molecule of one of the cells of my body? (Note by Père Teilhard.)

5. For the meaning of this expression, see 'The Spiritual Power of Matter', above, p. 67.

6. Its *noxious Materiality*, that is to say: conflicts, mutual exteriority of the parts, determinism. *Formal Materiality* ('capacity for Unification') does not disappear in Spirit, let me repeat, but finds its consummation in it. – Throughout this paragraph 5 we are concerned, it should be remembered, with Materiality *relative* to our soul. (Note by Père Teilhard.)

7. The inverse effect to that of chastity. (Note by Père Teilhard.)

8. The inverse effect to that of charity. – We may note that the first phase of all spiritualization – the constitution of a *multiple to be unified* – represents essentially a possibility of (a temptation to) materialization: *the multiple* when formed *can* dissociate itself instead of uniting itself. – Thus at every moment we are obliged to assert that Spirit and Matter, in any thing, are *complementary* or *inverse*. (Note by Père Teilhard.)

9. *Pro parte*. In addition to the individual determinisms we are concerned with here, the matter of the physicists includes (see above) determinisms whose origin is *collective* (= effect of large numbers). (Note by Père Teilhard.)

10. Here, it should be noted, there is a powerful principle of progress deposited in being. (Note by Père Teilhard.)

11. Cf. *Le Milieu Divin*, pp. 140–3: *The outer darkness and the lost souls*, and p. 148. (Note by Père Teilhard.)

12. That we confine this to atoms and molecules is the result of a false idea of the indestructibility and fundamental consistence of the lowest form of concrete Matter. (Note by Père Teilhard.)

CHRONOLOGICAL LIST OF WORKS*

1913 (5 January) 'The Progress of Prehistory' in *The Appearance of Man*. (*Oeuvres*, II)

1916 (24 April) 'Cosmic Life' in *Writings in Time of War*. (*Oeuvres*, XII)

1916 (17 May) Brief '*Nota* to Cosmic Life' in *Writings in Time of War*. (*Oeuvres*, XII)

1916 (20 September) 'Mastery of the World and the Kingdom of God' in *Writings in Time of War*. (*Oeuvres*, XII)

1916 (14 October) 'Christ in Matter. Three stories in the style of Benson' in *Hymn of the Universe* and extract in *The Heart of Matter*. (*Oeuvres*, XII, XIII)

1917 (26 February–22 March) 'The Struggle against the Multitude. A possible interpretation of the form of the world' in *Writings in Time of War*. (*Oeuvres*, XII)

1917 (13 August) 'The Mystical Milieu' in *Writings in Time of War*. (*Oeuvres*, XII)

1917 (September) 'Nostalgia for the Front' in *The Heart of Matter*. (*Oeuvres*, XII)

1917 (November) 'Creative Union' in *Writings in Time of War*. (*Oeuvres*, XII)

1918 (Epiphany: 6 January) 'The Soul of the World' in *Writings in Time of War*. (*Oeuvres*, XII)

1918 (15 January) 'The Great Monad (manuscript found in a trench)' in *The Heart of Matter*. (*Oeuvres*, XII)

1918 (19–25 March) 'The Eternal Feminine' in *Writings in Time of War*. (*Oeuvres*, XII)

1918 (14 April) 'My Universe' in *The Heart of Matter*. (*Oeuvres*, XIII)

1918 (8 July) 'The Priest' in *Writings in Time of War*. (*Oeuvres*, XII)

1918 (28 September) 'Operative Faith' in *Writings in Time of War*. (*Oeuvres*, XII)

1918 (13, not 22 December) '*Forma Christi*' in *Writings in Time of War*. (*Oeuvres*, XII)

* This list has been compiled from the 13 volumes of the *Oeuvres* (Editions du Seuil) and excludes all other published work. In most cases the dates are those inserted by Teilhard himself after finishing a paper. A few dates only indicate the time spent on a piece of writing. In the absence of any such indications the date of publication of an article in a periodical has been supplied. This, of course, merely affords a *terminus ad quem*. (Claude Cuénot)

1918 (22 December) 'Note on the "Universal Element" of the World' in *Writings in Time of War.* (*Oeuvres*, XII)

1919 (or early 1920?) 'On the Notion of Creative Transformation' in *Christianity and Evolution.* (*Oeuvres*, X)

1919 (or January 1920?) 'Note on the Physical Union between the Humanity of Christ and the faithful in the course of their sanctification' in *Christianity and Evolution.* (*Oeuvres*, X)

1919 (Epiphany, actually between 6 and 10 January) 'Note on the presentation of the Gospel in a new age' in *The Heart of Matter.* (*Oeuvres*, XII)

1919 (February) 'The Promised Land' in *Writings in Time of War.* (*Oeuvres*, XII)

1919 (21 February) 'The Universal Element' in *Writings in Time of War.* (*Oeuvres*, XII)

1919 (Easter: 20 April or very shortly after) 'The Names of Matter' in *The Heart of Matter.* (*Oeuvres*, XII)

1919 (August ?, doubtless before 5 September) 'What exactly is the human body?' not the author's title; opening words: 'Even a single attempt to determine exactly what the body of a living being consists in . . .' in *Science and Christ.* (*Oeuvres*, IX)

1919 (8 August) 'The Spiritual Power of Matter' in *The Heart of Matter* and also *Hymn of the Universe.*' (*Oeuvres*, XII, XIII)

1920 'Note on the Essence of Transformism' in *The Heart of Matter.* (*Oeuvres*, XIII)

1920 (early) cf.: 1919 (or early 1920?) 'On the Notion of Creative Transformation'.

1920 (January?) (or 1919) 'Note on the Physical Union between the Humanity of Christ and the faithful in the course of their sanctification' in *Christianity and Evolution.* (*Oeuvres*, X)

1920 (January) 'Note on the Universal Christ' in *Science and Christ.* (*Oeuvres*, IX)

1920 (January) 'Note on the modes of divine action in the Universe' in *Christianity and Evolution.* (*Oeuvres*, X)

1920 (20 July) 'Fall, Redemption and Geocentrism' in *Christianity and Evolution.* (*Oeuvres*, X)

1920 (10 August) 'A Note on Progress' in *The Future of Man.* (*Oeuvres*, V)

1921 (5 January) 'On my attitude to the official Church' in *The Heart of Matter.* (*Oeuvres*, XIII)

1921 (27 February) 'Science and Christ (or Analysis and Synthesis). Remarks on the way in which the scientific study of matter can and must help to lead us up to the Divine Centre' in *Science and Christ.* (*Oeuvres*, IX)

1921 (20 March) 'Fossil Men; Reflections on a recent book' in *The Appearance of Man*. (*Oeuvres*, II)

1921 (5–20 June) 'How the Transformist Question presents itself today' in *The Vision of the Past*. (*Oeuvres*, III)

1921 (5–20 December) 'Scientific Report. The Face of the Earth' in *The Vision of the Past*. (*Oeuvres*, III)

1922 (15 April or very shortly before) 'Note on some possible historical representations of Original Sin' in *Christianity and Evolution*. (*Oeuvres*, X)

1923 'The Mass on the World' in *Hymn of the Universe* and *The Heart of Matter*. (*Oeuvres*, XIII)

1923 (17 January) 'Pantheism and Christianity' in *Christianity and Evolution*. (*Oeuvres*, X)

1923 (March–April) 'Palaeontology and the Appearance of Man' in *The Appearance of Man*. (*Oeuvres*, II)

1923 (21 March) 'The Law of Irreversibility in Evolution' (not: 'On the Law . . .) in *The Vision of the Past*. (*Oeuvres*, III)

1924 (25 March) 'My Universe' in *Science and Christ*. (*Oeuvres*, IX)

1925 (January) 'The Natural History of the World. Reflections on the value and future of systematics' in *The Vision of the Past*. (*Oeuvres*, III)

1925 (January) The Transformist paradox. On the latest criticism of Transformism by M. Vialleton' in *The Vision of the Past*. (*Oeuvres*, III)

1925 (6 May) 'Hominization. Introduction to a scientific study of the Phenomenon of Man' in *The Vision of the Past*. (*Oeuvres*, III)

1926 (17 March) 'The necessarily discontinuous appearance of every evolutionary series' (not 'On the . . .) in *The Vision of the Past*. (*Oeuvres*, III)

1926 (Ascension Day: 14 May) 'The Basis and Foundations of the Idea of Evolution' in *The Vision of the Past*. (*Oeuvres*, III)

1926 (November–1927 (March)) (revised in 1932) *Le Milieu Divin (The Divine Milieu)*. (*Oeuvres*, IV)

1928 (April) 'The Movements of Life' in *The Vision of the Past*. (*Oeuvres*, III)

1928 (14 June) 'For Odette and for Jean' in *The Heart of Matter*. (*Oeuvres*, XIII)

1928 (September) 'The Phenomenon of Man' in *Science and Christ*. (*Oeuvres*, IX)

1929 (February–March) 'The Sense of Man' in *Toward the Future*. (*Oeuvres*, XI)

1930 (January) 'What should we think of Transformism?' in *The Vision of the Past*. (*Oeuvres*, III)

1930 (April) 'An Important Discovery in Human Palaeontology: *Sinanthropus Pekinensis*' in *The Appearance of Man*. (*Oeuvres*, II)

1930 (November) 'The Phenomenon of Man' in *The Vision of the Past*. (*Oeuvres*, III)

1931 (9 March) 'The Spirit of the Earth' in *Human Energy*. (*Oeuvres*, VI)

1932 'Man's Place in Nature' in *The Vision of the Past*. (*Oeuvres*, III)

1932 (8 September) 'The Road of the West: To a New Mysticism' in *Toward the Future*. (*Oeuvres*, XI)

1933 (1 April) 'The Significance and Positive Value of Suffering' in *Human Energy*. (*Oeuvres*, VI)

1933 (May) 'Christianity in the World' in *Science and Christ*. (*Oeuvres*, IX)

1933 (25 October) 'Modern Unbelief, its underlying cause and remedy' in *Science and Christ*. (*Oeuvres*, IX)

1933 (Christmas: 25 December) 'Christology and Evolution' in *Christianity and Evolution*. (*Oeuvres*, X)

1934 (February) 'The Evolution of chastity' in *Toward the Future*. (*Oeuvres*, XI)

1934 (20 March) 'The Prehistoric Excavations of Peking' in *The Appearance of Man*. (*Oeuvres*, II)

1934 (28 October) 'How I believe' (the rest of the title: 'This paper was written by Père Teilhard in answer to a request from Mgr Bruno de Solages, characteristic of the latter's deep concern for the apostolate' is obviously not Teilhard's) in *Christianity and Evolution*. (*Oeuvres*, X)

1935 'The Pleistocene Fauna and the Age of Man in North America' in *The Appearance of Man*. (*Oeuvres*, II)

1935 (15 June) 'Address given by the Rev. Fr Teilhard de Chardin on the occasion of the marriage of Monsieur and Madame de la Goublaye de Ménorval at the church of Saint-Louis des Invalides on 15 June 1935' in *The Heart of Matter*. (*Oeuvres*, XIII)

1935 (15 September) 'The Discovery of the Past' in *The Vision of the Past*. (*Oeuvres*, III)

1936 (4 May) 'Sketch of a Personalistic Universe' in *Human Energy*. (*Oeuvres*, VI)

1936 (9 October) 'Some Reflections on the conversion of the World. For the use of a Prince of the Church' in *Science and Christ*. (*Oeuvres*, IX)

1936 (11 November) 'The Salvation of Mankind. Thoughts on the present crisis' in *Science and Christ*. (*Oeuvres*, IX)

1937 (March) 'The Phenomenon of Spirituality' in *Human Energy*. (*Oeuvres*, VI)

1937 (5 July) 'The Discovery of Sinanthropus' in *The Appearance of Man*. (*Oeuvres*, II)

1937 (6 August–8 September) 'Human Energy' in *Human Energy*. (*Oeuvres*, VI)

1937 (20 October) 'The Principle of the conservation of personality', Appendix to 'Human Energy' in *Human Energy*. (*Oeuvres*, VI)

1938 'Social Heredity and Education. Notes on the humano-Christian value of teaching' in *The Future of Man*. (*Oeuvres*, V)

1938 (June, to June 1940) *The Phenomenon of Man*. (*Oeuvres*, I)

1939 (3 March) 'The Grand Option' in *The Future of Man*. (*Oeuvres*, V)

1939 (13 March) 'The Function of Art as an expression of Human Energy' in *Toward the Future*. (*Oeuvres*, XI)

1939 (20 March) 'The Mysticism of Science' in *Human Energy*. (*Oeuvres*, VI)

1939 (May) 'Some General Views on the essence of Christianity' in *Christianity and Evolution*. (*Oeuvres*, X)

1939 (5 July) 'The Natural Units of Humanity. An attempt to outline a racial biology and morality' in *The Vision of the Past*. (*Oeuvres*, III)

1939 (Christmas: 25 December) 'The Moment of Choice. A possible interpretation of War' in *Activation of Energy*. (*Oeuvres*, VII)

1940 (31 October) 'The Awaited Word' in *Toward the Future*. (*Oeuvres*, XI)

1941 (22 February) 'The Future of Man seen by a Palaeontologist', cf. 'Some Reflections on Progress' in *The Future of Man*. (*Oeuvres*, V)

1941 (30 March) 'On the possible bases of a universal human creed' cf. 'Some Reflections on Progress, II' in *The Future of Man*. (*Oeuvres*, V)

1941 (13 September) 'The Atomism of Spirit. An attempt to understand the structure of the stuff of the Universe' in *Activation of Energy*. (*Oeuvres*, VII)

1942 'A note on the concept of Christian perfection' in *Toward the Future*. (*Oeuvres*, XI)

1942 (20 January) 'The Rise of the Other' in *Activation of Energy*. (*Oeuvres*, VII)

1942 (13 February) 'The New Spirit. I. The Cone of Time. II. The "Conic" Transposition of Action' in *The Future of Man*. (*Oeuvres*, V)

1942 (20 March) 'Universalization and Union. An attempt at clarification' in *Activation of Energy*. (*Oeuvres*, VII)

1942 (8 October) Christ the Evolver or a logical development of the idea of Redemption. Reflections on the nature of Christ's "formal action" in the World' in *Christianity and Evolution*. (*Oeuvres*, X)

1942 (15 November) 'Man's Place in the Universe. Reflections on Complexity' in *The Vision of the Past*. (*Oeuvres*, III)

1942 (August) 'Super-Humanity, Super-Christ, Super-Charity. Some new dimensions for the future' in *Science and Christ*. (*Oeuvres*, IX)

1942 (15 September) 'The Question of Fossil Man. Recent discoveries and present-day problems' in *The Appearance of Man*. (*Oeuvres*, II)

1943 (28 December) 'Reflections on Happiness' in *Toward the Future*. (*Oeuvres*, XI)

1944 (29 June) 'Introduction to the Christian life. Introduction to Christianity' in *Christianity and Evolution*. (*Oeuvres*, X)

1944 (13 December) 'Centrology. An essay in the dialectics of union' in *Activation of Energy*. (*Oeuvres*, VII)

1944 (10 March) 'Life and the Planets. What is happening at this moment on earth?' in *The Future of Man*. (*Oeuvres*, V)

1945 (23 April) 'Can Moral Science dispense with a metaphysical foundation?' in *Toward the Future*. (*Oeuvres*, XI)

1945 (10 June) 'The Analysis of Life' in *Activation of Energy*. (*Oeuvres*, VII)

1945 (9 August) 'Action and Activation' in *Science and Christ*. (*Oeuvres*, IX)

1945 (11 November) 'Christianity and Evolution (suggestions for a new theology)' in *Christianity and Evolution*. (*Oeuvres*, X)

1945 (25 December) 'A Great Event Foreshadowed: The Planetization of Mankind' in *The Future of Man*. (*Oeuvres*, V)

1946 (August) 'Catholicism and Science', not Teilhard's title, any more than that in the periodical *Esprit*: 'Christianity and Science: P. Teilhard de Chardin'; opening words: 'It is always rash . . .' in *Science and Christ*. (*Oeuvres*, IX)

1946 (September) 'Some Reflections on the Spiritual Repercussions of the Atom Bomb' in *The Future of Man*. (*Oeuvres*, V)

1946 (15–20 November) 'Degrees of Scientific Certainty in the Idea of Evolution' in *Science and Christ*. (*Oeuvres*, IX)

1946 (25 November) 'Outline of a dialectic of Spirit' in *Activation of Energy*. (*Oeuvres*, VII)

1946 (15 December) 'Ecumenism' in *Science and Christ*. (*Oeuvres*, IX)

1947 (January) 'Faith in Peace' in *The Future of Man*. (*Oeuvres*, V)

1947 (January) 'A plausible biological interpretation of human history. The formation of the "Noosphere"' in *The Future of Man*. (*Oeuvres*, V)

1947 (16 January) 'The Place of Technology in a General Biology of Mankind' in *Activation of Energy*. (*Oeuvres*, VII)

1947 (February) 'Faith in Man' in *The Future of Man*. (*Oeuvres*, V)

1947 (10 February) 'The Spiritual Contribution of the Far East. Some Personal Reflections' in *Toward the Future*. (*Oeuvres*, XI)

1947 (March) 'Preface' to *The Phenomenon of Man*. (*Oeuvres*, I)

1947 (March) (?) 'Summary or Postscript: The Essence of the Phenomenon of Man' in *The Phenomenon of Man*. (*Oeuvres*, I)

1947 (22 March) 'Some Reflections on the Rights of Man' in *The Future of Man*. (*Oeuvres*, V)

1947 (April) 'Zoological Evolution and Invention' in *The Vision of the Past.* (*Oeuvres*, III)

1947 (20 August) 'The religious value of research', not Teilhard's title, any more than: 'Study week at Versailles: the importance of research'; opening words: 'In a recent letter our Fr General . . .' in *Science and Christ.* (*Oeuvres*, IX)

1947 (23 September) 'The Human Rebound of Evolution and its consequences' in *The Future of Man.* (*Oeuvres*, V)

1947 (2 November) 'Letter to Emmanuel Mounier' (not Teilhard's title); opening words: 'My dear friend, since it is now clear . . .' in *Science and Christ.* (*Oeuvres*, IX)

1947 (15 November) 'Reflections on Original Sin' in *Christianity and Evolution.* (*Oeuvres*, X)

1947 (20 December) 'Turmoil or Genesis? Is there in the Universe a main axis of Evolution? (An attempt to see clearly)' (title of manuscript) in *The Future of Man.* (*Oeuvres*, V)

1948 (February) 'Two Principles and a Corollary (or a *Weltanschauung* in three stages)' in *Toward the Future.* (*Oeuvres*, XI)

1948 (April) ' "My intellectual position" (In response to an "enquiry" and never published)' in *The Heart of Matter.* (*Oeuvres*, XIII)

1948 (23 April) 'On the nature of the phenomenon of human society and its hidden relationships with gravity' in *Activation of Energy.* (*Oeuvres*, VII)

1948 (30 June) 'The Directions and Conditions of the Future' in *The Future of Man.* (*Oeuvres*, V)

1948 (3 August) 'Note on the biological structure of mankind' in *Science and Christ.* (*Oeuvres*, IX)

1948 (12 August) 'My fundamental vision' in *Toward the Future.* (*Oeuvres*, XI)

1948 (26 August) 'Appendix (to 'My fundamental vision') I. Note to the Phenomenon of Man: on some analogies or hidden relationships between gravity and consciousness. II. Note to the Christian Phenomenon: on the "bi-axial" nature of the Incarnation. III. Note to Metaphysics on the notion of "paired entities" ' in *Toward the Future.* (*Oeuvres*, XI)

1948 (September) 'Qualifications, Career, Field-Work and Writings of Pierre Teilhard de Chardin' in *The Heart of Matter.* (*Oeuvres*, XIII)

1948 (23 September) 'Note on the teaching of Prehistory' in *The Heart of Matter.* (*Oeuvres*, XIII)

1948 (7 October) 'The basis of my attitude' (opening words) in *The Heart of Matter.* (*Oeuvres*, XIII)

1948 (17 October) 'My *"Phenomenon of Man"*: An Essential Observation' in *The Heart of Matter*. (*Oeuvres*, XIII)

1948 (28 October) 'Some remarks on the Place and Part of Evil in a World in Evolution': Appendix to *The Phenomenon of Man*. (*Oeuvres*, I)

1948 (21 December) 'Address for the wedding of Christine Dresch and Claude-Marie Haardt' in *The Heart of Matter*. (*Oeuvres*, XIII)

1949 (6 January) 'The Psychological Conditions of the Unification of Man' in *Activation of Energy*. (*Oeuvres*, VII)

1949 (26 January) 'A Phenomenon of Counter-Evolution in Human Biology or the existential fear' in *Activation of Energy*. (*Oeuvres*, VII)

1949 (2 February) 'The Essence of the Democratic Idea. A biological approach to the problem. In response to a questionnaire from UNESCO' in *The Future of Man*. (*Oeuvres*, V)

1949 (4 May) 'Galileo's question restated: Does Mankind move biologically upon itself?' in *The Future of Man*. (*Oeuvres*, V)

1949 (31 May) 'The Sense of the Species in Man' in *Activation of Energy*. (*Oeuvres*, VII)

1949 (4 August) *The Human Zoological Group. Evolutionary Structure and Directions*. The title *Le Groupe Zoologique Humain. Structure et Directions Evolutives* was used for the paperback edition (Albin Michel). The title of the subsequent edition (éd. du Seuil) *La Place de l'Homme dans la Nature. Le Groupe zoologique humain* is not Teilhard's; *Man's Place in Nature*. (*Oeuvres*, VIII)

1949 (8 September) 'The Heart of the Problem' in *The Future of Man*. (*Oeuvres*, V)

1949 (17–22 October) 'The Vision of the Past. What it brings to and takes away from Science' in *The Vision of the Past*. (*Oeuvres*, III)

1950 (6 January) 'On the probable coming of an "Ultra-Human". (Reflections of a biologist)' in *The Future of Man*. (*Oeuvres*, V)

1950 (8 January) 'The Spiritual Energy of Suffering' in *Activation of Energy*. (*Oeuvres*, VII)

1950 (18 January) 'How may we conceive and hope that human unanimization will be realized on earth?' in *The Future of Man*. (*Oeuvres*, V)

1950 (2 March) 'What is Life?' in *Science and Christ*. (*Oeuvres*, IX)

1950 (27 April) 'From the Pre-Human to the Ultra-Human or "The phases of a living planet"'; not Teilhard's title, the duplicated text is headed: 'Reflections on the Ultra-Human or "The phases of a living planet"'; in *The Future of Man*. (*Oeuvres*, V)

1950 (10 May) 'The Christian Phenomenon' in *Christianity and Evolution*. (*Oeuvres*, X)

1950 (June–July) 'Evolution of the idea of evolution' in *The Vision of the Past.* (*Oeuvres*, III)

1950 (June) 'The Australopithecines and the "Missing Link" in Evolution' in *The Appearance of Man.* (*Oeuvres*, II)

1950 (5 June) 'The Evolution of Responsibility in the World' in *Activation of Energy.* (*Oeuvres*, VII)

1950 (July) 'The Scientific Career of Fr Teilhard de Chardin' in *The Heart of Matter.* (*Oeuvres*, XIII)

1950 (25 July) 'A Clarification: Reflections on two converse forms of Spirit' in *Activation of Energy.* (*Oeuvres*, VII)

1950 (15 August–30 October) 'The Heart of Matter' in *The Heart of Matter.* (*Oeuvres*, XIII)

1950 (shortly after 22 August) 'Monogenism and Monophyletism: An Essential Distinction' in *Christianity and Evolution.* (*Oeuvres*, X)

1950 (November) 'The Zest for Living' in *Activation of Energy.* (*Oeuvres*, VII)

1951 (February) 'The Phyletic Structure of the Human Group' in *The Appearance of Man.* (*Oeuvres*, II)

1951 (15 March) 'A Mental Threshold across our Path: From Cosmos to Cosmogenesis' in *Activation of Energy.* (*Oeuvres*, VII)

1951 (Easter: 25 March) 'Reflections on the Scientific Probability and the Religious Consequences of an Ultra-Human' in *Activation of Energy.* (*Oeuvres*, VII)

1951 (5 May) 'Note on the present reality and evolutionary significance of a human orthogenesis' in *The Vision of the Past.* (*Oeuvres*, III)

1951 (probably May, certainly before 24 May) 'Can Biology, taken to its extreme limit, enable us to emerge into the Transcendent?'; not Teilhard's title, any more than 'Notes for the "Semaine des intellectuels catholiques français"' (preparatory meeting of 8 May?) 'Biology and Transcendence'; opening words: 'If biology is taken to its extreme limit . . .' in *Science and Christ.* (*Oeuvres*, IX)

1951 (23 July) 'The Convergence of the Universe' in *Activation of Energy.* (*Oeuvres*, VII)

1951 (winter) 'Some Notes on the mystical sense: an attempt at clarification' in *Toward the Future.* (*Oeuvres*, XI)

1951 (about November) 'Notes on South African Prehistory'; not Teilhard's title; opening words: 'Followed from afar, by way of the periodicals . . .' in *The Appearance of Man.* (*Oeuvres*, II)

1951 (19 November) 'The Transformation and Continuation in Man of the Mechanism of Evolution' in *Activation of Energy.* (*Oeuvres*, VII)

1951 (30 December) 'A major problem for Anthropology. Is there or is there not, in man, a continuation and transformation of the biological process of evolution?' in *Activation of Energy*. (*Oeuvres*, VII)

1952 (21 January) 'Australopithecines, Pithecanthropians and the Phyletic Structure of the Hominians' in *The Appearance of Man*. (*Oeuvres*, II)

1952 (March) 'Observations on the Australopithecines' in *The Appearance of Man*. (*Oeuvres*, II)

1952 (27 April) 'The Reflection of Energy' in *Activation of Energy*. (*Oeuvres*, VII)

1952 (14 September) 'What the world is looking for from the Church of God at this moment: A generalizing and a deepening of the meaning of the Cross' in *Christianity and Evolution*. (*Oeuvres*, X)

1952 (November–December) 'Hominization and Speciation' in *The Vision of the Past*. (*Oeuvres*, III)

1952 (9 December) 'The End of the Species' in *The Future of Man*. (*Oeuvres*, V)

1953 (18 January) 'Reflections on the Compression of Mankind' in *Activation of Energy*. (*Oeuvres*, VII)

1953 (April) 'On looking at a Cyclotron. Reflections on the folding-back upon itself of human energy' in *Activation of Energy*. (*Oeuvres*, VII)

1953 (1 May) 'The Contingence of the Universe and man's zest for survival or, How can one rethink the Christian notion of Creation to conform with the laws of Energetics?' in *Christianity and Evolution*. (*Oeuvres*, X)

1953 (24 May) 'The Energy of Evolution' in *Activation of Energy*. (*Oeuvres*, VII)

1953 (5 June) 'A Sequel to the Problem of Human Origins: The Plurality of Inhabited Worlds' in *Christianity and Evolution*. (*Oeuvres*, X)

1953 (14 July) 'The Stuff of the Universe' in *Activation of Energy*. (*Oeuvres*, VII)

1953 (October?) 'My Litany', not Teilhard's title; opening words: 'The God of Evolution, the Christic, the Trans-Christ'; in *Christianity and Evolution*. (*Oeuvres*, X)

1953 (Feast of Christ the King: 25 October) 'The God of Evolution' in *Christianity and Evolution*. (*Oeuvres*, X)

1953 (23 November) 'On the probability of an early bifurcation of the Human Phylum in the immediate neighbourhood of its origins' in *The Appearance of Man*. (*Oeuvres*, II)

1953 (6 December) 'The Activation of Human Energy' in *Activation of Energy*. (*Oeuvres*, VII)

1954 (14 January) 'A summary of my "Phenomenological" View of the World' in *Toward the Future*. (*Oeuvres*, XI)

1954 (25 March) 'The Singularities of the Human Species' followed by an 'Appendix: Complementary Remarks on the Nature of Omega Point or, the Unique Nature of the Christian Phenomenon' in *The Appearance of Man*. (*Oeuvres*, II)

1954 (June) 'The Search for the discovery of human origins in Africa south of the Sahara' in *The Appearance of Man*. (*Oeuvres*, II)

1954 (before June) 'The Phenomenon of Man (How can one go beyond a philosophico-juridico-literary "Anthropology" and establish a true Science of Man: an Anthropogenesis and an Anthropodynamics?)' in *The Heart of Matter*. (*Oeuvres*, XIII)

1954 (September) 'Africa and Human Origins' in *The Appearance of Man*. (*Oeuvres*, II)

1955 (January) 'A defence of Orthogenesis in the matter of patterns of speciation' in *The Vision of the Past*. (*Oeuvres*, III)

1955 (1 January) 'The Death-Barrier and Co-Reflection or, the imminent awakening of human consciousness to the sense of its irreversibility' (the Appendix: 'Science and Revelation' is dated 5 January 1955) in *Activation of Energy*. (*Oeuvres*, VII)

1955 (5 January) 'Science and Revelation: Appendix' to 'The Death-Barrier and Co-Reflection' in *Activation of Energy*. (*Oeuvres*, VII)

1955 (March) 'The Christic' in *The Heart of Matter*. (*Oeuvres*, XIII)

1955 (March) 'Research, Work and Worship' in *Science and Christ*. (*Oeuvres*, IX)

1955 (7 April) 'What I believe (Last page of the Diary)' in *The Heart of Matter*. (*Oeuvres*, XIII) (incomplete version printed in *The Future of Man*. (*Oeuvres*, V))

BIBLIOGRAPHY

1913

1.* *Sur une formation de Carbono-Phosphate de Chaux d'âge paléolithique.* (C.R. Acad. Sc., vol. 157, pp. 1077–9)

1914–15

2. *Les Carnassiers des Phosphorites du Quercy.* (Annales de Paléontologie, vol. IX, pp. 103–91, 13 fig., 9 pl., 8 tables)

1916

3. *Sur quelques Primates des Phosphorites du Quercy.* (Annales de Paléontologie, vol. X, pp. 1–20, 6 fig., 2 pl.)

1916–21

4. *Les Mammifères de l'Éocène inférieur français et leurs gisements.* (Doctoral thesis) (Annales de Paléontologie, vol. X, pp. 171–6–vol. XI, pp. 1–108, 8 pl., 42 fig.)

1919

5. *Sur la structure de l'Ile de Jersey.* (Bull. Soc. Géol. de France, 4th series, vol. 19, pp. 273–8, 2 fig., 1 map)

1920

6. *Sur la succession des Faunes de Mammifères dans l'Éocène inférieur européen.* (C.R. Acad. Sc., Paris, vol. 171, pp. 1161–2.)

1921

7. (and Fraipont) – *Note sur la présence dans le Tertiaire inférieur de Belgique d'un Condylarthré appartenant au groupe des Hyopsodus.* (Bull. Acad. Royale de Belgique, vol. VII, pp. 357–60.)

1922

8. *Sur une Faune de Mammifères Pontiens provenant de la Chine septentrionale.* (C.R. Acad. Sc., Paris, vol. 175, pp. 979–81.)

* In this Bibliography the numbers in italic (*2*) have been used to designate the longer papers or notes, the numbers in roman (1) less important writings. 'Pal. Sin' has been used as an abbreviation for 'Palaeontologica Sinica' (Palaeontological Memoirs of the Geological Survey of China).

9. (Jodot P., Joleaud L., Lemoine P.) – *Observations sur le calcaire pisolithique de Vertus et du Mont Aimé (Marne)*. (Bull. Soc. Géol. de France, Paris, 4th series, vol. 22, pp. 164–76, 6 fig.)

1923

10. *Cenozoic Vertebrate Fossils of E. Kansu and Inner Mongolia*. (Bull. Geol. Soc. China, vol. II, pp. 1–3.)

1924

11. *Note sur la structure des montagnes de l'Ouest du Linn-Ming-Kwan (Chihli Méridional)*. (Bull. Geol. Soc. China, vol. III, pp. 393–7.)
12. *Geology of Northern Chihli and Eastern Mongolia*. (Bull. Geol. Soc. China, vol. III, pp. 399–407, fig. maps.)
13. (and Licent) – *On the Geology of the Northern, Western and Southern Borders of the Ordos, China*. (Bull. Geol. Soc. China, vol. III, pp. 37–44, 5 fig.)
14. (and Licent) – *On the discovery of a Palaeolithic Industry in Northern China*. (Bull. Geol. Soc. China, vol. III, pp. 45–50, fig.)
15. (and Licent) – *Observations géologiques sur la bordure occidentale et méridionale de l'Ordos*. (Bull. Soc. Géol. de France, Paris, 4th series, vol. XXIV, pp. 49–91, 15 fig.)
16. (and Licent) – *Observations complémentaires sur la Géologie de l'Ordos*. (Bull. Soc. Géol. de France, Paris, 4th series, vol. XXIV, pp. 462–4, 2 pl.)
17. (and Dollo L.) – *Les gisements de Mammifères paléocènes de la Belgique*. (Quarterly Journal of the Géol. Soc., vol. 80, pp. 12–16.)

1925

18. *Le paradoxe transformiste – A propos de la dernière critique du Transformisme par M. Vialleton*. (Revue des Quest. Scient., Louvain, 32 pp.)
19. *Observations nouvelles sur les Mammifères du Tertiaire inférieur de Belgique*. (Bull. Acad. Royale de Belgique, series V, vol. XI, pp. 48–50.)
20. (and Licent) – *Note sur deux instruments agricoles du Néolithique de Chine*. (L'Anthropologie, vol. XXXV, pp. 62–74, 3 fig.)
21. (and Licent) – *Le Paléolithique de la Chine*. (L'Anthropologie, vol. XXXV, pp. 201–34, 16 fig.)
22. *Le Massif volcanique du Talaï-nor (Gobi orien.al)*. (Bull. volcanologique, Napoli, No. 3–4, pp. 100–8, 1 fig.)
23. (and Fritel) – *Note sur quelques grès mésozoïques à Plantes de la Chine septentrionale*. (Bull. Soc. Géol. de France, Paris, 4th series, vol. 25, pp. 523–40, 7 fig., 2 pl.)

1926

24. *Étude géologique sur la région du Dalai-Noor.* (Mémoires de la Soc. Géol. de France, Paris. New series, vol. III, No. 7, pp. 153, 21 fig., 2 pl.)

25. *Le Massif volcanique du Dalai-Noor (Gobi oriental).* (Congrès des Soc. Sav. et des Départements, Paris, pp. 460–3.)

26. *Description de Mammifères tertiaires de Chine et de Mongolie.* (Annales de Paléontologie, vol. XV, pp. 3–51, 25 fig., 5 pl.)

27. *Sur quelques Mammifères nouveaux du Tertiaire de la Belgique.* (Bull. Acad. de Belgique, Cl. Sciences, 5th series, vol. XII, pp. 210–15, 2 fig.)

28. *Palaeontological Notes.* (Bull. Geol. Soc. China, vol. 5, No. 1, pp. 57–9.)

29. *Le Néolithique de la Chine d'après les découvertes du Dr Andersson.* (L'Anthropologie, Paris, vol. XXXVI, pp. 117–24.)

30. *Sur l'apparence nécessairement discontinue de toute série évolutive.* (L'Anthropologie, Paris, vol. XXXVI, pp. 320–1.)

1927

31. *Les Mammifères de l'Éocène inférieur de la Belgique.* (Mém. Mus. R. Hist. Nat. Belg. No. 36, pp. 1–33, 29 fig., 6 pl.)

32. (and Licent) – *On the basal beds of the sedimentary series in Southwestern Shansi.* (Bull. Geol. Soc. China, vol. VI, No. 1, pp. 61–4, fig.)

33. (and Licent) – *On the recent marine Beds and the Underlying Freshwater Deposits, in Tientsin.* (Bull. Geol. Soc. China, vol. VI, No. 2, pp. 127–8.)

34. (and Licent) – *Observations sur les formations quaternaires et tertiaires supérieures du Honan septentrional et du Chansi méridional.* (Bull. Geol. Soc. China, vol. VI, No. 2, pp. 129–48, fig.)

35. (Licent and Black D.) – *On a presumably Pleistocene Human Tooth from the Sjaraosso-gol (South-eastern Ordos) deposits.* (Bull. Geol. Soc. China, vol. V, pp. 285–90, fig., 1 pl.)

36. (Barbour and Licent) – *Geological study of the deposits of the Sangkanho Basin.* (Bull. Geol. Soc. China, vol. V, pp. 263–78, fig.)

1928

37. *Quelques données nouvelles sur la mise en place de la Faune moderne (Mammifères) en Chine septentrionale.* (C.R. de la Société biologique, Paris, pp. 1–3.)

38. *Les couches de passage entre le Tertiaire et le Quaternaire en Chine septentrionale.* (C.R. Soc. Géol. de France, No. 1–2, pp. 12–14.)

39. *Observations sur la lenteur d'évolution des Faunes de Mammifères continentales.* (Palaeobiologica, Vienna, vol. I, pp. 55–60, 1 fig.)

40. *La Nature et la succession des Éruptions post-paléozoïques en Chine septentrionale.* (C.R. Acad. Sc., Paris, vol. 186, pp. 960–1.)

41. *Note complémentaire sur la Faune de Mammifères du Tertiaire inférieur d'Orsmael.* (Bull. Acad. Royale Belg., Cl. Sc., series 5, vol. XIV, pp. 471–4, 2 fig.)

42. *Les Roches éruptives post-Paléozoïques du Nord de la Chine.* (Bull. of the Geological Soc. of China, vol. VII, pp. 1–12.)

43. (Boule, Breuil, Licent) – *Le Paléolithique de la Chine.* (Arch. de l'Inst. de Pal. Hum., Paris, No. 4, 138 pp., 53 fig., 30 pl.)

1929

44. (and Young) – *On some traces of Vertebrate Life in the Jurassic and Triassic Beds of Shansi and Shensi.* (Bull. Geol. Soc. China, vol. VIII, pp. 173–202, 10 fig.)

45. (and Young) – *Preliminary report on the Chou-Kou-Tien fossiliferous Deposit.* (Bull. Geol. Soc. China, vol. VIII, pp. 173–202, 10 fig.)

46. *Le Paléolithique en Somalie française et en Abyssinie.* (L'Anthropologie, vol. 40, pp. 331–4.)

1930

47. *Que faut-il penser du Transformisme?* (Revue des Quest. Scient., Louvain, 4th series, vol. XVII, part I, pp. 89–99.)

48. *Le Sinanthropus de Peking. – État actuel de nos connaissances sur le Fossile et son gisement.* (L'Anthropologie, vol. XLI, No. 1–2, pp. 1–11.)

49. *Le phénomène humain.* (Revue des Quest. Scient., pp. 1–19.)

50. *Preliminary observations on the pre-Loessic and post-Pontian formations in Western Shansi and Northern Shensi.* (Mem. Geol. Surv. of China, series A, No. 8, pp. 1–54, 13 fig., 9 pl.)

51. *On the occurrence of a Mongolian Perissodactyle in the Red Sandstone of Sichuan, S.W. Honan.* (Bull. Geol. Soc. China, vol. IX, pp. 331–3, 1 fig.)

52. *Quelques observations sur les Terres jaunes (Loess) de Chine et de Mongolie.* (Soc. Géol. de France (jubilee volume) II, pp. 605–12, 12 fig.)

53. (and Piveteau J.) – *Les Mammifères fossiles de Nihowan (Chine).* (Annales de Paléontologie, vol. XIX, pp. 1–132, 42 fig., 23 pl.)

54. (and Licent) – *Geological observations in Northern Manchuria and Barga (Hailar).* (Bull. Geol. Soc. China, vol. IX, pp. 23–35, 4 fig.)

55. (and Young) – *Some correlation between the geology of China proper and the geology of Mongolia.* (Bull. Geol. Soc. China, vol. IX, No. 2, pp. 119–25.)

56. (and Lamare, Dreyfus, Lacroix, Basse) – *Études géologiques en Éthiopie, Somalie et Arabie méridionale.* (Mém. Soc. Géol. de France, N.S. vol. IV, No. 14, pp. 1–165, 29 fig., 5 pl.)

1931

57. *On an enigmatic Pteropod-like fossil from the lower Cambrian of Southern Shansi, Biconulites Grabaui, nov. gen., nov. sp.* (Bull. Geol. Soc. China, Vol. X, pp. 179–84, 2 fig., 2 pl.)

58. *Some observations on the archaeological material collected by Mr A. S. Lukashkin near Tsitsikar.* (Bull. Geol. Soc. China, vol. XI, pp. 183–93, 8 fig., 3 pl.)

59. (and Young) – *Fossil Mammals from the late Cenozoic of Northern China.* (Palaeontologia Sinica, series C, vol. IX, part I, pp. 1–188, 23 fig., 10 pl., 1 map.)

1932

60. *New observations on the Khangai series of Mongolia and some other allied formations.* (Bull. Geol. Soc. China, vol. XI, pp. 395–409.)

61. *The Geology of the Weichang Area.* (Geol. Bull. Geol. Surv. China, No. 19, pp. 1–49, fig., 1 pl.)

62. *Observations sur les changements de niveau marin dans la Région d'Obock.* (C.R.S. Soc. Géol. de France, No. 13, pp. 180–1.)

63. *Les résultats scientifiques de l'expédition (Citroën Centre-Asie).* (Terre, Air, Mer, Paris, pp. 379–90, 8 fig.)

64. (and Piveteau) – *Nouvelle étude sur le Cervus ertborni Dub. des argiles de la Campine.* (Mededeel. Kon. Natuurhist. Mus. Belgiï, vol. 8, No. 5, 12 pp., 5 fig.)

65. (and Pei W.C.) – *The lithic industry of the Sinanthropus deposits in Chou-Kou-Tien.* (Bull. Geol. Soc. China, vol. XI, pp. 315–58, 36 fig., 5 pl.)

66. (and Young) – *On some Neolithic (and possibly Palaeolithic) Finds in Mongolia – Sinkiang and West China.* (Bull. Geol. Soc. China, vol. XII, No. 1, pp. 83–104, 21 fig.)

1933

67. *The base of the Palaeozoic in Shansi: Metamorphism and Cycles.* (Bull. Geol. Soc. China, vol. XIII, pp. 149–53, 2 fig.)

68. *Les Cycles sédimentaires (pliocènes et plus récents) dans la Chine du Nord.* (Bull. Ass. Geol. Fr. Paris, No. 65, pp. 3–7, 1 fig.)

69. *Observations géologiques à travers les déserts d'Asie centrale de Kalgan à Hami (Mission Citroën Centre-Asie, 1931-2).* (Rev. Geogr. Phys., vol. V, pp. 365–97, 15 fig., 14 pl., 2 maps)

70. *Les graviers plissés de Chine.* (Bull. Soc. Géol. de France, series V, vol. II, pp. 527–31, 4 pl.)

71. *Les Bovinés fossiles en Chine du Nord.* (C.R. Soc. Biol., Paris, No. 79, pp. 1-2.)
72. (and Young) – *The late Cenozoic Formation of S.E. Shansi.* (Bull. Geol. Soc. China, vol. XII, pp. 207–41.)
73. (and Davidson Black, Young, Pei) – *Fossil Man in China. – The Chou-Kou-Tien cave deposits with a synopsis of our present knowledge of the late Cenozoic in China.* (Geological Memoirs, Peiping, Series A, No. 11, 158 pp, 81 fig., 3 tables, 6 maps.)
74. (and de Lapparent A.) – *Sur la découverte d'un Rongeur du genre* Paramys *dans l'Éocène inférieur de Provence.* (C.R.S. Soc. Géol. de France, pp. 26–7.)

1934
75. (and Pei W.C.) – *New discoveries in Choukoutien 1933–4.* (Bull. Geol. Soc. China, vol. XIII, pp. 309–89, 9 fig., 1 map, 3 pl.)
76. (and Stirton R.A.) – *A correlation of some Miocene and Pliocene Mammalian Assemblages in North America and Asia with a discussion of the Mio-Pliocene Boundary.* (Publ. Univ. Calif. Bull. Dept. Geol. Sc., Berkeley, vol. 23, pp. 277–90, 3 pl.)

1935
77. *La Faune pléistocène et l'ancienneté de l'homme en Amérique du Nord.* (L'Anthropologie, vol. 45, pp. 483–7.)
78. *Chronologie des alluvions pléistocènes de Java.* (L'Anthropologie, vol. 45, pp. 707–8.)
79. *Le Cénozoïque en Chine centrale et méridionale.* (C.R.S. Soc. Géol. de France, No. 11 and 12, pp. 150–2.)
80. (and Barbour G.B., Bien M.N.) – *A geological reconnaissance across the eastern Tsinling (between Leyang and Hsichuan, Honan).* (Bull. Geol. Surv. China, No. 25, pp. 9–38, 16 fig., 2 pl., 1 map.)
81. (and Young C.C.) – *The Cenozoic Sequence in the Yangtze Valley.* (Bull. Geol. Soc. China, vol. XIV, pp. 161–78, 12 fig.)
82. (and Young, Pei, Chang H.C.) – *On the Cenozoic Formations of Kwangsi and Kwangtung.* (Bull. Geol. Soc. China, vol. XIV, pp. 179–205, 14 fig., 2 pl.)
83. *Geological Observations in the Turfan Area.* (Geografiska Annaler [Stockholm], pp. 446–52.)

1936
84. *The significance of Piedmont gravels in continental Geology.* (Intern. Geol. Congress. Rep. XVI, Session U.S.A., Washington, vol. 2, pp. 1031–9, 2 fig.)

85. Fossil Mammals from Locality 9 of Choukoutien. (Palaeontologia Sinica, ser. C., vol. VII, part 4, 70 pp., 30 fig., 4 pl.)

86. (and Young C.C.) – *On the Mammalian remains from the archaeological site of Anyang.* (Palaeontologia Sinica, ser. C., vol. XII, part I, 78 pp., 26 fig., 8 pl.)

87. (and Young C.C.) –*A Mongolian Amblypod in the Red beds of Ichang (Hupeh).* (Bull. Geol. Soc. China, vol. XV, pp. 217–23, 3 fig.)

88. (and Licent) – *New remains of Postschizotherium from S.E. Shansi.* (Bull. Geol. Soc. China, vol. XV, pp. 421–7, 2 fig.)

89. (and Terra H. de) – *Observations on the upper Siwalik formation and later Pleistocene Deposits in India.* (Proc. Amer. Phil. Soc. Philadelphia, vol. 76, pp. 791–822, 14 fig.)

90. Notes on Continental Geology. (Bull. Geol. Soc. China, vol. XVI, pp. 195–220, 9 maps.)

1937

91. Ep-archaean and Epi-sinian Intervals in China. (Bull. Geol. Soc. China, vol. XVII, pp. 169–75.)

92. The Post-Villafranchian Interval in North China. (Bull. Geol. Soc. China, vol. XVII, pp. 169–75.)

93. Notes sur la Paléontologie Humaine en Asie Orientale. (L'Anthropologie, vol. 47. pp. 22–33, 6 fig.)

94. The Pleistocene of China: stratigraphy and correlations. (Early Man, Philadelphia, pp. 211–20, 3 fig.)

95. The structural Geology of Eastern Shantung (between Tsingtao and Yungch'eng). (Geol. Bull., Nanking, No. 29, pp. 85–105, 2 pl.)

96. (and Trassaert M.) – *The Proboscidians of Southern Shansi.* (Pal. Sin., Ser. C., vol. XIII, part 11, 58 pp., 6 fig., 13 pl.)

97. (and Trassaert M.) – *Pliocene Camelidae, Giraffidae and Cervidae of S.E. Shansi.* (Pal. Sin., New Series C, No. 1.)

1938

98. Deuxièmes Notes sur la Paléontologie Humaine en Asie Méridionale. (L'Anthropologie, vol. 48, pp. 449–56.)

99. The Fossils from Locality 12 of Choukoutien. (Pal. Sin., New Series C, No. 5.)

100. (and Trassaert M.) – *Cavicornia of S.E. Shansi.* (Pal. Sin., New Series C, No. 6.)

101. A Map of the younger eruptive rocks in China. (Bull. Geol. Surv. China, Nanking.)

101a. *Le Villafranchien d'Asie et la question du Villafranchien.* (C.R.S. Soc. Géol. Fr., pp. 325-7.)

1939

102. *Two skulls of* Machairodus *from Choukoutien.* (Bull. Geol. Soc. China, vol. XIX, pp. 235-56.)
103. *New observations on the genus* Postschizotherium. (Bull. Geol. Soc. China, vol. XIX, p. 257-68.)
104. *The Miocene Cervids from Shantung.* (Bull. Geol. Soc. China, vol. XIX, pp. 269-78.)
105. (and Breuil, Wernert) – *Les industries lithiques de Somalie française.* (L'Anthropologie, vol. 49, pp. 497-522, 13 fig.)

1940

106 *The Fossils from Locality 18, near Peking.* (Pal. Sin., New Series C, No. 11.)
107. *The Granitisation of China.* (Publications de l'Institut de Géobiologie de Pékin, No. 1, 33 pp., 10 fig., 1 map.)

1941

108. *Early Man in China.* (Publ. Inst. Géobiol. Pékin, No. 7, 112 pp., 51 fig., 5 maps.)
109. *The Fossils of Locality 13 in Chou-Kou-Tien.* (Pal. Sin., New Series C, No. 11.)

1942

110. (and Leroy P.) – *Chinese fossil Mammals.* (Publ. Inst. Géobiol. Pékin, No. 8, 142 pp., 1 map.)
111. *New Rodents of the Pliocene and Lower Pleistocene of North China.* (Publ. Inst. Géobiol. Pékin, No. 9, 100 pp., 61 fig.)

1943

112. *The Genesis of the Western Hills of Peking.* (Geobiologia, vol. I, pp. 17-49, 12 fig., 1 map.)
113. *Contorted figures in the Sinian limestone.* (Geobiologia, vol. I, pp. 53-5, 1 fig., 1 pl.)

1944

114. *Le Néolithique de la Chine.* (Publ. Inst. Géobiol. Pékin, No. 10, 112 pp., 48 fig., 2 maps.)

1945

115. *Un problème de Géologie asiatique: le faciès Mongol.* (Geobiologia, vol. 2, pp. 1–12, 5 fig.)
116. *The Geology of the Western Hills, – additional Notes.* (Geobiologia, vol. 2, pp. 13–18, 1 fig.)
117. *The geological structure of the Shihmenchai Basin near Shanhaikwan.* (Geobiologia, vol. 2, pp. 19–26, 3 fig.)
118. (and Leroy P.) – *Les Félidés de Chine.* (Publ. Inst. Géobiol. Pékin, No. 11, 70 pp., 20 fig., 2 maps.)
119. (and Leroy P.) – *Les Mustélidés de Chine.* (Publ. Inst. Géobiol. Pékin, No. 12, 56 pp., 24 fig., 2 maps.)

1946

120. *La Planétisation Humaine.* (Cahiers du Monde Nouveau, August 1946.)
121. *Remarques sur les Flexures continentales de Chine.* (Bull. Soc. Géol. Fr., series 5, vol. XVI, pp. 497–502.)

1947

122. *La Question de l'Homme Fossile.* (Éditions Psyché, Paris, 33 pp., 12 fig.)
123. *Une interprétation biologique plausible de l'Histoire humaine: la formation de la Noosphere.* (Revue des Quest. Scient., January 1947, pp. 1–35.)
124. *La structure de l'Asie Centrale, d'après le Dr Norin.* (Revue Scientifique, 1947.)

1948

125. *Le rebondissement humain de l'Évolution, et ses conséquences.* (Revue des Quest. Scient., April 1948, pp. 166–85.)*
* September 1948.

The list drawn up by Teilhard includes only a portion of his scientific writings. These have been gathered by Dr Karl Schmitz-Moormann into a Corpus of 11 volumes, *Pierre Teilhard de Chardin: L'Oeuvre Scientifique* (Walter-Verlag, Olten und Freiburg im Breisgau, W. Germany, 1971). Previously, M. Claude Cuénot had compiled a bibliography of Teilhard's works (in French), which was published in the Spanish Edition of his *Pierre Teilhard de Chardin. Les Grandes Étapes de son évolution* (Madrid, Taurus Ediciones)

INDEX

stuff; of the cosmos, 26–7, 29, 30,
52, 143; of the noosphere, 32–5;
of things, 17, 23, 33, 35, 82, 86;
of the universe, 21, 84
Suess, Eduard, 30, 182
suffering, 52, 119
super-centration, 60
super-charity, 55
super-Christ, 55
supernatural, the, 221, 223
Sussex, 21, 26, 152, 158
synthesis, era of, 8

Tavannes tunnel, 176, 180
technology, 37, 98
tectonics, 159
Teilhard de Chardin, Pierre; early
attraction for rocks and natural
history, 19–23, 46, 152; mother's
influence, 17, 41–2, 44; effect of
War, 29, 31, 47, 192; loyalty to
Church, 116–17, 209; spirit of
discovery, 133, 170–1; professional
career, 152–4, 157–64; restrictions
on writing, 8, 11; Rome visit,
147–50; exile in New York, 80;
fundamental vision, 8, 15–16, 83,
101, 196–208; influence since
death, 8–10. *See also* separate
subject headings
Writings:
Address to International Congress
S.J., 210
Address at the wedding of
C. Dresch and C. M. Haardt,
150–1
Address at the wedding of M. and
Mme de la Goublaye de
Ménorval, 140–2

'Atomism of Spirit, The', 193, 194,
223
'Awaited Word, The', 210
'Basis of my Attitude, The', 147–
8
'Christic, The', 7, 8, 80–102, 193,
222
'Cosmic Life', 192, 195, 196, 203
'Creative Union', 9, 193, 198, 205
'*Crise Présente, La*', 180
'Death-barrier and co-reflection',
193
Diary, last page, 103–4. *See also Journal*
'End of the species, The', 193, 194
'Eternal Feminine, The', 79, 223
'Faith in Man', 210
'Faith in Peace', 180
'For Odette and for Jean', 135–9,
195
'*Forma Christi*', 209
'Great event foreshadowed, A',
192
'Great Monad, The', 78, 181,
182–95, 223
'Heart of Matter, The', 7, 15–55,
80, 81, 102
'Heart of the Problem, The', 210
'Hominization', 78, 181
'How I believe', 36, 78, 192, 222
'How may we conceive and hope
that human unanimity will be
realized on Earth?', 194
'How the Transformist Question
presents itself', 107
'Human Energy', 180, 193, 223
'Human rebound of evolution,
The', 193
'Hymn to Matter', 75–7, 79

PIERRE TEILHARD DE CHARDIN was born and raised in Auvergne, France. A lifelong member of the Society of Jesus, he also studied physics, chemistry, geology, and palaeontology. He was a volunteer stretcher bearer in the First World War and received the Military Medal and the Legion of Honor.

Following the war, he lived for many years in China and was a major participant in the discovery and classification of Peking Man. His academic distinctions included a professorship in geology at the Catholic Institute of Paris, and directorships of the National Geographic Survey of China and the National Research Center of France.

Teilhard lived in New York City after the Second World War and continued his philosophic work there under the auspices of the Wenner-Gren Foundation until his death. He is buried in the United States.

During his lifetime Père Teilhard was barred by his religious superiors from teaching and publishing his philosophical and religious works. His manuscripts, which he bequeathed to a friend, were published posthumously—among them such major works as *The Phenomenon of Man* and *The Divine Milieu*. The latest works of Père Teilhard published in the United States are *Human Energy, Activation of Energy, Christianity and Evolution*, and *Toward the Future*.